ARTISAN CHEESE MAKING AT HOME

Reblochon at 2 months (page 172)

ARTISAN CHEESE MAKING AT HOME

Techniques & Recipes for
Mastering World-Class Cheeses

Mary Karlin

Photography by Ed Anderson

Foreword by Peter Reinhart

TEN SPEED PRESS
Berkeley

Leaf-Wrapped Goat Cheeses (page 59). Clockwise from bottom: peach, maple, persimmon, fig

CONTENTS

Double-Milled Stout Cheddar at 2 weeks (page 124)

FOREWORD

Most people know me as a bread guy, but some who knew me back when remember me also as a cheese guy. Yes, before embarking on the baking career that has defined my professional life, I thought I might instead be a cheese maker, fermenting milk rather than grain. I had studied a small book on making cheese at home and worked out a deal with a local raw milk dairy to buy all their unsold milk for one dollar a gallon, about thirty gallons a week.

I borrowed a stainless steel, double-jacketed cheese maker on wheels from the same dairy, and every week I rolled it out into the driveway of the ranch where I lived with thirty other people in a Christian community (I was known as Brother Peter back then), and transformed that milk into six small wheels of cheddar-style cheese that, after some aging, was pretty tasty. We called it Abbey Jack even though it wasn't anything like other Jack cheeses, because we liked the sound of the name.

Soon I was looking at a space in a converted wine building (I lived in Sonoma County in the heart of wine country, so old wine buildings were abundant) to set up what I intended to call the Forestville Creamery. After we measured the one stall in the building that was still available amidst the other businesses—the existing winery, a gem and crystal seller, a silk screen T-shirt shop, a comic book collector, and scattered offices—I studied the board of health requirements for cheese making operations. I looked, too, at the requirements for bread bakeries, since I also was a serious amateur baker at the time. It was a no-brainer—the rules governing a cheese operation were far more stringent and costly than those for bread, and so I took the path of least resistance. Had I chosen the creamery path, who knows: perhaps I'd have written a few books like the one you are now holding instead of

bread books. But, as we all know, there are no coincidences, and this is why I am so grateful to Mary Karlin, whom I have known for several years and who I consider one of the godmothers of the artisan food movement in Sonoma County, with her popular classes on cheese making and wood-fired cooking and her many years of studying and working side by side with the finest chefs and cheese makers in America (even I had the honor of working numerous times with Mary at the award-winning Ramekins Culinary School in Sonoma). Here, she demystifies essential processes for a new generation of artisans in this, the most comprehensive book ever written for home cheese makers.

There are two key words in the previous sentence that I'd like to revisit: "demystifies" and "artisan." The category of fermented foods includes bread, wine, beer, spirit beverages, cheese, pickles, cured meats, sauerkraut, kimchi, and more. They all evoke an ancient lineage of mystery that, until modern science grabbed hold, had an aura of alchemy and magic. This is because, in my opinion, each of these foodstuffs represents a type of transformation of one thing into something totally new and different. And the artisans who knew how to perform those transformations attained a vital, honored, and almost shamanistic role in their communities. They had, or so it seemed, a mysterious power. But as science and technology deconstructed the transformational steps into very nonmagical, mechanical processes, an important trade-off occurred: volume production supplanted small-scale artistry.

However, as anyone interested in this book probably knows, we are now in the midst of an artisanal renewal. We saw it happen with bread, wine, and beer in the 1980s, followed by a flowering of amazing domestic farmstead cheeses in the 1990s. Lately it's showing up in *salumi* and charcuterie. And where the professionals dare to go, home cooks soon follow. This book celebrates these artisan mysteries, if I can be so bold as to resurrect that mystical image. I think it's allowable, because things exist on many levels, and while alchemy is no longer the rulebook of the day, the yearning for the transformations that it symbolically points to never has and never will depart from us. And so I believe that all of us, whether professional or home cooks, long for the kind of empowerment that comes with the ability to transform one thing into something else.

In my cheese making days I marveled at how milk could become so many different other things and how, if I learned how to properly control the environment in which I performed my transformations, I could tease out flavors and textures that weren't there in the original source product; I could effect a radical change in the elements, bringing joy to others. I viewed my stainless steel cheese vat as a kind of altar, and my aging room as a sacred, veiled chamber. I believe it is in making connections like this—in seeing the implications embedded in fermented and thus transformational foods (and in all things, for that matter, but it's so much easier to grasp with fermented foods)—that we do attain a type of veil-splitting empowerment and thus begin to scratch the itch of our deeper yearnings.

So a book like this one, which demystifies and simplifies, also leads us deeper into mystery, because it gives us the tools to effect transformations and to experience the joy of such creation, and also the joy of giving joy. Every now and then I get the urge to track down some rennet and make another batch of Abbey Jack, and with this book in hand, I've already begun designating my aging cellar. But more important,

because I have the privilege of traveling frequently, I look forward to tasting the cheeses made by you, of sharing in your joy by being the recipient of it.

One final anecdote: During the height of my Abbey Jack days I decided to make small, twelve-ounce wheels to give as Christmas gifts. I even dipped them in beeswax and tied them up with twine, with a little nub of string dangling off the top to facilitate untying them, and happily gave them to my friends to send to their families across the country. I couldn't wait to hear how everyone liked it (this was in the early 1980s when many people had never eaten homemade, aged cheese). A few days after Christmas I heard one of my friends, who was talking on the telephone, laughing hysterically. He kept looking at me and laughing again. When he got off the phone he said, "My folks wanted me to tell you thank you for all your hard work, but to also let you know that it was smelliest candle they'd ever burned."

Over the next few days I heard this same response from three other people. Of course, those who figured out that it was cheese raved about it, but, frankly, I still get notes from old friends reminding me of my days as the smelly candle maker.

So as you dive into the world that Mary Karlin describes in the following pages, I leave you with this thought: Know that you are entering a long tradition of multidimensional artisanship, with all that the term implies. As you become adept in your transformations of milk into curds and whey, and thus into cheeses of many types, and as you learn how to evoke every subtle nuance of flavor trapped in those curds through proper temperature control, acid balancing, and aging, and as you begin spreading the joy you have created by sharing the cheese you create, remember, above all else, to always label your cheese.

Peter Reinhart
Charlotte, North Carolina
September 2010

INTRODUCTION

I am thrilled to invite you on a rewarding journey, one that starts with a simple ingredient, milk, which is transformed through a few fundamental practices into glorious cheese. Whether you are a curious novice or an experienced hobbyist, you are part of a culture with a seemingly insatiable appetite for hand-crafted cheese, always yearning to discover yet another treasure at the local cheese shop or as part of a restaurant's cheese plate. Maybe you are like me:

when I encounter a new, remarkable artisan cheese, it makes an indelible mark, and I think to myself, "I want to make a cheese like *that*!" The enthusiasm comes easy when there are so many cheeses to be inspired by and so many excellent reasons to make your own. Perhaps you are motivated by the guaranteed freshness of homemade cheese or want to save money through DIY production, or maybe you are lured by the age-old tradition of homestead cheese making as a means to feed your family.

I've worked with some of the most influential cheese makers and authorities in the field, and now, in this comprehensive book, I share with you the collective expertise and knowledge of the American cheese making community—a dedicated segment of the burgeoning artisan food movement. As a passionate cook, educator, and hobbyist cheese maker, I adore both making hand-crafted cheeses and cooking with the results, and I'm very keen to pass on what I know. This book is my offering, filled with formulas for making more than eighty cheeses, including longtime favorites, and more than two dozen newer contemporary cheeses.

We are lucky that the appreciation for hand-crafted cheeses, in the recent past a rather rarefied interest, is now part of mainstream culture. There is growing and widespread interest in hand-crafted foods and the do-it-yourself experience—all part of what Peter Reinhart calls the artisan

renewal. But it is also worth noting that a mere century ago cheese was still a relatively regional—and European—phenomenon and that cheese making techniques were limited by climate, geography, and technology in a way that modernity has rendered obsolete. For example, bloomy-rind cheeses like Camembert and Brie were first created in northwestern France because cows were prevalent, cheese was made for home or village consumption, and a specific acid-tolerant mold flourished in that region. High in the mountains, fewer cows were grazed and their milk was pooled cooperatively. Therefore, large wheels of low-moisture cheeses like Comté and Emmental were created to be shared and to last through the winter months. In the United States, cheese production first emulated regional European cheeses, made by and for specific immigrant audiences. Hard Italian-style cheeses were crafted in California, Germanic washed-rind cheeses like Limburger were produced in Wisconsin, and cheddar was produced in New York.

Yet today, cheese makers have nearly unfettered access to the specialized equipment and molds and cultures needed to produce any type of cheese; the boundaries that once kept cheeses regionalized no longer exist. This has resulted in what cheese authority Liz Thorpe notes is a significant blurring of and riffing on tradition where Old World meets New. And though technology has increased our access to supplies, one of the most enjoyable parts of cheese making is decidedly unmodern: you still can't rush cheese. It slows down the pace of daily life by requiring our attention and patience; waiting is essential to its success.

Knowing this, I should not be surprised that my joyful journey to writing this book has taken fifteen years in the cheese world, organizing culinary tours to various farms and creameries, teaching cooking classes using artisan cheeses, and sharing the hand-crafted babies of passionate artisan producers in Northern California. These award-winning craftspeople inspire me, and their dedication has shaped my career and provided motivation for writing this book.

But maybe the most generous educator is cheese itself. Each time I make cheese, the process teaches me something valuable. I can also say to you, with certainty, expect the unexpected. Cheese making is an unending learning process, even for those who do it daily. My job in this book is to demystify and simplify that process enough that you can confidently venture forth into this exciting, mystical world. Once your hands are on the wheel, the road to proficiency is simple: keep making more cheese and joyfully share it!

In addition to the more than eighty tested cheese making formulas, I have included two dozen savory and sweet recipes inspired by the ethnic or cultural origins of the featured cheeses—the Mediterranean, Northern Africa, India, and Latin and North America. Helpful at-a-glance charts, worksheets, guides for aging, and steps for making your own versions of new artisan cheeses can be found on this book's companion website, www.artisancheesemakingathome.com.

I encourage you to visit my blog, *Artisan Cheese Making at Home* (http://homecraftedcheese.com), so that together we may share updates, discussions, recipes, new developments, and discoveries. Now, let's get started on this magical journey!

A note on the photography: All of the cheeses photographed for this book by the gifted Ed Anderson were made either by me or by my team of skilled hobbyist cheese heads. Additional photos were taken by me on field trips to cheese makers and in my home cheese making kitchen. Most of the cheeses are perfectly beautiful; some are less so. I hope showing them to you warts and all proves a valuable tool for gaining knowledge of what transpires (even unexpectedly) in the cheese making process. Trust me, even the ugly ducklings can be delicious! The breads in the photographs are courtesy of Della Fattoria, Petaluma, California.

Young Buttermilk Blue at 4 weeks (page 180)

CHAPTER 1
Cheese Making Basics
Equipment, Ingredients, Processes, and Techniques

Curds draining on rack prior to applying designated pressure (see Halloumi, page 70)

Though there are more than two thousand varieties of cheese hailing from ethnic cultures around the world, on the most basic level cheeses all rely on the same components: milk, starters (whether naturally occurring bacteria or starter cultures), coagulants (such as rennet), and salt.

The process always begins with milk. Then either natural bacteria start to work on the milk, or a starter culture is added. These act on the milk sugar (lactose), converting it to lactic acid. A coagulant is then added to this hospitable environment, causing the milk protein casein to curdle, or coagulate, forming a solid mass of curds. From there, the curds are cut into a specific size, depending on the style of cheese being made. Then they are stirred, drained, and salted; molded or pressed; and, finally, ripened or aged. Voilà: cheese, in all its variety.

In my beginning cheese making class, we start with simple fresh cheeses as the first step in demystifying how cheese happens. Queso blanco (page 38), for example, is a very simple cheese made with whole cow's milk and coagulated with vinegar. The milk is heated to a specific temperature, then the acid (vinegar) is added and stirred to distribute. Like magic, curds begin to appear from the depths of the white liquid. Suddenly, with only a little stirring, there are fluffy curds floating in clear, yellowish whey. Drain the curds and toss them with salt, and you've got cheese. Queso blanco is not complex in terms of flavor, but its simplicity demonstrates the fundamental action that takes place in transforming milk into cheese. Not all cheeses are formed as easily, but by following the steps and stages presented in this book, you'll gain a rounded understanding of how cheeses of varying degrees of complexity stem from this common foundation.

Building Your Skills: The Habits of Successful Cheese Making

This book is structured to let you develop your skills progressively. We'll start with the easiest fresh cheeses and add complexity from there. If you are a beginner, I encourage you to start at the beginning and build your skills as you go, because the key to successful cheese making is to start with small, manageable steps. With each success, you'll want to make more cheese. As you develop your skills and gain an understanding of and level of comfort with the cheese making process, you will build your repertoire on a solid foundation. Be patient. You may be successful the first time you make a cheese, but then again, you may not be. It takes time to master the skills; however, even mistakes can be delicious!

Here are some practices and habits of mind that will help you succeed, whatever your level of cheese making experience.

1. Make Small Batches

Regardless of which cheese you are attempting, make an amount that you have the equipment to handle and the room to ripen, and that you can store and consume within a couple of weeks of its readiness. By making small batches, you have the opportunity to make and taste a variety of cheeses rather than a larger amount of only one. The cheese making recipes presented in this book are geared for small batches, using mostly 1 or 2 gallons of milk. As a general rule, 1 gallon of milk yields 1 pound of firm or hard cheese and up to 2 pounds of fresh cheese. Note that all the yields for the cheeses are approximate.

As I worked on this book, I often had a dozen different cheeses ripening in my cheese refrigerator "cave" at any given time. I worked in small batches, and because the cheeses were aged for different amounts of time, at least one of them was always ready to taste and enjoy. This may be too complicated an undertaking for beginners, but for me it was a perfect arrangement.

2. Set Your Expectations

Before you jump in to make any given cheese for the first time, familiarize yourself with what that cheese *looks* like and, better still, what it *smells* and *tastes* like. It's important to have a frame of reference for the cheese you are trying to create before you make it, and with such a wealth of information available, both from reference works like this one and from your own senses as you taste and smell a sample, there's no need to work in the dark. Taking a photograph of the sample cheese before you taste it will guide your endeavors.

3. Plan and Prepare

Wouldn't you love to make cheese once a week or twice a month and have that to share with family or friends? Once you become proficient, you can make not just one but two or three cheeses in the same session, especially if they are cheeses of the same style. That's an efficient use of your time, and it allows you to make enough cheese for your own use and some to age or share. Here are some basic steps to help you manage the project and be successful, whether you are making one cheese or several:

- Plan ahead. Some cheeses can be ready in an hour, while some need a 6-month lead time and lots of attention. Determine a realistic scope of work.
- Have your work space, equipment, and tools prepped and sanitary before you begin.

- Keep a notebook to record your thoughts and observations. This is a great catchment system for valuable information that you can apply to subsequent cheese making sessions or use in problem solving. Detailed checklists, worksheets, guides, and observation forms are available for download on this book's companion website at www.artisancheesemakingathome.com.

4. Keep It Safe and Sanitary

When using your kitchen to make any food, but perhaps especially cheese, it is imperative to ensure your space is safe to work in (no clutter or pets around) and is sanitary. While bacteria is part of cheese making, it needs to be the right kind! Don't try to cook anything else while making cheese. This can lead to cross contamination and also distract your attention from the cheese.

Before you begin:

- Sanitize your work station with a commercial cleaner or a bleach-water sanitizing solution of 2 tablespoons household bleach dissolved in 1 gallon of water.
- Keep a roll of paper towels within reach and a small trash receptacle next to it.
- Sanitize your cheese making pots, equipment, and utensils before and after using. To sanitize properly, wash with hot soapy water, rinse with water, then rinse again with 2 tablespoons household bleach dissolved in 1 gallon of water. Allow to air-dry on a rack set on a sheet pan rather than in your dish drainer to minimize contact with bacteria.
- Consider using dedicated plastic buckets as your sanitary curd-draining "sinks."
- Keep two clean cotton kitchen towels handy, one for laying out your working tools on and one for drying your hands.
- Do not wear any fragrance while making cheese, as it masks your ability to use your sense of smell to guide the process.
- Wash your hands thoroughly before starting and after handling any nonsterile items.

Equipment and Supplies

When you're getting started, you can take much of your basic equipment from your existing kitchen arsenal of pots, colanders, measuring cups, measuring spoons, whisks, rubber spatulas, ladles, and slotted spoons. Once you are totally immersed in making cheese in your own kitchen, you may want to put pots aside that are dedicated to this function. Think of cheese making in the same way you would canning. Equipment set aside for that purpose is always easier to keep stored, clean, and collected.

Before making any cheese in the book, first read the recipe carefully and collect and sanitize all needed equipment. I have noted in the body of each formula which specialty equipment is needed, but will count on your having the following foundational supplies in your kitchen. If you are using specialty equipment or dedicated utensils and make cheese often, store them in a lidded box to protect them from dust and keep them ready for your next session.

The basic equipment and supplies you'll need for nearly all the cheeses in this book include:

- Butter muslin (4 to 6 yards) and cheesecloth (4 to 6 yards)
- Colander or strainer (made of plastic or another nonreactive material) for draining curds
- Curd cutting knife or 10-inch cake decorating spatula
- Cutting boards or cheese boards: food-grade boards to fit draining trays
- Disposable vinyl or food-service gloves
- Draining bowl or bucket: a large, nonreactive, food-grade vessel for catching up to 2 gallons of whey
- Cheese mats (plastic): to drain molded curds
- Draining rack: nonreactive material, to sit inside draining tray
- Draining trays: food-grade plastic trays or rimmed quarter-sheet or half-sheet baking pans
- Flexible wire stainless steel whisk with a long handle

Improvising Cheese Draining and Shaping Equipment

Be inventive and recycle other food containers to drain and shape your curds. Some produce containers already have drain holes or slots and function quite nicely for draining curds. Prepared foods sometimes come in containers with interesting shapes. The shape of cut-off flat-bottomed plastic milk containers works for some cheeses (use them in place of square molds of about the same size). These you'll need to punch with drain holes, but it's worth the (mimimal) effort.

Cheesecloth and Butter Muslin

Both cheesecloth and butter muslin are necessary supplies in cheese making. Butter muslin has a tighter weave than cheesecloth and is my choice when draining curds, especially small ones, since the goal is to capture as many curds as possible in that cloth. Cheesecloth works well for lining cheese molds, bandaging cheese, and covering air-drying cheeses and can be made into sacks for smoking cheese. Think about the properties of the cloth (open or tighter weave) and apply those in choosing the better cloth for the task at hand.

You can reuse cheesecloth and butter muslin. In fact, once-used pieces are even better than new ones, because the weave will become tighter once the cloth is used or washed, so the cloth will be able to capture curds more efficiently.

To care for your used cloth, first rinse out any curd residue in clear water. Then wash by hand in warm soapy water and rinse thoroughly in water to remove any detergent. As a final step, rinse in a sterilizing solution to remove any residue. To make the solution, in a glass jug or food-grade plastic container with a lid, mix 2 tablespoons each of household bleach and distilled vinegar into 1 gallon of cool tap water. Pour whatever amount you are going to use into a stainless steel or glass bowl and rinse the cloth. Air-dry the cloth, then fold and store it in a resealable plastic bag. Storing cheesecloth in one bag and butter muslin in another keeps things simple. It is also a good idea to keep the cloths batched by milk type and style of cheese they were used on.

- Flexible blade rubber spatulas
- Instant-read kitchen or dairy thermometers
- Ladle or skimmer (stainless steel or other nonreactive material) for removing curds from whey
- Molding and shaping devices (see below)
- Paper towels
- Ripening boxes: food-grade storage boxes with lids
- Spoons: large nonreactive metal, wood, or plastic spoons for stirring; one slotted and one not
- Stainless steel pots: a 6-quart pot for working with 1 gallon of milk; a 10-quart pot for working with 2 gallons; a 12-quart pot for making a water bath for indirect heating
- Stainless steel measuring spoons that include the very important ⅛ teaspoon
- Wrapping materials: resealable bags, plastic wrap, and aluminum foil
- Weights: such as foil-wrapped bricks, heavy skillets, or empty milk containers filled with water (see page 22)

For a number of the formulas, you will also need the following:

- An atomizer or fine spray bottle: used for spraying mold solution on surface-ripened cheeses
- A cheese press (see page 21): 2-gallon capacity
- Cheese wax (see page 28)
- Heat-resistant waterproof gloves of rubber or neoprene: used for handling hot curds for stretched-curd cheeses
- Hygrometer: a tool for measuring relative humidity; very helpful for monitoring the environment in which cheeses ripen
- pH strips or pH meter: used to measure the acidity of curds in some recipes, especially stretched-curd cheeses
- Specialty wrapping materials: cheese paper

MOLDING, SHAPING, AND PRESSING DEVICES

Most of the cheese recipes in this book call for particular cheese molds, in which the curds are drained and shaped before aging. Like any cookware, these require a small investment, but with proper care they will last well past your cheese making lifetime. As you begin to make cheese, I recommend you first get a sense of the styles of cheeses you prefer making. You can build your collection of molds as you go, and you can find a more comprehensive list of molds and photos of these molds on this book's companion website at www.artisancheesemakingathome.com.

For fresh cheeses, you can buy a few reusable (but called disposable) ricotta baskets from cheese making suppliers for only a few dollars. Recycled plastic berry and tomato baskets also work well for some fresh cheeses. Once you are established in and committed to your cheese making, invest in a few shapes of professional molds that can be used for making a number of different cheeses. These molds include a 4-inch-diameter Camembert mold with a follower (a snug-fitting plug or cap inserted into a cheese mold on top of the curds), a 5-inch-diameter tomme mold with a follower, a crottin mold, and a chèvre mold. Purchase two of any of these configurations to be able to make batches larger than 1 gallon or two cheeses at once. Dedicate a lidded plastic tub to house your collection and keep the molds protected from dust.

Other molds used in this book include:

- 8-inch-diameter Brie mold with a follower
- 4-inch-square mold with no bottom
- Saint-Maure or bûche (log) mold with no bottom
- Saint-Marcellin mold with a rounded bottom
- 7-inch-square, 5-inch-high Taleggio mold with no bottom
- 8-inch-diameter tomme mold with a follower
- Truncated pyramid mold with no bottom

Firm and hard cheeses also require a period of controlled pressing to expel whey and compact the curds. For this process, it is preferable to use a dedicated cheese press—one that you purchase or build. However, you can also use weights to improvise a cheese press (see pages 21–22).

Many plans and schemes for improvising cheese pressing equipment can be found online, but a specially designed mechanical cheese press is beneficial for creating the highest-quality firm or hard cheeses, because it distributes the pressure evenly and consistently onto the curds. If you make hard cheese regularly, a press will be worth the investment. One of my favorite presses is the Schmidling Cheesypress; other favorite cheese presses are available from the Beverage People, or you can purchase plans for building your own press from New England Cheesemaking Supply (see Resources).

Ingredients: The Building Blocks of Cheese

As with all foodstuffs made with a very few ingredients, the quality and characteristics of the ingredients of cheese are very important. In fact, getting the ingredients right not only makes the difference between a good cheese and an unappealing one, but also determines whether crucial cheese making processes work at all.

It all starts, of course, with milk.

MILK

Milk possesses a unique protein structure that enables coagulation, which allows for the preservation of milk as a food source in the form of cheese. Understanding the components of milk and how they behave is critical to understanding the process of coagulation. Milk is composed of water; proteins, including caseins; lactose, or milk sugar; and milk fat (also known as butterfat), those lovely taste globules that contribute so much to your cheese's final flavor. Because milk is the primary ingredient in cheese, choosing high-quality producers and buying as close to the source as possible will help ensure a great final product.

The primary animal milks used for cheese making come from cows, goats, sheep, and water buffalo (although water buffalo's milk is rather difficult to obtain and is not featured in this book). However, the type of milk used for cheese making does not determine the style of cheese; in fact, all of these varieties of milk are used for all styles of cheese. That said, there are general differences among the milks produced by different animals. Cow's milk is sweet, creamy, and buttery, with a fat content of 3.25 percent by weight. Goat's milk has a tangy, citrusy, almost barnyard quality with a slightly higher fat content than cow's milk. Sheep's milk is the richest, at 7.4 percent milk fat by weight, appears golden and oily, and has a gamey flavor. The milks always have a fuller flavor when the animals are fed their natural diet.

Nearly all the cheeses in this book call for cow's milk, goat's milk, or a combination of the two. Sometimes sheep's milk is given as an alternative. If you have a reliable local source, give it a try with the needed adjustments, described below.

Milks can be substituted in the formulas, though adjustments to the amount of coagulant (rennet) may be necessary. You may wish to test the formula as written before making any milk substitutions. The textures and yields of the cheeses will differ from one milk to another. Goat's milk, having smaller fat particles than cow's or sheep's milk, will produce smaller and softer curds. Sheep's milk will produce a higher yield than the other two milks. If you are substituting sheep's or goat's milk for cow's milk, reduce the amount of rennet by 10 to 15 percent. If you are substituting cow's milk for goat's milk, increase the amount of rennet by 10 to 15 percent.

Whether you are working with raw or pasteurized milk (see page 10), find a reputable source for locally produced, high-quality milk. Once you have a source you like for making cheese, stick with it. Always read the labels for processing procedures and sell-by dates, and always buy the freshest milk available and keep it refrigerated at 40°F. Avoid milks or creams that have stabilizers or thickeners added,

Pasteurizing Your Own Milk

If you are able to attain raw milk, you can use a hot water bath and an ice bath to safely pasteurize your milk at home.

Put the milk in the top of a stainless steel double boiler or nonreactive pot. Fill the bottom of the double boiler with water or fill a larger pot with a few inches of water and insert the smaller pot into it. Insert a thermometer into the milk and gently heat the milk to 145°F over the course of no less than 30 minutes, cover, then hold that temperature for 30 minutes. Immediately put the pot of milk into an ice bath to chill rapidly. Keep it in the ice bath until the milk temperature registers 40°F to 45°F. This milk will keep for up to 3 weeks in the refrigerator. It is critical that you follow this procedure precisely. If too little heat or too little time is applied, the possible undesirable pathogens in the raw milk may not be totally destroyed, making the milk unsafe to consume. If too much heat is applied or if the milk is held at temperature for too long, the desirable flora and the proteins in the milk needed for cheese making may be destroyed.

Cow's Milk and Milk Fat

The cow's milks called for in this book range in fat content from skimmed (nonfat) milk to heavy cream:

- Nonfat or skimmed milk: 0 to 0.5 percent milk fat
- Low-fat milk: 1 percent milk fat
- Reduced-fat milk: 2 percent milk fat
- Whole milk: 3.25 percent milk fat
- Half-and-half: 10.5 to 18 percent milk fat
- Light whipping cream: 30 to 36 percent milk fat
- Heavy cream: 36 to 40 percent milk fat

as these additives can inhibit proper coagulation and curd development.

The way milk is processed can have profound impacts on how well it's suited to cheese making and on the characteristics of the cheeses you make from it. By familiarizing yourself with milk processing terms and ingredients, you can better understand their effects on the milk and, in turn, on the cheese.

RAW Raw milk is milk that has not been processed at all; as such, it contains all of its natural bacteria and flavorful flora, resulting in cheeses with more complex and layered flavors than those made with standard pasteurized milks. Of benefit in cheese making, raw milk will curdle and separate if left at room temperature, as lactic bacteria in the air will produce a culture. Thus, when you're using raw milk, the amount of starter culture needed may differ, and the character of raw milk cheese will therefore differ from that made with pasteurized milk that has been inoculated only with laboratory-produced cultures.

If using raw milk, observe a few precautions. Unless you know your animal, pasteurize raw milk to kill any harmful pathogens before consuming (see sidebar); however, it can safely be used to make cheese if the cheese is aged to 60 days or more. Raw milk will keep about a week; note it also will not be available to many cheese makers, as it is illegal for sale in a number of states. Where legal, look for local cow or goat herd shares (see Resources).

PASTEURIZED If you're not using raw milk, this is the best choice for cheese making. Pasteurized milk will coagulate better than homogenized milk, and will in fact curdle and separate if left at room temperature, as lactic bacteria in the air produce a culture in the milk. Pasteurization destroys dangerous pathogens, including salmonella and *E. coli*. However, it also destroys, to a degree, vitamins, useful enzymes, beneficial bacteria, texture, and flavor.

HOMOGENIZED This milk has been processed to break up the fat globules and force them into suspension in the liquid. Meant to prohibit the separation of milk and cream, this process changes the molecular structure of the milk and renders it incapable of producing a culture if left out at room temperature. Homogenized milk sours more quickly than nonhomogenized milk.

PASTEURIZED AND HOMOGENIZED Most milk available at retail is in this form. Some calcium chloride and valuable bacteria are destroyed with each of these processes (homogenization and pasteurization) and in cheese making must be replaced with added calcium chloride and bacteria. In the recipes in this book, it is assumed that the milk used is pasteurized or both pasteurized and homogenized; if you are using raw milk, you may omit the calcium chloride called for in the ingredient list.

ULTRA-PASTEURIZED (UP) OR ULTRA-HIGH TEMPER-ATURE (UHT) These milks are exposed to extreme heat and cold shock processes to denature the milk to the point that it is shelf stable, allowing it to last longer in transport to the market as well as in the dairy case. Unfortunately, this process is used for many organic milks because they are purportedly more fragile to transport and may sell more slowly at retail. Ultra-pasteurized milk and cream do *not* work at all for setting proper curds in making cheese and are to be avoided. Ultra-pasteurized milk is heat-treated to 191°F for at least 1 second and ultra-high temperature milk has been heat treated to 280°F for 2 seconds. Then both are instantly stored at cold temperatures (40°F) for a prolonged time.

STARTER CULTURES

Starter cultures (starters) are specifically chosen bacterial cultures that are added to warmed milk to start the process of cheese making by acidifying the milk, creating the proper environment for the cultures to grow and flavor to develop. This process of acidification is called ripening the milk, and it includes controlling ripening time and temperature to increase acidity. Different strains of bacteria in a given culture contribute specific flavors, textures, and aromas to the final cheese. One culture might help produce holes or "eyes" in one cheese, for example, while another culture would encourage buttery flavors.

There are two basic types of working cultures responsible for converting lactose into lactic acid, with the main difference being the optimum temperature at which they work. Mesophilic cultures have an optimum temperature of 86°F and a working range of 68°F to 102°F, while thermophilic cultures have an optimum temperature of 108°F to 112°F and a working range of 86°F to 122°F. Within these types of cultures, there are different bacterial strains that work at moderate to rapid rates of acid production.

All of these bacteria are currently isolated in pure form by culture-producing labs for sale to cheese makers. Before making a cheese in this book, look at the ingredient list to ascertain which types of starter or secondary cultures are required. In creating the formulas for this book, I chose specific cultures that I trust and that are readily available in small quantities from cheese making supply companies (see the chart on pages 12–13 for cultures used and the Resources section for suppliers). For detailed information on the various starter and secondary cultures used in this book, refer to the more comprehensive cultures chart online at www.artisancheese-makingathome.com. As you gain experience, branch out and try variations on these cultures to produce your own unique results, keeping in mind that it is always advisable to use as little starter culture as is necessary to make a cheese successfully, instead extending the ripening time, just as a baker might use longer fermentation to develop flavor and structure instead of rushing the process with too much yeast. Less is more.

SECONDARY CULTURES: MOLDS AND BACTERIA

Most frequently used in bloomy-rind and washed- or smeared-rind cheeses, secondary cultures are bacteria, molds, and yeasts that act in the cheese ripening phase. The veins of mold and the distinct flavors of a blue cheese are caused by secondary cultures, as is the fuzzy white rind on a Brie. These cultures are either added directly to the milk, added between layers of curds, or sprayed or rubbed on the surface of the cheese as it ripens. In washed-rind cheeses, the ripening cultures are also rubbed onto the surface of the rind periodically as the cheese ages. Many cheeses utilize a combination of secondary cultures and enzymes. Flavor-enhancing bacteria such as *Propionibacterium shermanii* are also useful as ripening cultures.

CULTURES CHART

Cultures are classified based on their temperature of growth, flavor, and acid production features. Culture companies put together specific blends depending on the style of cheese being made. Most of the blends are standard and can contain anywhere from two to six different types (strains) of cultures in varying ratios. Below, you will see some cultures listed that contain the same strains of bacteria; however, those cultures are not identical. They each have a different ratio or percentage of strains based on the desired results.

Note these important reference terms regarding cultures: **Acidifier:** lactic acid producer; **Proteolysis:** an important process that refers to the breakdown or fermentation of milk proteins; **Proteolytic (protein-degrading) enzymes:** contribute to development of desirable flavor and texture in virtually all aged cheeses; **Diacetyl:** a fermentation compound that contributes a desirable buttery aroma to a cheese; **Gas production:** refers to cultures that produce CO_2.

Culture name	Type	Active ingredients	Suppliers	Notes and uses
Meso I	Mesophilic starter culture	*Lactococcus lactis* ssp. *lactis*	Glengarry Cheesemaking and Dairy Supply	Low level acidifier. Cheddars and Jacks.
Meso II	Mesophilic starter culture	*Lactococcus lactis* ssp. *cremoris*	The Beverage People, Glengarry Cheesemaking and Dairy Supply	Salt sensitive. moderate to high acidifier with no gas or diacetyl production. Brick, Brie, Camembert, Cheddar, Colby, farmer's cheese, Jack, stretched-curd cheeses, Parmesan, Provolone, Romano, and some blue cheeses.
Meso III	Mesophilic starter culture	*Lactococcus lactis* ssp. *lactis* *Lactococcus lactis* ssp. *cremoris*	The Beverage People, Glengarry Cheesemaking and Dairy Supply	Moderate to high acidifier with no gas or diacetyl production. Creates a clean flavor and very closed texture, and is proteolytic during aging. Edam, Gouda, Havarti.
MA 011	Mesophilic starter culture	*Lactococcus lactis* ssp. *lactis* *Lactococcus lactis* ssp. *cremoris*	Dairy Connection, Glengarry Cheesemaking and Dairy Supply, New England Cheesemaking Supply	Moderate to high acidifier with no gas or diacetyl production. Creates a clean flavor and very closed texture, and is proteolytic during aging. Cheddar, Colby, Monterey Jack, feta, chèvre.
C101	Mesophilic starter culture	*Lactococcus lactis* ssp. *lactis* *Lactococcus lactis* ssp. *cremoris*	New England Cheesemaking Supply	Premeasured blend used in a variety of hard, moderate temperature cheeses including cheddar, Jack, Stilton, Edam, Gouda, Munster, blue, Colby.
MM 100	Mesophilic starter culture	*Lactococcus lactis* ssp. *lactis* *Lactococcus lactis* ssp. *cremoris* *Lactococcus lactis* ssp. *lactis* biovar. *diacetylactis*	Dairy Connection, Glengarry Cheesemaking and Dairy Supply, New England Cheesemaking Supply	Moderate acidifier with some gas production and high diacetyl production. Brie, Camembert, Edam, feta, Gouda, Havarti, and other buttery, open-textured cheeses, including blue cheeses and chèvre.
MA 4001 Farmhouse	Mesophilic starter culture	*Lactococcus lactis* ssp. *lactis* *Lactococcus lactis* ssp. *cremoris* *Lactococcus lactis* ssp. *lactis* biovar. *diacetylactis* *Streptococcus thermophilus*	The Beverage People, Dairy Connection, Glengarry Cheesemaking and Dairy Supply, New England Cheesemaking Supply	Moderate acidifier with some gas and diacetyl production; similar to the bacteria balance in raw milk. Creates a slightly open texture. The culture used for most types of cheese. Caerphilly, Brin d'Amour, Roquefort.
Aroma B	Mesophilic starter culture	*Lactococcus lactis* ssp. *lactis* *Lactococcus lactis* ssp. *cremoris* *Lactococcus lactis* ssp. *lactis* biovar. *diacetylactis* *Leuconostoc mesenteroides* ssp. *cremoris*	The Beverage People, Dairy Connection, Glengarry Cheesemaking and Dairy Supply	Moderate acidifier with some gas production and high diacetyl production. Cream cheese, crème fraîche, cottage cheese, cultured butter, fromage blanc, sour cream, Camembert, Havarti, Valençay.

Culture name	Type	Active ingredients	Suppliers	Notes and uses
C20G	Mesophilic starter culture	*Lactococcus lactis* ssp. *lactis* *Lactococcus lactis* ssp. *cremoris* *Lactococcus lactis* ssp. *lactis* biovar. *diacetylactis* Rennet	New England Cheesemaking Supply	Premeasured blend chèvre starter containing rennet. Used for making chèvre and other fresh goat cheeses.
Thermo B	Thermophilic starter culture	*Streptococcus thermophilus* *Lactobacillus delbrueckii* ssp. *bulgaricus*	The Beverage People, Dairy Connection, Glengarry Cheesemaking and Dairy Supply	More proteolytic than *S. thermophilus* alone. Italian-style cheeses including mozzarella, Parmesan, Provolone, Romano, and various soft and semisoft cheeses.
Thermo C	Thermophilic starter culture	*Streptococcus thermophilus* *Lactobacillus helveticus*	The Beverage People, Dairy Connection, Glengarry Cheesemaking and Dairy Supply	Used in Italian and farmstead-type cheeses. More proteolytic than *S. thermophilus* alone. Emmental, Gruyère, Romano, Swiss.
Bulgarian 411 yogurt starter	Nondairy culture	*Streptococcus thermophilus* *Lactobacillus delbrueckii* ssp. *Bulgaris*	The Beverage People	For making yogurt.
Brevibacterium linens	Secondary culture	*B. linens*	The Beverage People, Dairy Connection, Glengarry Cheesemaking and Dairy Supply, New England Cheesemaking Supply	High pH is required for growth of this bacteria. Used to create red or orange rinds on smeared-rind or washed-rind cheeses including Muenster.
Geotrichum candidum	Secondary culture	*G. candidum*	The Beverage People, Dairy Connection, Glengarry Cheesemaking and Dairy Supply, New England Cheesemaking Supply	Rapid-growing mold that prevents unwanted mold growth in moist cheeses, for use in cheeses made with *P. candidum* or *B. linens*. Several varieties are available. Geo 13 produces intermediate flavors, Geo 15 is mild, and Geo 17 is very mild.
Penicillium candidum	Secondary culture	*P. candidum*	The Beverage People, Dairy Connection, Glengarry Cheesemaking and Dairy Supply, New England Cheesemaking Supply	Produces fuzzy, white mold on the surface of bloomy-rind cheeses including Brie, Camembert, Coulommiers, and a variety of French goat cheeses. Various strains are used to produce a range of flavors from mild to very strong. Strains available include ABL, HP6, Niege, SAM3, and VS.
Penicillium roqueforti	Secondary culture	*P. roqueforti*	The Beverage People, Dairy Connection, Glengarry Cheesemaking and Dairy Supply, New England Cheesemaking Supply	Creates colored veins and surfaces and is a major contributor to flavor in blue cheeses including Gorgonzola, Roquefort, and Stilton. Various strains are used for a range of colors, with variations of gray, green, and blue. Strains available include PA, PJ, PRB18, PRB6, PV Direct, and PS.
Propionic bacteria	Secondary culture	*P. shermanii*	The Beverage People, Dairy Connection, Glengarry Cheesemaking and Dairy Supply, New England Cheesemaking Supply	Used for eye formation, aroma, and nutty or buttery flavor production in Swiss-type cheeses.
Choozit CUM	Yeast	*Candida utilis*	Glengarry Cheesemaking and Dairy Supply	Acid neutralizer. Moderate aroma development. Promotes surface and interior growth.

COAGULANTS

Whereas starters acidify the milk, coagulants are used to solidify the milk protein (casein) and form the curds. Coagulants work in concert with bacteria, temperature, and time to curdle, or coagulate, ripening milk. The most basic cheeses use coagulants you probably already have in your home, such as lemon juice or vinegar; these coagulants work at high heat, as do citric acid and tartaric acid. Other coagulants—chiefly rennet—work as the milk is kept at a moderate temperature for an extended period of time.

Animal rennet (containing the enzyme rennin, or chymosin) is naturally found in the stomachs of calves, kids, or lambs, with calf rennet used most often. It is generally recognized that calf rennet produces superior aged cheeses, and for many cheese makers it is their rennet of choice. It is the only animal rennet a home cheese maker will need (see the sidebar for vegetarian options), and is available from cheese making suppliers (see Resources).

Rennet comes in liquid or tablet form. Liquid rennet is easier to measure, dissolve, and distribute into the milk than tablets, and the recipes in this book call for it. Half a tablet is equivalent to ¼ teaspoon of regular-strength liquid rennet; to use tablet rennet, crush the tablet and dissolve in the same amount of water called for in the recipe. Liquid rennet often comes in double strength, so read the label to know the ratio of dilution needed. Rennet should always be diluted in nonchlorinated water because chlorine will kill the enzyme and make it ineffective. Liquid rennet will keep for 3 months, refrigerated. Tablets may be stored in the freezer for up to 1 year.

SALT

Salt is a key ingredient in cheese making, added for a number of reasons. It is a natural antibacterial, preservative, desiccant, and flavor carrier and enhancer. In cheese making it improves the draining of the curds, adding body to them; it controls moisture; it controls undesirable bacteria and nurtures the growth of desirable bacteria; it contributes to surface dehydration and rind formation; it deactivates the

Vegetarian Cheese

There are a number of coagulation options available to you if you desire to create a cheese where milk is the only ingredient sourced from an animal. Vegetable rennet is extracted from a variety of plants (such as thistles, nettles, fig bark, fig leaves, and safflower seeds) and is almost as powerful as animal rennet (see Resources). It can be used in any cheese.

Microbial or fungal rennets are made from the fermentation of fungi or bacteria, most typically the mold of *Rhizomucor miehei*. This rennet is often the choice when making a cheese to be labeled "vegetarian."

cultures and stops the acidification process; it slows the aging process so cheese can be held long enough to develop the desired texture; and it enhances the inherent flavors by affecting the formation of flavor compounds in the cheese.

Coarse noniodized salt is used in cheese making and is almost always introduced into the process after the whey is drained and at the beginning of or during the ripening process, depending on the style of cheese. Cheese salt is available from cheese supply companies; for the recipes in this book you may also use Diamond Crystal brand kosher salt or fine or flake sea salt. Never use iodized salt.

WATER

Water is integral to nearly every cheese in this book. It's used to dissolve coagulants and other additives, like rennet and calcium chloride, and it's used to make the brine in which many of the cheeses spend some time. It's also used to wash curds in a number of recipes. Always use cool (50°F to 55°F) nonchlorinated water to dissolve rennet, calcium chloride, or other additives to ensure their effectiveness, as chlorine not only has an undesirable flavor and odor, but will also make a coagulant ineffective. Bottled or filtered water is your best option for all applications other than for rinsing curds.

However, if the only water available is chlorinated tap water, boil it first, cool to 50°F to 55°F, then use at the temperature designated in the recipe.

CALCIUM CHLORIDE

Pasteurization and homogenization change the structure of milk, removing some of the calcium and destabilizing it slightly. When using any milk that is not raw milk to make cheese, add calcium chloride to increase the number of available calcium ions and help firm up the curds. Calcium chloride is added to the milk before the coagulant. Purchase calcium chloride from a cheese making supplier (see Resources) and store it in the refrigerator according to the supplier's directions, generally up to 12 months.

LIPASE POWDER

Lipase is an enzyme found in raw milk; it is often added in powder form to processed cow's milk to impart a stronger, tangy flavor to the cheese along with a distinctive aroma. It is used in two degrees of potency: Italase (calf enzyme), considered mild, and Capalase (goat enzyme), considered sharp. When used in combination with certain cultures, the resulting cow's milk cheese mimics the rich flavor of a sheep's milk cheese. If using, add lipase powder to the milk before adding the rennet. It can be purchased from cheese making suppliers (see Resources) and should be stored in the freezer and used within 12 months.

VEGETABLE ASH

Also sometimes called activated charcoal, the finely ground powdered ash used in cheese making is a food-grade charcoal available from cheese making suppliers (see Resources). It is mixed with salt and sprinkled or rubbed on the surfaces of some soft cheeses (primarily goat) to encourage desirable mold growth and discourage unwanted bacteria. The ash neutralizes the surface acidity, allows moisture to be drawn out, protects the exterior, firms up the cheese, and allows the interior (paste) to ripen and stay soft.

Because ash is very messy to apply and stains on contact, use disposable gloves and work carefully. Transfer some of the ash powder to a dedicated salt shaker and add the amount of salt called for in the recipe you are using. To apply ash, place the cheese in the bottom of a plastic tub and sprinkle the surface to be coated with the ash and salt, patting with your hands to distribute and adhere the mixture to the surface of the cheese. Clean the ash from the tub using soapy water and repeating as necessary to remove any oily residue.

ANNATTO

Annatto is a dark orange natural food coloring product derived from the seeds of the achiote tree. In its liquid form it is added to cheddars and other cheeses to create their orange color and is also used in washes to create a blush on the surface of some cheeses. Liquid annatto can be purchased from cheese making suppliers (see Resources) and should be stored in the refrigerator and used within 12 months. Ground annatto seed and achiote paste can be found in the spice section of many supermarkets, or in Latin American or Caribbean markets.

HERBS AND SPICES

There's a world of culinary herbs and spices that can be used to flavor or add color to cheeses. They are best used in their dried form in flavor-added pressed or aged cheeses, but fresh herbs are also wonderful tossed into the curds or rolled on the exterior of fresh cheeses. As with any ingredient, you want to make sure they are free of pesticides, dirt, and other contaminants. If you are unsure of the source, first boil the herbs or spices in nonchlorinated water for 5 minutes, then let drain and cool on paper towels before adding to the curds.

Processes and Techniques

In this section, I'll walk you through the basic processes and techniques of cheese making—and some more advanced techniques as well. The formulas for individual cheeses will teach variations on these techniques, but the same basic set of processes applies across the spectrum of cheese making, from the simplest fresh cheeses to the fussiest long-aged washed-rind cheeses. These are preparation; ripening milk; coagulation and curd finishing; draining, shaping, and pressing; salting; drying; affinage, or cheese ripening; and storage. These processes can overlap and even swap places in the order of cheese making steps, depending upon the cheese.

Here you will find descriptions of basic processes and specific instructions for the techniques that make up those processes, like cutting curds or controlling the humidity in a cheese ripening box.

PREPARATION

In cheese making, preparation has two components. The first involves reading the recipe through carefully and familiarizing yourself with any terms or techniques that aren't familiar to you. If it's a cheese you haven't tried before and you don't already have an extensive collection of molds and starter cultures, it may involve ordering some equipment and supplies. Think about timing, too: the creation of a cheese requires performing a series of tasks over a period of hours or days, and ripening tasks can require you to focus on the cheese for weeks or months.

The second part of getting ready involves assembling your equipment, ingredients, and supplies and making sure everything is squeaky clean. Cheese making involves manipulating the microbial content of milk, and your chances of getting a successful result will be aided greatly if you eliminate undesirable microbes from the cheese making environment before you start. Sterilize all your equipment before you use it. Wipe everything else, including work surfaces, with bleach solution or a commercial sterilizing spray, then rinse thoroughly with very hot water to wash away any residue of the bleach or other cleansing chemicals. Air-dry everything rather than wiping it with a cloth, and use clean kitchen towels. Always wash your hands well before you touch your equipment or ingredients, or your curds or cheese (or you may like to use disposable food preparation gloves instead).

Whichever pieces of your equipment are solely for cheese making (as opposed to being taken from your usual kitchen equipment) should be sterilized and air-dried before you put them away. If possible, store them all together in one place—a lidded box is perfect—so they're collected with easy access when you need them next.

Keep good records of each session using the charts and forms available on my website (www.artisancheesemaking athome.com), such as Planning Your Cheese Making Session Checklist and the Cheese Making Form. Set up a binder for collecting these forms.

Keep a notebook or cheese journal to record your thoughts and observations. This is a great system to retain valuable information that you can apply to other sessions or consult to seek out needed answers.

RIPENING MILK

For every recipe in this book, the first step is to prepare the milk for acidification by warming it to a specified temperature. The general range is from 86°F to 92°F, though some cheeses will require a temperature outside of this range. A slow, steady increase in temperature is crucial to proper milk ripening: too much heat too fast can destroy the proteins you are depending upon to build your curds and can create a hostile atmosphere for the microflora you're trying to foster.

At the beginning of the cheese making process, start with milk that has been removed from refrigeration and left at room temperature (68°F to 72°F) for 1 hour. Place the milk in the pot and slowly raise the temperature to the specified level before adding the culture or acid coagulant.

Always begin with a sterilized, nonreactive stockpot or pan equipped with a dairy thermometer. For many cheeses, the milk is heated directly and slowly over low heat until the desired temperature is reached. Most of the recipes in this book instruct you to heat the milk directly in this manner. A good general rule to follow for slowly heating milk over low, direct heat is to raise the milk temperature 2°F per minute. For example, if the milk is 50°F when added to the pot and the specified temperature to reach before adding the culture or bacteria is 86°F, it should take no less than 18 minutes to reach temperature.

But sometimes it's desirable to heat the milk indirectly, using a water bath. This slows the ripening time, heats the milk evenly, and prevents the milk from scorching. If your stove burners are not easily kept at a very low heat, you may prefer using this indirect method instead. When heating milk in a water bath, the time needed to reach temperature can be reduced by half because the water bath is 10°F warmer than the milk temperature you need to reach, and the milk pot is warmed from the bath, heating the milk more quickly yet more gently and evenly than over direct heat.

Technique: Making and Using a Hot Water Bath

To make a water bath, nest a 4- to 10-quart stockpot (depending on the quantity of milk you are heating) inside a larger pot and pour water into the larger pot to come as far up the side of the smaller pot as the milk level will be (for example, if you are heating 1 gallon of milk in a 6-quart pot, the water should come two-thirds of the way up the inner pot). Remove the smaller pot and place the larger pot over low heat. When the water reaches a temperature 10°F warmer than you want the milk to be, put the smaller pot back in the water to warm slightly, then pour the milk into the smaller pot and slowly warm to temperature over the period of time specified in the recipe. If the milk is heating too fast, adjust the burner heat, add cool water to lower the water bath temperature, or remove the pot of milk from the water bath.

Maintaining Milk Temperature

In different phases of cheese making you will allow the mixture to sit while maintaining the milk at a particular temperature. There are several ways to accomplish this:

- In order to best maintain the temperature of milk or curds, use the water bath method to heat the milk. The residual heat will dissipate more slowly.
- Always cover the pot.
- Use ceramic-coated cast-iron Dutch ovens or stockpots; these hold the heat better and longer than stainless steel pots.
- If using a stainless steel heavy-bottomed pot, also use a cast-iron simmer plate to maintain heat.
- A towel wrapped around the sides of the pot will help hold in the heat.
- If temperatures under 95°F are required, setting the pot under the light of your stove hood should be sufficient to maintain the temperature.
- If you live in a very cool or cold environment, place the pot on a warmed heating pad to maintain the needed temperature.

Adding Starter Cultures

Time, temperature, and microbial action are the keys to successfully ripening or acidifying the milk in preparation for proper curd formation. For most cheeses, this involves the addition of one or more starter cultures (see page 11). After the milk has reached its proper ripening temperature, a small quantity of powdered culture is sprinkled over the milk's surface and allowed to rehydrate for 5 minutes before being incorporated throughout the milk using a whisk in an up-and-down motion from top to bottom of the pot. This technique is a valuable one: using an up-and-down rather than a circular motion draws the additives down into the milk for more even distribution. It also allows the milk to settle in a shorter period of time and contributes to a more even consistency in the developing curds. Note that if a mold such as *Penicillium candidum* is to be introduced to the curds, it's usually added at the same time as the starter culture and incorporated along with the culture.

Technique: Whisking in Starter Cultures and Other Additives

After adding any culture or coagulant to the milk, mix well, using a long-handled whisk in an up-and-down motion at least twenty times, or for the time period specified in the recipe. At a minimum, rennet should be stirred in using an up-and-down motion for 30 seconds to fully distribute it throughout the milk.

COAGULATION AND CURD FINISHING

The ripened milk begins its turn toward becoming recognizable cheese when a coagulant is added and the milk coagulates or curdles, separating into liquid whey and solid curds. Most cheeses use rennet (either animal or vegetable rennet) as a coagulant (see page 14), while direct-acid cheeses use lemon juice, vinegar, citric acid, tartaric acid, or even buttermilk. All coagulants are incorporated with a whisk using the same up-and-down motion used to stir in starter cultures (see above). If calcium chloride, lipase, or certain flavorings or colorings are to be added to the milk, they're stirred in before the rennet, using the same technique. Then, usually, the pot is covered and the milk is left at a specific temperature for a specific period of time until the curds and whey have separated from each other and the curds are firm and give what is called a clean break: when cut with a knife, the cut is clean and not soft or mushy, and some clear whey accumulates in the cut. This means the curds are ready to be cut and finished or washed if necessary, and then drained.

Technique: Testing for a Clean Break

Using a sanitized long-blade curd cutting knife (or 10-inch cake decorating spatula, chef's knife, or bread knife—anything with a blade long enough to reach to the bottom of the pot), make a short test cut at a 45-degree angle and observe the firmness of the curds. If the cut edge is clean and there's some accumulation of light-colored whey in the cut area, the curds are ready to be cut into their proper size. If the cut edge is soft and the curds are mushy, the curds are not ready. Allow them to sit 15 minutes longer before testing again.

Cutting Curds

Curds are cut into varying sizes, from slabs down to rice-size pieces, depending upon the style and desired moisture content of the finished cheese. Larger pieces retain more whey, resulting in a moister cheese. Smaller pieces expulse more whey, resulting in a drier cheese.

Technique: Cutting the Curds

To cut the curds into uniform pieces (rather than into the large slices or slabs suitable for some soft cheeses), use a 10-inch cake decorating spatula or curd cutting knife to make vertical cuts of the designated size all the way down through the curds from surface to bottom. Repeat this across the entire mass of curds. Turn the pot 90 degrees and repeat the process to create a checkerboard of square, straight cuts. Then, using the straight cuts as a guide, cut down through the curds at a 45-degree angle, from one side of the pot to the other. Then turn the pot 45 degrees and make angled cuts down through the curd, working in diagonal lines across the squares of the checkerboard. Turn the pot 45 degrees two more times for two more sets of angled cuts. You will now have cut the curds in six directions total: two vertical and four at a 45-degree angle. Your goal is to cut them quickly and with as much uniformity as possible throughout.

Using a rubber spatula, gently stir the curds to check for larger curds below those at the surface. Cut any larger curds into the proper size.

When making some soft-curd cheeses, after the curds form a solid mass in the pot, gently cut ½-inch-thick slices of the curds using a ladle or skimmer and gently place them in a strainer or layer them in a cheese mold as directed.

Cooking the Curds

After they're cut, the curds often need to be cooked, or alternately be very, very gently stirred and then be allowed to rest while at a rather higher temperature than they were kept at during coagulation. This process expulses whey from the curds, allowing them to shrink a bit and firm up, and keeps them from matting together. It is important in establishing the texture of the finished cheese. It also affects the acidity of the curds, which in turn impacts the flavor of the finished cheese, which will be bland with too little acid and bitter with too much. So it's important to carefully follow directions for temperature and timing for this process. At the end of the cooking process, the cut curds have typically sunk in a mass to the bottom of the pot, with the whey floating above them.

Alternatively, the curds may be washed, if that's necessary to create the cheese they're destined to become, or they may simply be ready to drain. Washing curds reduces the lactose level of the finished cheese, making it less acidic, with a smooth texture and a mild flavor. (Gouda is an example of a washed curd cheese.) It is usually done by replacing some of the whey with water that's either warmer or cooler than the whey (the temperature affects the moisture level of the curds and thus the final texture of the cheese) and alternating gentle stirring and resting to firm the curds.

Or the curds may be set; that is, transferred after a cooking period to a lined colander and immersed in ice water to halt development.

Left: Cutting curds; Center: Checking for uniform curd size;
Right: Stirring the curds to expel whey and prevent matting

DRAINING, SHAPING, AND PRESSING CURDS

When the cooked or washed curds are sitting at the bottom of the pot covered with whey, the excess whey is sometimes ladled out to expose the tops of the curds, which affects the temperature and the acidity of the curds. Any removed whey can be used for another purpose—the most common being as part of the brine used for that given cheese or as the foundation for making Whey Ricotta (page 41). Then the curds are very gently transferred to a cloth-lined strainer or colander, or directly into lined or unlined molds or the barrel of a cheese press, to drain. Curds may be drained entirely in molds, or they may be drained first in a colander or draining sack, then transferred to molds for further draining and shaping and, in the case of firm and hard cheeses, pressing.

Draining, molding, and pressing curds are all processes to expulse more whey and knit the curds together in a solid, whole cheese. As such, these processes have a great impact on the final texture and other characteristics of a cheese.

....

Left: Gently spooning curds into strainer; Center: Draining curds in a colander; Right: Draining curds in a sack

Technique: *Draining Curds in a Colander*

Place a plastic or mesh strainer over a bowl or plastic bucket large enough to capture the whey. Line the strainer with clean, damp butter muslin or cheesecloth and gently ladle the curds into it. Let the curds drain for the time specified in the recipe. Discard the whey or reserve it for another use.

Technique: *Making and Using a Draining Sack*

Line a colander with damp butter muslin and gently ladle the curds into it. Tie two opposite corners of the butter muslin into a knot close to the surface of the curds and repeat with the other two corners. Slip a dowel or wooden spoon under the knots to suspend the bag over the whey-catching receptacle, or suspend it over the kitchen sink using kitchen twine tied around the faucet.

Technique: *Draining Curds in a Mold*

Line the mold with damp butter muslin and set it on a rack over a baking sheet or other draining tray. Gently ladle the curds into the mold and let drain for the time specified in the recipe. At the specified time, lift the sack of curds from the mold

and place on a clean cutting board. Open the sack, gently lift the cheese, flip it over, and return it to the cloth. Redress and return to the mold. Place back on the draining rack and continue to drain as instructed in the recipe.

For some mold-ripened cheses, use this method of draining in a mold: Set a draining rack over a tray or baking sheet, put a cutting board on the rack and a cheese mat on the board, and, finally, place the mold or molds on the board. Ladle the curds into the cheese mold (or molds) and let drain for the time specified in the recipe. Then place a second mat and cutting board over the top of the mold. With one hand holding the board firmly against the mat and mold, lift and gently flip the bottom board and mat with the mold over and place it back on the draining rack. The second board and mat will now be on the bottom, and the original mat and board will be on top. Continue draining as instructed in the recipe.

Left: Placing partially drained curds in a mold; Center: Gently pressing down curds; Right: Covering curds with tails of cloth

Pressing Cheese

Compressing the curds in a press releases moisture, helping create a smooth interior texture (paste) and smooth rind in firm and hard cheeses. A mold or press is lined with cheesecloth and filled with curds. The tails of the cloth are folded over the top of the curds, and a follower—a piece of wood or plastic that fits inside the mold or press and covers the whole surface of the curds—is inserted. The follower distributes the force of the press evenly over the curds, helping the final cheese achieve uniform shape and texture. Whey runs out of the bottom of the mold or press, which typically has a draining tray or other means of catching the whey.

The amount and duration of pressure is determined by the style and size of the cheese and the desired final texture of the cheese. For the purposes of cheese making, pressure is measured in pounds per square inch (psi) of the surface area. This pressure can best be obtained by using a cheese press, which is designed to apply a specified amount of pressure. However, cheese can be successfully pressed at home using any number of simple weights (see below). The formulas in this book specify the amount of weight needed, not the pressure or psi. It is expressed like this: "press with 5 pounds for 15 minutes." Typically, light pressure or weight is applied at

first, and then the pressure is increased as the curds expulse more whey and become firmer and more cohesive.

Partway through the pressing process, the cheese is flipped one or more times. It's removed from the mold or press, unwrapped from its cloth, turned over, and redressed in the same cheesecloth before being returned to the mold for more pressing. Flipping helps make the cheese uniform in texture and shape. If you encounter a recipe for a firm or hard cheese that has no instruction for how much pressure should be applied, here is a general rule you can follow with success: Apply enough pressure to compress the curds into a smooth surface without squeezing the curds out. Press until the whey stops draining. Or you can lightly press for 1 hour at 8 to 10 pounds, then flip, redress, and apply medium pressure overnight at 20 to 30 pounds of pressure. Then flip, redress, and press for 8 to 12 hours at the same pressure.

There are a number of simple weights for pressing that you can create from your home kitchen. Water-filled milk containers or buckets and other pantry items will work for the home-batch quantities of cheese presented in this book. Be resourceful with what you have available, but consider the size and shape of the weight or container to ensure the weight will stay put. Here are some examples:

LIGHT PRESSURE: 5 TO 10 POUNDS
- A jar (2 cups) of tomato sauce = 15.5 ounces—about 1 pound
- 1-quart plastic milk container filled with water = 2 pounds
- Marble mortar (without the pestle) = about 2½ pounds
- A brick = 4 to 5 pounds
- ½-gallon plastic milk container filled with water = 4 pounds
- 1-gallon plastic milk container filled with water = 8 pounds

MEDIUM PRESSURE: 11 TO 20 POUNDS
- A cement block = 10 to 20 pounds

HEAVY PRESSURE: 21 TO 40+ POUNDS
- 5-gallon bucket filled with water = 40 pounds

How to Use Whey

Whey may be saved and reused in a number of practical and tasty ways. Because it is acidic, it can sour fairly quickly, so it should be refrigerated within 2 to 3 hours. It can be frozen and used within a couple of months. It makes terrific soup stock, it can be all or some of the liquid for cooking beans or rice, and it is fun to use when making bread. If you raise pigs, feed it to them; they'll love you forever. Additionally, whey can be fed to acid-loving plants, such as tomatoes.

Technique: Filling a Cheese Mold or Press for Pressed Curds

Ladle the curds into a mold or press lined with a single layer of damp cheesecloth and use your hands to distribute the curds evenly; pull up on the cheesecloth to eliminate any folds. Smooth out the top tails as best you can to prevent indentations in the surface of the cheese. Excess tails of cloth can be cut off to ensure a smoother surface. Gently press down on the curds with your hand to close up some of the gaps; if left, gaps are not only unattractive but are likely homes for unwanted bacteria and mold; exceptions to this process include both Stilton (page 190) and Cabra al Vino (page 157), where gaps are part of their craggy style. Place the follower on top of the wrapped cheese in the press and press according to the recipe and the press manufacturer's instructions.

Technique: Flipping Cheese During Pressing

Partway through the pressing period and as specified in the recipe—usually soon after the curds are solid enough to be handled without falling apart—lift the cloth-covered cheese from the mold, unwrap it, turn it over, redress it in the same cloth, and return it to the mold, so that the surface of the cheese formerly on top is on the bottom.

Technique: Cheddaring

In the process known as cheddaring, warm curds are drained over heated whey to further expel whey from the curds and knit them together to form a slab. The slab is then carefully milled, or cut into uniform pieces or broken into small chunks, without removing any whey. The milled curds are then salted and placed in the mold or press and are flipped at least one time during pressing to create an even shape.

SALTING

Salt—usually coarse salt, and always uniodized salt—is a crucial element of cheese making (see page 14). There are two basic methods of adding salt to a cheese: dry salting, which can happen before or after pressing, after the curds have been drained; and brining, which typically happens after the curds have been drained and shaped. Dry salting and brining are often used in combination.

In addition to adding flavor to cheese, salt aids in rind development, which is necessary to allow the interior, or paste, to ripen properly. During brining or surface dry salting, salt dissolves into the moisture at the surface of the cheese, and water is drawn to the surface and evaporates, leaving behind a layer of dehydrated cheese, which is the rind. In semisoft, firm, and hard cheeses, the rind acts as a barrier protecting the paste development, and it also influences what can grow on the surface. On surface-ripened cheeses, dry salting promotes the growth of desirable microorganisms needed for ripening, and some of the salt passes into the cheese as well.

The thickness and strength of the rind can be controlled by the brining conditions and the humidity and temperature during and after dry salting. Hard-rind cheeses are kept at a lower humidity (85 to 90 percent) after salting to allow moisture to evaporate more quickly, leaving a layer of rind behind. The application of salt to the exterior of the cheese is repeated until the desired firmness of rind is achieved. Soft-rind cheeses are kept at a high humidity (95 percent) after salting to prevent too much evaporation and rind formation, and to allow desirable bacteria and molds to grow and migrate into the cheese.

Too much salt can inhibit bacteria growth and slow down the ripening process, and too little salt can allow unwanted bacteria to grow. This delicate balance takes time and skill to master. The information here is based on guidelines used by professional cheese makers. However, I often make adjustments to brine strength, the duration of brining, or the amount of salt rub when using other cheese makers' or my own formulas, using my experience as a guide. After testing a few recipes that call for brining or salting, you may choose to make adjustments as well, based on your own growing body of experience.

Technique: Dry Salting

Sprinkling salt directly on the cheese, referred to as dry salting, can occur before or after pressing, depending upon the cheese. The curds should be between 87°F and 92°F at the time of salt application; this helps some of the salt penetrate the interior of the curds. If you are tossing curds with salt, divide the salt into two or three batches and gently toss the curds after each addition for uniform salt distribution.

Here are some general rates of dry salting:

- 1 teaspoon per 3- to 4-ounce cheese, sprinkled evenly on top and bottom of the cheese
- 1½ teaspoons per 8- to 10-ounce cheese, sprinkled evenly on top and bottom of the cheese
- 2 teaspoons per 14- to 16-ounce cheese, sprinkled evenly on top and bottom of the cheese
- 1 teaspoon per 1-gallon batch of milk for dry salting cheddar curds

Flavored salts (smoked, herbed, porcini, lavender, green tea, and even chocolate, for example) and various fleur de sel from all over the world can be used to dry salt cheeses with amazing results (see Honey-Rubbed Montasio, page 130).

Technique: Brining

Most firm and hard cheeses are salted using brine, with cheddar as one notable exception. A brine can be flavored with spices, beer, ale, wine, or spirits and can be applied either by soaking certain cheeses or as a wash that is rubbed or brushed onto a cheese's surface to flavor its exterior and develop its rind. Bacterial brines or surface-ripening solutions of varying formulas listed in the recipes are washed or sprayed on certain surface-ripened cheeses to promote the growth of surface bacteria. Some cheeses, such as feta, are salted and then preserved in brine. For those just starting to make rinded cheeses, you may fear the brining process will create an overly salty finished product. However, at that point the salt has only begun to make its contribution and will dissipate with time; let the salt do its job.

To make brine, dissolve salt thoroughly in cool water, cover, and chill to 50°F to 55°F before using. Keeping the brine at this temperature throughout the brining process aids in uniform salt absorption and optimum rind formation. The cheese should be brought to the same temperature as the brine beforehand, with some exceptions; for example, Gouda and feta are placed in the brine directly after pressing, while still warm. Unripened stretched-curd cheeses like mozzarella may be cold brined (below 50°F) to cool them quickly and help them avoid excessive moisture loss.

Use a nonreactive container and make enough brine to surround the cheese and allow it to float. As a rule of thumb, 3 to 4 quarts of brine will float two 2-pound cheeses and will fit into a container that's of a manageable size. All cheeses should

BRINE CHART

Simple brine

2 percent salinity: 1 1/2 teaspoons salt to 1 cup water, cooled to 55°F
Used as a wash.

Light brine

10 percent salinity: 13 ounces salt to 1 gallon water
Used to flavor soft or stretched-curd cheeses (like mozzarella or bocconcini) that stay in a lightly salted solution for a short period of a few hours to a few days before consumption.

Medium brine

15 percent salinity: 19 ounces salt to 1 gallon water
Considered a pickling brine used for a salty profile. A cheese such as feta or Halloumi may be stored in this brine after a short time in saturated brine.

Medium-heavy brine

20 percent salinity: 26 ounces salt to 1 gallon water
Used to preserve cheese and add distinct salty flavor.

Near-saturated brine

22 percent salinity: 28 ounces salt to 1 gallon water
Used for firm, hard, and washed-rind cheeses to draw in salt, draw out moisture, and set up rind development.

Saturated brine

25 percent salinity: 32 ounces salt to 1 gallon nearly boiling water; some salt will remain undissolved
Used for firm, hard, and washed-rind cheeses to draw in salt, draw out moisture, and set up rind development; excessive moisture may be lost too quickly at this level if brined for too long a time; some cheese makers prefer to use the 22 percent level.

be turned over at least once during the brining time indicated to ensure even salt intake and evaporation.

Brine can be kept and reused for up to 1 month if filtered of solids. If it exceeds 55°F for any length of time, make a fresh batch to ensure maximum effectiveness.

DRYING

All cheeses other than fresh cheeses benefit from some degree of air-drying before they enter their ripening stage. In soft cheeses, a degree of drying sets the surface of the cheese, allowing it to hold its shape in preparation for the next stages of ripening. In semisoft, firm, or hard cheeses air-drying is essential in setting the surface of the cheese, preparing it for rind development and aging.

Technique: Air-Drying

After draining in a mold or brining, place the cheese on a mat or rack set over a baking sheet, loosely cover with cheesecloth, and air-dry at room temperature (68°F to 72°F) until the surface is dry to the touch—usually no less than 6 hours and up to a couple of days—before placing it in its ripening box or cave. A fan can be used to improve air circulation and inhibit mold growth.

Soft-ripened cheeses are dried in a well-ventilated room for 1 to 3 days, ideally at 58°F to 60°F with 85 percent relative humidity (RH). These conditions help ensure the drying process does not happen too quickly, which could cause the surface to crust and inhibit even ripening. With soft cheeses, the way to check for satisfactory dryness is to press the cheese with your finger. If the cheese is resilient and keeps its shape, it is dry enough. At this point the cheese is ready for final ripening.

RIPENING OR AGING

Ripening the cheese—also called aging or affinage—is the final, and for many cheeses the most critical, step of the cheese making process. It involves holding a cheese for a designated period of time to develop its flavor, texture, and final personality. A controlled combination of temperature, humidity, and air circulation is needed for the proper ripening of any given style of cheese.

For the home-based cheese maker, this important final stage can also be the most challenging. The cheese will indeed ripen, but not always at the pace or with the results anticipated. Ripening can oftentimes be difficult and frustrating to manage and, with some cheese making episodes,

result in disappointment. The road to success takes time and practice. This is where the craft of cheese making takes its place alongside the science. Refer to the companion website www.artisancheesemakingathome.com for aging charts by style of cheese.

If the cheese didn't come out the way you intended, a valuable lesson has been presented. Maybe you really *enjoyed* the problem cheese. In that case, you've discovered a new one. But whether you found the cheese enjoyable or unappealing, you can analyze both the results and the steps you took to arrive at it to help you make adjustments for the next time you attempt that cheese. Be sure to keep good notes of what you did and when and how you did it every step of the way in making the cheese, and refer to the troubleshooting guide on pages 32–33 to help figure out what may have gone amiss. For a sample cheese making form, refer to www.artisancheese makingathome.com.

I describe here the general environment and equipment you will need for proper and successful ripening; specific cheese formulas have more precise instruction.

Technique: Controlling Unwanted Growths

Mold and bacteria *will* grow on your cheeses. During the ripening process the surface will show a bit of fuzz or become slightly slimy from bacteria. Any black fuzz, blue or greenish molds, or yellow-colored growth other than what is described in the development of the surface is undesirable. What do you do? Remove it by rubbing with a small piece of cheesecloth dipped in a vinegar-salt solution (a 1-to-1 solution of distilled vinegar and salt), then wiping clean with a piece of washed, dry cheesecloth. Hand wash and rinse out the cheesecloth, dry, and store in a jar in refrigeration along with your stored washes and brines. Reuse this rag for the same function.

Ripening Boxes

Used to provide the perfect controlled environment for ripening, a ripening box can be as simple as a food-storage vegetable keeper with adjustable vent holes, though there is a dedicated box called the Cheese Saver that works well for small wheels of cheese and for storing cheeses (see Resources).

As a general rule, choose a ripening box that's more than twice as big as the cheese it will contain to provide for good air circulation and inhibit mold. You will also need a rack or tray on which the ripening mat and cheese can sit for drainage and a piece of moistened natural sponge or paper towel to introduce moisture as a humidity contributor.

Understand that this ripening system has many variables. It is up to you to monitor the progress of the ripening. Being able to properly ascertain by sight, smell, and touch what is going on with the cheese takes practice. Use your senses from the very beginning, and you will learn from each session.

Technique: Using a Ripening Box

Insert the rack or tray into your box. Place a small bowl with a chunk of natural sponge in the box at one end and add just enough water to wet the sponge. This will contribute humidity. Place the cheese on a mat set on top of the rack, then loosely cover the box for the first few days of ripening; this helps keep the humidity in check—you want it just right. Once whey stops draining from the cheese, secure the lid. As the cheese ripens, open the box daily to provide for air exchange and to wipe out any moisture from the inside surfaces of the box. A small bowl of salt placed inside the box can also act as a desiccant. The air should be moist; the cheese should not be. If it is, wipe any excess moisture from the cheese and the box and adjust the lid for more air circulation and to adjust the humidity.

Ripening Caves

Ripening rooms or caves with controlled conditions are used by professional cheese makers, but a temperature- and humidity-controlled refrigerator or wine cooler works just fine. Even home basements or protected corners of garages can be outfitted to function as ripening "caves."

To dedicate a home refrigerator to cheese ripening, retrofit it with a hygrometer to help you maintain a given temperature and humidity. You can also adjust humidity more simply by lining a sheet pan with a kitchen towel and filling it with water, then placing it in the fridge. I have found that this method increases the humidity enough to support the needs of cheeses in their individual ripening boxes. I keep track of the temperature and humidity inside my cheese refrigerator with a wireless device that tells temperature and relative humidity.

Note that unless you are ripening cheeses of the same type outside of individual boxes, needing the same temperature and humidity within this regulated space, you will most importantly need to carefully monitor the humidity within each ripening box—that is the more critical environment to manage.

You can also purchase a wine cellar refrigerator. They are manufactured to maintain the cellar temperatures needed for cheese making. Some even come with humidors. These are perfect ripening caves that need no reprogramming or additional attachments. You'll still need to use ripening boxes if you are aging more than one variety of cheese at the same time. Shop for these wine cellars at your local home improvement store.

Spirited Ripening

In addition to being dry salted or brined, some cheeses are soaked, washed, or rubbed with alcohol or wrapped in spirit-macerated leaves as a means of preservation, as a ripening vehicle, and as a flavor contributor. Armagnac, beer or ale, bourbon or other whiskeys, brandy, Calvados, cider, cognac, eau-de-vie, grappa, vodka, and walnut liqueur are the most widely used spirits, though flavored vodkas and nontraditional spirits can be used as well. See O'Banon (page 60), Lemon Vodka Spirited Goat (page 163), and Époisses (page 166) for examples of cheeses washed in spirits or wrapped in spirit-macerated leaves. The sidebar on page 59 gives instructions for using leaves—macerated or otherwise—to wrap cheeses for ripening.

Smoking

Low-temperature cold smoking (50°F to 60°F) is used for cheeses because the goal is not to cook or melt the cheese; the smoke acts as a flavoring. The smoke evaporates moisture, causing the milk fat in the cheese to rise to the surface. When combined with the smoke, the milk fat forms a thin skin on the surface, which acts as a preservative. The smoke just kisses the exterior of the cheese but does not infuse it and will not impart much if any color to the surface of the cheese.

Stovetop wok-smoking Scamorza (page 88)

Many smoked cheeses available at retail have a darkly colored rind and an overpowering smoked flavor due to liquid smoke being added to the curds in the cheese making process or rubbed onto the rind. You can try this method on your hand-crafted cheeses, but I strongly suggest the superior and more delicate flavor cold smoking achieves. Mozzarella, Scamorza, cheddar, Provolone, Gruyère, and Gouda work best for smoking: look for several of these and other smoked variations in the following chapters.

Woods used to smoke cheese often reflect the local region and terroir; however, any of the readily available aromatic fruit woods and nut woods (or shells) will impart light flavor and work well for smoking cheese: apple, cherry, peach, pear, citrus, fig, grape, plum, almond, pecan, or walnut. Avoid woods that impart intense flavor, such as hickory, mesquite, and oak. Tea can also be used to smoke cheese (see page 103).

Technique: Smoking Cheeses

Dry the cheese, uncovered, in the ripening cave or ripening refrigerator overnight. Before smoking, bring the cheese to room temperature, making sure it keeps a dry surface.

Using an outdoor smoker, wood-burning oven, bamboo steamer and wok (see page 103), or other smoking device, smoke the cheese, monitoring and maintaining the temperature carefully so that the cheese does not melt. A pan or pie tin of ice water slightly smaller in diameter than the smoking rack or steamer should be placed between the smoke source and the cheese. The pan of water acts as a barrier to the heat and keeps the cheese cool enough to absorb the smoke properly without melting.

Cheese will take only 1 to 2 hours to take on the smoking flavors of the aromatic fuel of choice, though some old-world cheeses such as ricotta affumicata (see page 40) are hung in cheesecloth to smoke for multiple days. Once the surface of the cheese has absorbed the desired amount of smoke, remove from the smoker and cool to room temperature, then wrap in cheese paper or vacuum seal and refrigerate. Smoked cheeses can be kept for up to 3 months or more.

Waxing, Cloth Bandaging, and Vacuum-Sealing

Waxing and cloth bandaging are two methods used for protecting a cheese from unwanted bacteria and mold while it's ripening. Wax is typically applied to cheeses that age for a few months, such as Gouda, while cloth bandaging is used with cheeses such as cheddars that age for several months up to several years. Vacuum-sealing functions as airtight protection on cheeses that are either partially ripened and awaiting finishing at a later time, or are finished.

Waxing is traditionally used for firm, semihard, and hard cheeses as a protective casing and ripening enclosure. It is an alternative to developing a natural rind when the needed environment for natural rind ripening is not available or long-term aging is the goal. Cheese wax is a reusable, food grade paraffin–based product that acts as a mold deterrent. The wax both creates a barrier against undesirable bacteria and protects the cheese against drying out.

The waxing process entails two steps. First, a coating of one or two layers of liquid wax is applied directly to the dry rind of the cheese to protect it from the penetration of unwanted molds. When this is set, a layer of hard cheese wax is added.

Hard cheese wax typically comes in 1-pound slabs, enough for double coating three 2-pound cheeses. Liquid wax or "coating" comes in a 500-gram jar, enough for double coating ten 2-pound wheels. Any leftover hard cheese wax (wax that was melted but did not end up coating the cheese) can be saved and used later. Place bits of wax in a resealable bag and store in a cool place. When ready to use, just melt it and strain it through butter muslin to remove any unwanted particles. Add new wax as needed.

Use disposable materials when waxing—gloves, plates, paper towels—to make cleanup easier. If you need to remove spilled wax, it is best to let the wax fully harden and then scrape it off with a butter knife. Use a dedicated pastry brush for waxing. After applying the wax, wipe the brush clean of any residual wax on a dry paper towel. Any wax that remains on the brush will harden but will melt away when placed in hot wax the next time. Any equipment that is used for liquid wax should be washed right away with warm, soapy water. Don't put any wax down the drain of your sink, as it will damage the plumbing.

Technique: Waxing Cheese

Refrigerate the cheese overnight before waxing. Working over a paper plate, apply liquid wax to the cooled cheese in a thin coating using a pastry brush or your fingertips, alternating sides as the coating dries. Place on a rack to dry. The coating will take 1 to 2 hours at room temperature to set up, at which point you may handle the cheese.

Refrigerate the cheese to set the wax coating. While in this environment, the waxy membrane will allow some of the cheese's moisture to evaporate, creating the desired flavor and texture. Turn the cheese every day for 5 to 7 days prior to hard waxing.

One hour prior to dipping in the hard wax, the coated cheese should be left at room temperature. Place 2 to 3 ounces of hard cheese wax in a stainless steel bowl sitting in simmering water. As the wax melts, ensure the depth of the liquefied wax is approximately half the diameter of the cheese. It's best to melt slightly more wax than you think you will need.

Hold one side of the cheese and dip half of the cheese directly into the melted wax for 2 seconds. Take the cheese out of the melted wax and allow the wax to harden for about 30 seconds, then flip and repeat with the other half of the cheese. Place the waxed cheese on a sheet of parchment paper to cool. Use a dedicated pastry brush dipped in melted wax to touch up any exposed areas. Write a label for your cheese and affix it to the waxed surface with a dab of melted wax.

Note: You may choose to bypass the liquid wax stage and go straight to the hard wax layer, though the liquid wax coating will better protect the cheese from any air holes that may develop in the hard wax.

Cheesecloth bandaging or wrapping has traditionally been used on cheddars for assisting in their rind formation and in creating their unique texture and flavor profile. The entire surface of the pressed cheese wheel is first rubbed (larded) with a thin coat of butter, lard, or vegetable shortening as a deterrent to excessive mold growth. The wheel is then carefully wrapped with two layers of cheesecloth, larding again between the layers. The cheesecloth is pressed against the cheese, adhering to the coating as a protective barrier. Mold then grows on the cloth instead of on the cheese, and the cheese underneath is prevented from drying out while allowing it to develop flavor to its fullest potential. After ripening, the bandage is removed and discarded.

Cloth bandaging allows the cheese to breathe, releasing moisture and concentrating the flavor, and produces a drier, flaky texture under the natural rind. Though not traditional, this same technique can be applied to other hard cheeses to create a protective casing and ripening enclosure. Bandaging works especially well if your cellar or basement maintains a temperature of 55°F to 60°F and 65 to 75 percent humidity. Follow the humidity guidelines stated in each recipe.

Technique: Bandaging Cheese

Lay out a four-layer-thick square of cheesecloth that's 2 inches larger than the wheel of cheese in all directions. Place the cheese in the center and, using clean kitchen scissors, cut around the wheel, leaving a 1 1/2-inch border. These rough circles will cover the top and bottom of the wheel. Cut or tear strips from a sheet of butter muslin to use as edge banding. They should be as wide as the thickness of the cheese and long enough to wrap around the circumference of it one and a half times.

Rub the cheese with a thin coat of your fat of choice and lay one cheesecloth cap on each end. Press the cap onto the surface, rub the area touching the cheese with more fat, and press the second

Left: Rubbing surface with butter; Center: Determining size of cheesecloth; Right: Rubbing cloth smooth on surface of cheese

circle of cheesecloth onto it. Rub the entire cloth circle smooth onto the surface of the cheese, then wrap the edge with the strips of butter muslin, covering the edges, pressing to affix, and smoothing as you lay it down. You want a smooth seal. Place the cheese in the ripening space for 3 to 6 months or the designated duration on your recipe.

Note: Some softer cheeses use cheesecloth or bands of lace around the edge to provide support as the cheese ripens. Examples include Serra da Estrela from Portugal and Torta de los Pedroches from Spain.

A home food storage vacuum-sealing system can be used very successfully for storing many styles of cheeses firm enough to withstand the pressure of the vacuum, primarily semifirm, firm, and hard cheeses. Unless they are first wrapped securely in materials forming a rigid barrier around the cheese (such as a wooden box), vacuum-sealing should not be used for soft cheeses.

This system can also be used to hold and store unfinished cheeses in refrigeration until a later date when they might be washed, rubbed, leaf-wrapped, or finished by any other method. The stage for vacuum-sealing the cheese is the same as for waxing the cheese: after air-drying.

STORING

Whether you make your own cheese or purchase cheese at its peak, eat it right away for fullest enjoyment. However, immediate consumption isn't always possible. Knowing that cheese is a living, breathing thing, you want to keep it alive and ripening (however slowly) in the best environment possible.

In general, an environment that is 45°F to 60°F and 80 percent relative humidity is best for storing most cheeses. If you don't have the ideal setting available, you do have options.

Storing your cheese in the vegetable drawer of your home refrigerator allows for its contents to share their moisture and create a more humid home for the cheese, and also protects cheese from the drying air circulating in the general refrigerator.

Beyond the home refrigerator, here are the best storing conditions, by style. Once you've begun making and ripening cheeses, you may have these environments already set up, or you may have the elements at hand for easy setup. If you have a cellar, wine cave, beverage cooler, or ripening refrigerator that can be used to fulfill these optimum conditions, by all means store your cheeses accordingly after properly wrapping (see page 29).

FRESH: 38°F to 40°F;
75 to 80 percent relative humidity

BLUES: 42°F to 46°F;
85 to 95 percent relative humidity

SOFT, RIPENED: 50°F to 52°F;
80 to 90 percent relative humidity

WASHED-RIND: 50°F to 55°F;
90+ percent relative humidity

HARD, AGED: 55°F to 60°F;
80+ percent relative humidity

General Guidelines for Wrapping and Storing Cheeses

All styles referred to here may be stored in the vegetable drawer of your refrigerator.

1. If a cheese comes packed in water or brine, leave it there. Water-packed cheeses are fresh and should be eaten within 1 week. Brined cheeses can be stored in their brine until it becomes a bit cloudy, at which point the cheese should be stored in a fresh light brine solution (see page 24). If a brined cheese is too salty for your taste, it can be rinsed in water to remove some of its salt and then packed in a light brine solution for up to 2 more weeks.

2. If a fresh cheese comes in a vacuum-sealed package, transfer it to an airtight container after opening.

What's a Mother Culture?

Much like a mother starter used for making bread, you can prepare a mother culture for cheese making that you replenish for ongoing use, using cow's or goat's milk. You can make either a mesophilic or thermophilic mother culture, though not all starter cultures will work for creating a mother that can be propagated from one batch to another. Ask your supplier for good choices. If properly attended to, a mother can be replenished and last up to 6 months.

The following method for making a starter culture is recommended for the most consistent and reliable results. The process is rather like canning jam and uses the same sanitation standards. Sterilize 1-quart jars and lids, fill them with milk to 1 inch below the rim, secure the lids, and submerge the jars in a warm water bath. Bring to a slow boil and boil for 30 minutes. Remove the jars and cool to 72°F for a mesophilic starter, and 110°F for a thermophilic one. Remove the lids and test the temperature with a thermometer. When the milk reaches temperature, add $1/4$ teaspoon of culture to each jar. Return the lids to the jars, gently agitate to incorporate the culture, and leave at a warm ambient temperature, 70°F to 72°F. The culture will ferment the lactose to lactic acid and the milk will thicken after 15 to 20 hours for a mesophilic starter, and 6 to 8 hours for a thermophilic starter. Refrigerate after the designated ripening time, or as soon as the milk has thickened to the consistency of pancake batter or thick yogurt. At this point it should taste acidic but slightly sweet. Use within 2 weeks, or within 3 days after the jar has been opened, or portion into 1-ounce cubes in sterilized ice cube trays, wrap, seal, and freeze for up to 1 month. Use to make a new batch of starter (2 ounces, $1/4$ cup, or 2 cubes per batch), or use 1 ounce or 2 tablespoons of this mother culture for every $1/4$ teaspoon of culture listed in a recipe to make cheese.

3. High-moisture cheeses should be wrapped in double-layer cheese paper (which is specially designed to allow the cheese to breathe freely; see Resources) or loosely wrapped in waxed paper, allowing the cheese to breathe, followed by a loose wrap of plastic to keep moisture in.

4. Place soft-ripened and surface-ripened cheeses, unwrapped, in an airtight container with a few holes poked in the lid to allow the cheese to breathe. If the cheese is firm, place a small damp wad of paper towel off to one side away from the cheese to create a small amount of humidity in the container.

5. Washed-rind cheeses are happiest wrapped in cheese paper and housed in boxes. If you have no box, wrap the cheese in waxed paper followed by plastic wrap.

6. For semifirm, firm, hard, and aged cheeses, wrap in waxed paper, allowing the cheese to breathe, then snugly in plastic wrap to keep moisture in. To best retain what little moisture a hard cheese has, wrap then place in an airtight container before refrigerating.

7. For classic blue cheeses, you want to keep them away from oxygen, which will promote more blue mold growth. If a blue cheese is stored in a home refrigerator at below 42°F, the blue mold growth will be retarded. After opening the cheese, rewrap with plastic wrap directly on the surface followed by tightly wrapped foil. If a purchased blue came in cheese paper, rewrap it in a clean piece of the same, then cover with plastic wrap.

TROUBLESHOOTING

We all encounter surprises when making cheese, not all of them ideal, though they do lessen with practice. I've listed below some of the most common issues that hobbyist cheese makers encounter, along with some remedies you might try. If you have a specific problem that you don't see here, visit my blog at homecraftedcheese.com. The experts will chime in as needed!

Problem	Possible reason	Action to try
Milk coagulates immediately.	Milk is too acidic due to too much starter after adding rennet or too lengthy ripening time.	Reduce starter next time or shorten ripening time.
Milk did not coagulate.	Milk is old or excessively heat-treated.	Change milks.
	Lactic bacteria is inactive.	Try fresh milk and starter.
	Too little rennet was used.	Use a few drops more next time.
No clean break achieved.	Needs longer ripening.	Ripen longer.
	Too little rennet was used.	Start over with a few drops more rennet.
	Outdated or inactive starter.	Use a fresh starter.
Curds too soft.	Needs longer ripening.	Ripen longer.
	Milk has been heat-treated at too-high temperatures.	Try other brands of pasteurized milk.
	Too little rennet was used.	Use a drop or two more next time.
	Not enough starter was used.	Add a pinch more next time.
Curds won't stretch.	The pH is not correct.	Watch for 5.0 to 5.2 pH. If too low, ripen longer but watch rise of pH. If too high, next time shorten ripening.
Curds are difficult to press.	Too much moisture lost in stirring or cooking curds, making them too dry to bind together in pressing.	Test curds for moisture during cooking.
Pressed curds show undesired cracks.	Pressure was not strong enough to press the curds together to remove spaces.	Increase pressure and pressing time.
Pressed cheese is growing undesired mold in crevices.	Pressure was not strong enough to press the curds together to remove spaces for mold to grow.	Increase pressure and pressing time.
Cheese surface is oily when air-drying.	Air-drying temperature is too high, bringing fat to the surface.	Place in a cooler environment (not exceeding 66°F).
Cracks appear in the rind while ripening.	Humidity is too low while air-drying.	Cover cheese with cheesecloth and air-dry on a rack with a bit of water below for added moisture.
	Temperature is too high while air-drying, removing moisture too quickly.	Place in a cooler environment (not exceeding 66°F) to slow down moisture release.
Finished cheese is too hard.	Too much rennet was used.	Use less rennet.
Finished cheese is too dry and crumbly.	Curds were cooked at too high a temperature.	Lower temperature by a few degrees next time. Check for rate of temperature increases.
	Curds lost too much whey or moisture.	Check curds for the correct texture.
Finished cheese has a rubbery texture.	Too much rennet was used.	Use less rennet.
	Too little lactic bacteria.	Remove less whey when washing curds or add less water when removing whey.
Finished cheese tastes bitter.	Too much rennet was used.	Use less rennet.
	Excessive acidity developed.	Reduce ripening time.
	Too little salt was added.	Add more salt.

Problem	Possible reason	Action to try
Finished cheese has little flavor.	Too much moisture in cheese; too much whey was trapped in the curds.	Cut the curds into smaller pieces.
	Curds heated too rapidly.	Raise the heat by only 2°F every 5 minutes.

FOR MOLD-RIPENED OR BLOOMY CHEESES

Problem	Possible reason	Action to try
Mold development takes too long to develop.	Ripening temperature was too low.	Raise the ripening temperature.
	Humidity was too low.	Increase humidity.
	Too much salt slowed development.	Reduce salt.
Pink mold on surface.	Too much moisture surrounding the cheese.	Give the cheese breathing space: use a larger box and wipe out moisture daily.
	Humidity too high.	Reduce humidity.
Dark brown or black mold on surface.	Too much moisture surrounding the cheese.	Rub the surface with the salt-vinegar solution to remove mold.
Rind is too thick.	Too much mold powder added.	Reduce the amount of mold powder used; add a pinch of *Geotrichum candidum.*
Finished cheese is too firm.	Too much whey expelled in stirring.	Reduce the amount of stirring.
Finished cheese is too runny.	Too much moisture left in the curds.	Stir longer to release more whey.
Finished cheese ripened too quickly.	Too much moisture left in the curds.	Stir longer to release more whey.
	Temperature too high in the ripening area.	Reduce the temperature to slow down ripening.

FOR WASHED-RIND CHEESES

Problem	Possible reason	Action to try
Rind is sticky.	Too much humidity or too little air space in the ripening area.	Reduce humidity; rub off the surface with a dry cloth or dry rub with salt to remove sticky surface.
Rind is too thin and doesn't hold its shape.	Not brined long enough or not air-dried long enough.	Extend brining time or air-drying time.
	Humidity in the ripening area is too high.	Reduce humidity.
	Rind washing leaves the surface too wet.	Dry-rub the surface or wring the rag dry of solution before rubbing.
Cheese is soft before end of ripening period.	Too much moisture is left in the curds.	Stir longer or drain longer to remove more whey.
	Too much humidity in the ripening area.	Reduce humidity.
	Curds are too acidic.	Ripen the milk longer before adding rennet.

FOR BLUE CHEESES

Problem	Possible reason	Action to try
Little or no blue mold developed in interior.	Not enough space and oxygen for mold to develop.	Check piercing holes while cheese is developing and repierce as needed to keep vein passages open.
	If the cheese is not pierced, curds were packed too firmly, closing spaces for mold to grow or there was too little mold powder between layers of curds.	Pack curds less firmly or add more mold powder when ladling the curds into the mold.
Blue mold takes too long to develop on the surface.	Humidity is too low or the curds are too dry.	Increase humidity or stir less to retain moisture in the curds.

CHAPTER 2

Beginning Cheese Making

Fresh Direct-Acidification Cheeses, Cultured
Dairy Products, Fresh Culture-Ripened Cheeses, and
Salt-Rubbed and Brined Cheeses

I f you've never made cheese before, this chapter is the place to start. Experienced cheese makers will also find recipes here to try, but this chapter is structured to introduce the novice to some of the basics of cheese making: handling equipment; heating milk and maintaining its temperature as it ripens; incorporating coagulants and other additives; draining and cutting curds; molding and brief aging; and so on. Work your way through these recipes, referring

back to the "Processes and Techniques" section (pages 16–33) as needed, and you will have a good grounding in the dairying arts.

In that spirit, the chapter opens with recipes for fresh unripened cheeses. These are the simplest cheeses to make successfully in your own kitchen, and they're delicious. As the category name implies, these cheeses are young, usually ready within one to fourteen days from the time of production, and are best consumed within a few days of ripening. With little or no aging, they have a creamy texture and relatively mild, milky flavor and aroma. These direct-acidification cheeses use acids such as vinegar and lemon juice to coagulate hot milk, which will give you a basic understanding of the processes of heating milk and draining curds.

Next follows a group of recipes for noncheese dairy products like cultured butter, crème fraîche, yogurt, and more. These are among the most satisfyingly delicious kitchen staples to make by hand, and they will introduce you to using cultures.

The third group of recipes, fresh culture-ripened cheeses, allows you to master gentle heating and gradual milk ripening, using starter cultures and rennet to coagulate ripened milk, and draining and setting curds using a variety of techniques. Modern examples include Laura Chenel's cabécou

and chèvre, Cowgirl Creamery clabbered cottage cheese, Vermont Butter & Cheese fromage blanc, Mozzarella Company queso blanco and goat ricotta, and Lucky Layla Farms yogurt cheese.

The chapter ends with a handful of recipes for simple salt-rubbed or brined cheeses like feta and Halloumi; the techniques used to make these cheeses will also be used in later chapters for cheeses such as Saffron-Infused Manchego (page 106) and Kasseri (page 84).

Profile: Vermont Butter & Cheese Creamery

Vermont Butter & Cheese Creamery is an award-winning creamery that was born out of a chef's request for fresh chèvre in 1984. Allison Hooper (founder and co-owner along with Bob Reese) had studied cheese making in France. She knew how to make chèvre and did so for the chef. The cheese got rave reviews, requests for more came in, and voilà: VB&CC was born. Over its more than twenty-five years, the creamery has built its fine reputation on thoughtfully executed handcrafted goat's and cow's milk cheeses and cultured butter, all made in the European tradition.

Fresh Direct-Acidification Cheeses

These fresh cheeses are made by adding a simple acid such as buttermilk, citrus juice, citric acid, vinegar, or tartaric acid to the milk to cause coagulation. In this introduction to cheese making, you'll be using accessible kitchen equipment, basic cheese making ingredients, and simple heating, draining, and salting methods to learn how easy and magical it is to make these basic everyday cheeses.

MASCARPONE

MAKES 12 ounces
MILKS Pasteurized heavy cream, powdered skim milk
START TO FINISH Less than 1 day

Originating in Italy, mascarpone is a mild and creamy fresh cheese with a consistency similar to soft butter or thick crème fraîche and a fat content between 70 and 75 percent. You may know it as the key ingredient in the decadent Italian dessert tiramisu. This recipe hails from Allison Hooper, award-winning cheese maker and co-owner of the notable Vermont Butter & Cheese Creamery (see page 35). The overnight process is virtually effortless, and the resulting cheese may very well be the best mascarpone I've ever tasted.

2 cups pasteurized heavy cream without thickeners
1/3 cup powdered skim milk
1 lemon, cut in half

1. Read through the recipe and review any terms and techniques you aren't familiar with (see chapter 1). Assemble your equipment, supplies, and ingredients, including a dairy or kitchen thermometer; clean and sterilize your equipment as needed and lay it out on clean kitchen towels.

2. In a nonreactive, heavy 2-quart saucepan with a lid, whisk together the cream and powdered milk. Place over low heat and slowly bring to 180°F, stirring constantly to prevent scorching. It should take about 40 minutes to come to temperature. Turn off the heat.

3. Slowly squeeze the juice from half of the lemon into the cream. Switch to a metal spoon and keep stirring; do not use a whisk, as that will inhibit the curd formation. Watch carefully to see if the cream starts to coagulate. You will not see a clean break between curds and whey. Rather, the cream will coat the spoon and you will start to see some flecks of solids in the cream.

4. Add the juice from the remaining lemon half and stir with the spoon to incorporate. Cover the pan and cool the cream in the refrigerator for 8 hours or overnight.

5. When the cream is firm to the touch, transfer it to a bowl or colander lined with clean, damp butter muslin. Draw the ends together and twist into a ball to squeeze out the excess moisture. This last step will make the mascarpone thick.

6. This cheese is now ready to eat. It has a very short shelf life, so refrigerate what you don't eat immediately and use it within 2 days.

LOW-FAT PANIR

MAKES 12 to 14 ounces
MILKS Reduced fat (2 percent) cow's milk, buttermilk
ALTERNATIVE MILK Pasteurized or raw whole cow's milk to replace the reduced fat milk
START TO FINISH Less than 1½ hours: 30 minutes to make the cheese; 20 minutes to drain; 30 minutes to press

Panir (often spelled "paneer") is indigenous to India and is the featured ingredient in the classic spinach and cheese dish saag panir (page 217), among many others. Panir is traditionally made with whole cow's milk; this is a lower-fat version using 2 percent milk and buttermilk to help coagulate the curds. The finished shape is a solid pressed brick about ³/₄ inch thick, which is then cut into cubes to use in cooking. Panir does not melt easily, which makes it perfect for grilling and stir-fries.

2½ quarts reduced fat (2 percent) pasteurized or raw
    cow's milk
5 cups buttermilk, homemade (see page 44)
    or store-bought
¹/₂ teaspoon fine sea salt

1. Read through the recipe and review any terms and techniques you aren't familiar with (see chapter 1). Assemble your equipment, supplies, and ingredients, including a dairy or kitchen thermometer; clean and sterilize your equipment as needed and lay it out on clean kitchen towels. For this recipe, you will need a 4-pound weight, such as a ¹/₂-gallon jug filled with water or a cast-iron skillet.

2. Put the reduced fat milk in a nonreactive, heavy 4-quart stockpot over medium-low heat and slowly bring it to 175°F to 180°F. It should take about 40 minutes to come to temperature. Turn off the heat.

3. Pour in the buttermilk and gently stir with a whisk just to combine. Coagulation will start to occur immediately, and the curds will begin to form after about 2 minutes. Slowly raise the temperature to 195°F, gently stirring with a spatula. You will see an obvious separation of curds and whey. Using a rubber spatula, gently stir until the majority of the floating curds have attached to the larger mass, about 10 more minutes. Remove from the heat and gently stir around the edge of the curds with the rubber spatula. Cover and allow the milk to ripen for 5 minutes.

4. Place a nonreactive strainer over a nonreactive bowl or bucket large enough to capture the whey. Line it with clean, damp butter muslin and gently ladle the curds into it. Make a draining sack: Tie two opposite corners of the butter muslin into a knot and repeat with the other two corners. Slip a dowel or wooden spoon under the knots to suspend the bag over the whey-catching receptacle, or suspend it over the kitchen sink using kitchen twine tied around the faucet. Let the curds drain for 10 minutes, then open the cloth, distribute the salt over the curds, and gently toss the curds with your hands to incorporate. Tie closed and let drain for 10 minutes more, or until the whey stops dripping. Discard the whey or reserve it for another use.

5. Open the cloth and flatten and shape the curds into a brick about ³/₄ to 1 inch thick. Wrap the curds snugly in the same cloth to hold the shape. Place the packet of curds on a draining rack set over a tray and set the weight on top. Press and drain for at least 30 minutes, or longer for a drier cheese.

6. Remove the cloth. The cheese will be dry and will have formed into a solid brick. If you are not using it the same day, tightly wrap the cheese in plastic wrap and store refrigerated for up to 4 days or vacuum-seal and freeze for up to 2 months.

VARIATION
Add 1 teaspoon of cumin seeds to the curds with the salt.

QUESO BLANCO

MAKES 1 pound
MILK Pasteurized whole cow's milk
ALTERNATIVE MILKS Raw cow's milk; pasteurized or raw goat's milk
START TO FINISH 2 hours: 1 hour to make the cheese; 1 hour to drain

Translated as "white cheese," queso blanco is one of the fresh cheeses found all over Latin America that are similar to farmer's cheese. Because queso blanco doesn't melt completely when heated, it makes a perfect finishing or garnishing cheese, or you can incorporate it into dishes where you want chunks of cheese to remain intact.

1 gallon pasteurized whole cow's milk
About 1/3 cup cider vinegar or distilled white vinegar
1 teaspoon kosher salt (preferably Diamond Crystal brand)

1. Read through the recipe and review any terms and techniques you aren't familiar with (see chapter 1). Assemble your equipment, supplies, and ingredients, including a dairy or kitchen thermometer; clean and sterilize your equipment as needed and lay it out on clean kitchen towels.

2. Heat the milk in a nonreactive, heavy 6-quart stockpot over medium heat to 195°F, stirring occasionally to prevent the milk from scorching. It should take about 25 to 30 minutes to bring the milk to temperature. Turn off the heat.

3. Stir in 1/3 cup vinegar using a whisk. Cover, remove from the heat, and let sit for 10 minutes. The milk protein will coagulate into solid curds and the liquid whey will be almost clear and light green in color. Depending upon the milk used, if the whey is still a bit cloudy or there are small bits of curd visible in the whey, you may need to add a bit more vinegar to fully coagulate the curds. If so, add 1 teaspoon at a time and stir the vinegar in with a rubber spatula until the remainder of the curds are formed. Too much vinegar will negatively flavor the curds.

4. Place a nonreactive strainer over a nonreactive bowl or bucket large enough to capture the whey. Line it with clean, damp butter muslin and gently ladle the curds into it. Let the curds drain for 5 minutes.

5. Distribute the salt over the curds and gently toss the curds with your hands to incorporate. Be careful not to break up the curds in this process.

6. Make a draining sack: Tie two opposite corners of the butter muslin into a knot and repeat with the other two corners. Slip a dowel or wooden spoon under the knots to suspend the bag over the whey-catching receptacle, or suspend it over the kitchen sink using kitchen twine tied around the faucet. Let the curds drain for 1 hour, or until the whey has stopped dripping. Discard the whey or reserve it for another use.

7. Remove the solid mass of cheese from the cloth and place in an airtight container or wrap tightly in plastic wrap and refrigerate until ready to use. Fresh cheeses such as queso blanco are best when eaten within 24 hours, though queso blanco may be stored for up to 1 week.

WHOLE MILK RICOTTA

MAKES 1 pound
MILKS Pasteurized or raw whole cow's milk, heavy cream
ALTERNATIVE MILK Pasteurized or raw goat's milk
START TO FINISH About 1½ hours: 1 hour to make the cheese; 20 to 30 minutes to drain

Ricotta is a simple, fresh cheese that takes little time to make. It is best when used within a few days while its flavor is bright and the texture is still moist and creamy. Traditionally, ricotta is made by reheating whey (*ricotta* means "recooked" in Italian) after making other cheeses such as mozzarella, though it takes a fair amount of whey to yield a usable amount of ricotta. This home-crafted formula using whole milk and citric acid is very basic. If you like an even richer and creamier ricotta, try replacing the milk with more heavy cream. In place of citric acid, lemon juice may be used to coagulate.

1 gallon pasteurized or raw whole cow's milk
½ cup heavy cream
1 teaspoon citric acid powder
2 teaspoons kosher salt (preferably Diamond Crystal brand)

1. Read through the recipe and review any terms and techniques you aren't familiar with (see chapter 1). Assemble your equipment, supplies, and ingredients, including a dairy or kitchen thermometer; clean and sterilize your equipment as needed and lay it out on clean kitchen towels.

2. In a nonreactive, heavy 4-quart stockpot, combine the milk, cream, citric acid, and 1 teaspoon of the salt and mix thoroughly with a whisk. Place over medium-low heat and slowly heat the milk to 185°F to 195°F. This should take about 15 to 20 minutes. Stir frequently with a rubber spatula to prevent scorching.

3. As the milk reaches the desired temperature, you will see the curds start to form. When the curds and whey separate and the whey is yellowish green and just slightly cloudy, remove from the heat. Gently run a thin rubber spatula around the edge of the curds to rotate the mass. Cover the pan and let the curds set without disturbing for 10 minutes.

4. Place a nonreactive strainer over a nonreactive bowl or bucket large enough to capture the whey. Line it with clean, damp butter muslin and gently ladle the curds into it. Use a long-handled mesh skimmer to capture the last of the curds. If any curds are stuck to the bottom of the pan, leave them there. You don't want scorched curds flavoring your cheese.

5. Distribute the remaining 1 teaspoon salt over the curds and gently toss the curds with your hands to incorporate. Be careful not to break up the curds in the process.

6. Make a draining sack: Tie two opposite corners of the butter muslin into a knot and repeat with the other two corners. Slip a dowel or wooden spoon under the knots to suspend the bag over the whey-catching receptacle, or suspend it over the kitchen sink using kitchen twine tied around the faucet. Let the curds drain for 20 to 30 minutes, or until the desired consistency has been reached. If you like moist ricotta, stop draining just as the whey stops dripping. If you like it drier or are using it to make ricotta salata, let the curds drain for a longer period of time. Discard the whey or keep it for another use.

(continued)

7. Transfer the cheese to a lidded container. Cover and store, refrigerated, for up to 1 week.

VARIATIONS

To make goat ricotta, substitute goat's milk and use 1½ teaspoons of citric acid, adding an additional ½ teaspoon of citric acid if needed to cause coagulation. The curds will be softer and more delicate than the cow's milk curds and the whey will be slightly cloudy.

To make smoky ricotta affumicata, place the curds in a plastic Italian draining basket lined with butter muslin or cheesecloth and let drain on a rack for 24 hours (see page 20). Remove the cheese from the cloth, then dry salt it with 2 teaspoons sea salt (see page 23), wrap it in a dry cheesecloth sack, and cold smoke it in a cool wood-fired oven or smoker for 3 days (see page 27). Remove the cheese from the smoker and allow to air-dry for at least 1 week and up to 1 month. Use it right away, or vacuum-seal and refrigerate for up to 1 month.

WHEY RICOTTA

MAKES 3 cups
MILKS Fresh cow's milk whey, pasteurized whole cow's milk, pasteurized heavy cream
START TO FINISH About 1¼ hours: 1 hour to make the cheese; 10 minutes to drain

This formula from Robin Rosemon at the Beverage People reflects the traditional method for making ricotta. When making other cow's milk cheeses, the fresh whey is reserved and combined with fresh whole milk and cream, and vinegar is used as the coagulant. Any fresh whey should be used within a few hours of collecting it because it can go sour if left for too long. Always smell and taste the whey before using; if it's sour, toss it into the garden to feed your acid-loving plants. You will need to make a 2-gallon batch of mozzarella or other cow's milk cheese to have enough whey to make this ricotta.

1 gallon fresh cow's milk whey from making a cow's
   milk cheese using 2 gallons of milk
1 gallon pasteurized whole cow's milk
3½ tablespoons distilled vinegar
1 tablespoon fine sea salt
¼ cup pasteurized heavy cream without additives

1. Read through the recipe and review any terms and techniques you aren't familiar with (see chapter 1). Assemble your equipment, supplies, and ingredients, including a dairy or kitchen thermometer; clean and sterilize your equipment as needed and lay it out on clean kitchen towels.

2. Assemble a water bath using a 6-quart stockpot set inside a larger pot. Pour water into the larger pot to come two-thirds of the way up the side of the smaller pot. Remove the smaller pot and place the pot of water over low heat. When the water reaches the boiling point (212°F), put the smaller pot back in the water to warm slightly, then pour the whey into the smaller pot. Gently stir the whey with a whisk using an up-and-down motion for 20 strokes to evenly distribute the heat (see page 17). Add the cow's milk, cover the pot, and slowly warm the milk to 192°F over the course of about 20 minutes, lowering the heat, adding cool water to the water bath, or removing from the heat if the temperature is rising too quickly. Turn off the heat.

3. Slowly pour the vinegar over the surface of the milk. Using a whisk, thoroughly incorporate the vinegar into the milk using an up-and-down motion for 20 strokes. Small curds will begin to form. Cover the pot and let stand for 10 to 15 minutes, stirring once around the edge of the curds with a rubber spatula. The curds will settle down into the pot. Ladle off the whey until you can see the curds.

4. Place a nonreactive strainer over a nonreactive bowl or bucket large enough to capture the whey. Line it with clean, damp butter muslin and gently ladle the curds into it. Let the curds drain for 10 minutes. Distribute the salt over the curds and gently toss the curds with your hands to incorporate. Be careful not to break up the curds in this process. Discard the whey or reserve it for another use.

5. Transfer the ricotta to a bowl and gently mix in the cream using a rubber spatula, being careful not to break up the curds. Serve while warm, or refrigerate for up to 3 days.

Cultured Dairy Products

Cultured dairy products—including yogurt, sour cream, cultured butter, and buttermilk—are related to cheese because of the cultures used. However, the process of making them differs from cheese making in that there is no coagulation and formation of curds, but rather fermentation of the milk or cream. All of these products are easy to make and far more flavorful than their store-bought counterparts.

Sour cream, cultured buttermilk, and crème fraîche form after milk or cream is inoculated with cultures and left to develop overnight, and cultured butter can be made in a food processor while you prepare a meal. Yogurt is made from milk inoculated with strains of thermophilic bacteria. A few artisan American examples include Kendall Farms crème fraîche, Redwood Hill goat yogurt, and Vermont Butter & Cheese cultured butter.

Cultured Butter

CULTURED BUTTER

MAKES 1 pound (6 ounces if starting with raw milk)
MILK Pasteurized heavy cream or raw cow's milk
START TO FINISH About 24 hours: 12 hours to make the butter; 12 hours to chill

Cultured butter has a more pronounced flavor than plain butter because it is made from cream ripened with a lactic bacterial culture. Basically, you make crème fraîche, then use a food processor to churn it into rich, flavorful butter. Choose the highest-fat, freshest raw or pasteurized cream you can find to make this butter. The recipe will not work with homogenized or ultra-pasteurized cream or cream with additives or thickeners; check the label carefully.

1 quart pasteurized heavy cream or raw cow's milk
1/8 teaspoon Aroma B powdered mesophilic starter culture

1. Read through the recipe and review any terms and techniques you aren't familiar with (see chapter 1). Assemble your equipment, supplies, and ingredients, including a dairy or kitchen thermometer; clean and sterilize your equipment as needed and lay it out on clean kitchen towels.

2. To start with pasteurized cream, pour the cream into a nonreactive 2-quart saucepan and bring to 68°F over low heat. This should take 8 to 10 minutes. Turn off the heat.

3. Sprinkle the starter over the cream, and let it rehydrate for 5 minutes. Whisk the starter into the cream to incorporate, using an up-and-down motion for 20 strokes. Cover and set aside for 12 hours at room temperature, then chill in the refrigerator for an additional 12 hours. Allow the cream to come to 54°F before churning.

4. To start with raw milk, pour the milk into a shallow stainless steel bowl and cover with cheesecloth. Place in a warm (70°F to 72°F) part of your kitchen to stand and ripen for 24 hours. Refrigerate for 12 hours to firm the milk fat, then, using a skimmer, remove the cream layer from the top of the milk. Allow the cream to come to 54°F before churning.

5. To churn, fill the bowl of a food processor halfway with cream and start churning continuously. Do not overload the processor, because the cream needs expansion room. After 5 to 7 minutes, the cream will become very stiff and yellowish in color. Keep going; gradually, over the course of about 10 minutes, the volume of the cream will reduce and the texture will become grainy with small flecks of butter. Next, the mixture will become more liquid and the flecks of butter will separate from the buttermilk. Do not over-churn: stop when there's a slight splashing sound from the buttermilk.

6. Place a strainer over a bowl and pour the butter and buttermilk into it. Reserve the buttermilk for another use. Rinse the butter under very cold running water to wash off any milk residue. Return the butter to the strainer and place the strainer over a chilled bowl to keep the washed butter cool. Quickly knead the butter with your fingertips to remove any excess water. Form the butter into a ball or log, wrap in foil, and refrigerate until firm. Repeat the churning, straining, rinsing, kneading, and rolling with any remaining cream.

CRÈME FRAÎCHE

MAKES 4 cups
MILK Pasteurized heavy cream
ALTERNATIVE MILK Half-and-half
START TO FINISH 18 to 48 hours: 30 minutes to make the crème fraîche; 18 to 48 hours to ripen

Crème fraîche is a cultured cream similar to sour cream but not as tangy. This easy version comes from the Beverage People, who smartly suggest you make it overnight in glass canning jars. Excellent dolloped on fresh fruit or fruit desserts, crème fraîche is also a miraculous cooking ingredient that can, for example, be stirred into tomato sauce for a tomato-cream sauce, blended with curry powder and stirred into pasta with peas, or drizzled over roasted salmon. One of its best qualities is that it doesn't curdle when heated. The recipe will not work with ultra-pasteurized cream or cream with additives or thickeners; check the label carefully.

1 quart pasteurized heavy cream
¼ teaspoon Aroma B powdered mesophilic
    starter culture

1. Read through the recipe and review any terms and techniques you aren't familiar with (see chapter 1). Assemble your equipment, supplies, and ingredients, including a dairy or kitchen thermometer and 2 pint-size glass canning jars with lids; clean and sterilize your equipment as needed and lay it out on clean kitchen towels.

2. Pour the cream into the 2 sterilized pint jars and place in a 4-quart stockpot. Fill the pot with warm water to halfway up the sides of the jars. Over low heat, slowly heat the cream to 86°F. This should take about 15 minutes. Turn off the heat.

3. Sprinkle the starter over the cream and let it rehydrate for 5 minutes, maintaining the temperature. (Refer to page 17 for tips on maintaining milk or curds at a steady temperature over a period of time.) Then thoroughly incorporate the starter into the cream using a whisk in an up-and-down motion for 20 strokes.

4. Place the lids loosely on the jars, and leave the jars in the warm water bath to ripen for 12 hours or overnight. The water bath will cool slowly, keeping enough warmth to develop the culture.

5. Take the jars out of the water bath, tighten the lids, and continue to ripen at room temperature for at least 6 more hours and up to 48 hours total. The cream should be as thick as creamy yogurt at the point of full development.

6. Refrigerate overnight or for up to 2 weeks. Refrigeration thickens the crème fraîche further and improves its flavor.

VARIATION
To make cultured buttermilk, follow the method for making crème fraîche with these changes: substitute whole, 2 percent, or 1 percent milk for the cream, and inoculate and ripen at room temperature rather than first heating the milk.

BUTTERMILK SOUR CREAM

MAKES 3½ cups
MILKS Pasteurized heavy cream, pasteurized whole cow's milk, cultured buttermilk
START TO FINISH About 24 hours: 30 minutes to make the sour cream; 24 hours to ripen

Buttermilk sour cream is made with a blend of whole milk and cream that is acidified by adding cultured buttermilk. It is thinner in consistency than cultured sour cream (page 46) but can be whipped to become thicker. The acidity of the buttermilk makes this sour cream extra tangy and delicious. Try making it with homemade cultured buttermilk (see page 44).

1½ cups pasteurized heavy cream
1½ cups pasteurized whole cow's milk
¾ cup cultured buttermilk, homemade (see page 44)
    or store-bought

1. Read through the recipe and review any terms and techniques you aren't familiar with (see chapter 1). Assemble your equipment, supplies, and ingredients, including a dairy or kitchen thermometer and 2 pint-size glass canning jars with lids; clean and sterilize your equipment as needed and lay it out on clean kitchen towels.

2. While the pint jars are still warm from sterilizing, whisk together the cream, milk, and buttermilk and pour into the jars. Put the jars in a 4-quart stockpot and fill the pot with warm water to halfway up the sides of the jars. Over medium-low heat, slowly heat the milk to 75°F. This should take about 15 minutes. Turn off the heat.

3. Place the lids loosely on the jars, and leave the jars in the warm water bath to ripen for 12 hours or overnight. The water bath will cool slowly, keeping enough warmth to develop the culture.

4. Take the jars out of the water bath, tighten the lids, and continue to ripen at room temperature for 24 hours total. The sour cream should have the consistency of thick yogurt at this point.

5. Refrigerate for up to 3 weeks. The sour cream is better after 2 days, as refrigeration thickens it further and enhances the flavors.

CULTURED SOUR CREAM

MAKES 4 cups
MILK Pasteurized light whipping cream
START TO FINISH 12 to 36 hours: 30 minutes to make the sour cream; 12 to 36 hours to ripen

Cultured sour cream is far superior in taste to store-bought sour cream, which often has stabilizers added for firmer texture and extra thickness. This sour cream is similar to but thicker than crème fraîche (page 44) and is made with light whipping cream instead of heavy cream. The recipe will not work with ultra-pasteurized cream or cream with additives or thickeners; check the label carefully.

....

1 quart pasteurized light whipping cream
^{1}/$_8$ teaspoon Aroma B powdered mesophilic starter
    culture

1. Read through the recipe and review any terms and techniques you aren't familiar with (see chapter 1). Assemble your equipment, supplies, and ingredients, including a dairy or kitchen thermometer and 2 pint-size glass canning jars with lids; clean and sterilize your equipment as needed and lay it out on clean kitchen towels.

2. While the pint jars are still warm from sterilizing, pour the cream into them and place in a 4-quart stockpot. Fill the pot with warm water to halfway up the sides of the jars. Over medium-low heat, slowly heat the cream to 86°F. This should take about 15 minutes. Turn off the heat.

3. Sprinkle the starter over the cream and let it rehydrate for 5 minutes, maintaining the temperature. (Refer to page 17 for tips on maintaining milk or curds at a steady temperature over a period of time.) Then thoroughly incorporate the starter into the cream using a whisk in an up-and-down motion for 20 strokes.

4. Place the lids loosely on the jars, and leave the jars in the warm water bath to ripen for 12 hours or overnight. The water bath will cool slowly, keeping enough warmth to develop the culture.

5. Take the jars out of the water bath, tighten the lids, and continue to ripen at room temperature for up to 36 hours total. The sour cream should have the consistency of creamy yogurt at this point.

6. Refrigerate for up to 2 weeks. The sour cream is better after 2 days, as refrigeration thickens it further and enhances the flavors.

YOGURT

MAKES 2 cups
MILK Pasteurized whole cow's milk
ALTERNATIVE MILK Pasteurized or raw goat's milk
START TO FINISH 5½ to 7½ hours: 1 hour to make the yogurt; 4 to 6 hours to ripen;
20 to 30 minutes to drain (optional)

Yogurt can be made from just about any milk; if goat's milk is used, the yogurt will be softer than if made with cow's milk. In this recipe, you can use either commercial powdered yogurt starter or a quantity of cultured yogurt plus rennet. If you like, use the commercial starter for the first batch, then save 2 to 3 tablespoons of the finished yogurt to use as a starter for the next batch. If you're using the powdered starter with cow's milk, you won't need to use any rennet. If you're making goat's milk yogurt, use rennet regardless of whether you are starting the yogurt with powdered starter or with cultured yogurt.

The natural bacterial cultures in homemade yogurt have general health benefits and make this yogurt more digestible, even for people who are lactose intolerant. The live lactic bacteria do the job of converting the lactose into lactic acid before you eat it.

---

1 quart pasteurized whole cow's milk
1 teaspoon Bulgarian 411 powdered yogurt starter, or 2 tablespoons plain yogurt with live cultures at room temperature
1 drop liquid rennet diluted in ¼ cup cool nonchlorinated water (omit if using powdered starter)

1. Read through the recipe and review any terms and techniques you aren't familiar with (see chapter 1). Assemble your equipment, supplies, and ingredients, including a dairy or kitchen thermometer; clean and sterilize your equipment as needed and lay it out on clean kitchen towels.

2. Place the milk in a nonreactive, heavy 4-quart stockpot over medium-low heat and slowly heat it to 115°F to 116°F over the course of about 40 minutes.

3. Keeping the milk at temperature, sprinkle the starter, if using, over the milk and let it rehydrate for 5 minutes. (Refer to page 17 for tips on maintaining milk or curds at a steady temperature over a period of time.) Then thoroughly incorporate the starter into the cream using a whisk in an up-and-down motion for 20 strokes. If you are not using yogurt starter culture, whisk in 1 tablespoon of the rennet solution using an up-and-down motion for 20 strokes, then stir in the 2 tablespoons of cultured yogurt and mix well. (This amount of rennet will create a soft yogurt. For a firmer yogurt, use the entire ¼ cup of diluted rennet.)

4. Cover the pot, remove it from the heat, and let sit for 4 hours at room temperature, until a solid mass of curds forms. If a more tart flavor is desired, let the curds develop for another 2 hours. Gently stir with a rubber spatula for 20 seconds to slightly break up the mass into large chunks. Cover and let sit for 10 minutes.

5. Place a nonreactive strainer over a nonreactive bowl or bucket large enough to capture the whey. Line it with clean, damp butter muslin and gently ladle the curds into it. Let the curds drain for 20 minutes, or until the whey stops dripping. Discard the whey or reserve it for another use.

6. Transfer the yogurt to a container, cover, and store refrigerated for up to 2 weeks. The yogurt will firm up when refrigerated.

YOGURT CHEESE WITH MINT

MAKES 1½ cups

START TO FINISH About 14 hours: 12 hours to drain; 2 hours to set

Yogurt cheese is essentially well-drained yogurt. The cultures present in the yogurt are the flavor contributors, so start with very good-quality yogurt, preferably homemade. Yogurt cheese is delicious plain or can be flavored with any of your favorite dried herbs and used as a spread. It can also be used to top Moroccan Chickpea Soup (page 213).

3 cups Greek-style yogurt (page 49) or plain whole or 2 percent cultured yogurt

1 teaspoon kosher salt (preferably Diamond Crystal brand)

1½ tablespoons dried mint

Zest from 1 lemon

1. Place the yogurt in a bowl, then sprinkle the salt over it and gently fold it in using a rubber spatula. Set a plastic strainer over a bowl and line it with clean, damp butter muslin, then pour the yogurt into it. Make a draining sack (see page 20) and leave the yogurt to drain for 12 hours or overnight. Discard the liquid.

2. Combine the drained yogurt with the mint and lemon zest and leave it at room temperature for 2 hours, or refrigerate uncovered overnight to dry it out a bit and firm it up. Bring to room temperature and stir before using. Yogurt cheese may be refrigerated for up to 5 days.

GREEK-STYLE YOGURT

MAKES 2 cups
MILKS Pasteurized half-and-half, plain cultured yogurt
ALTERNATIVE MILK Pasteurized reduced fat (2 percent) cow's milk
START TO FINISH 9½ hours: 1 hour to make the yogurt; 8 hours to ripen; 20 to 30 minutes to drain

This style of yogurt is typically richer than plain whole milk yogurt due to the fat content of the milk used: either half-and-half or, in Greece, sheep's milk. The method for growing the desired bacteria to create this style of yogurt is to inoculate the milk with live cultures from a premade yogurt, such as in the recipe on page 47. You may also use store-bought plain yogurt with live active cultures and no stabilizers. The rennet helps to set up the curds. The recipe will not work with ultra-pasteurized half-and-half; check the label carefully. You can save ¼ cup of the finished yogurt as a starter for the next batch.

1 quart pasteurized half-and-half
1 drop liquid rennet diluted in ¼ cup cool
    nonchlorinated water
¼ cup plain cultured yogurt, homemade (page 47) or
    store-bought

1. Read through the recipe and review any terms and techniques you aren't familiar with (see chapter 1). Assemble your equipment, supplies, and ingredients, including a dairy or kitchen thermometer; clean and sterilize your equipment as needed and lay it out on clean kitchen towels.

2. Place the half-and-half in a nonreactive heavy 4-quart stockpot over medium-low heat and slowly heat the half-and-half to 180°F. This should take about 55 minutes. While the half-and-half is heating, fill a large pot or bowl with cold water and ice.

3. When the half-and-half is at temperature, put the pot in the ice bath and whisk the half-and-half to cool to 100°F to 105°F.

4. Using a whisk, stir in 1 tablespoon of the rennet solution using an up-and-down motion to incorporate, then stir in the yogurt and mix well. Cover and let sit for 8 hours or overnight at room temperature, until a solid mass of curds forms. As soon as the curds are set, gently stir with a rubber spatula for 20 seconds to slightly break up the mass into large chunks. Cover and let sit for 10 minutes.

5. Place a nonreactive strainer over a nonreactive bowl or bucket large enough to capture the whey. Line it with clean, damp butter muslin and gently ladle the curds into the strainer. Let the curds drain for 20 minutes, or until the whey stops dripping. Discard the whey or reserve it for another use.

6. Transfer the yogurt to a container, cover, and store refrigerated for up to 5 days. The yogurt will firm up when refrigerated.

Fresh Culture-Ripened Cheeses

At the next level of making fresh cheeses, starter cultures and enzyme coagulants are used. Though still young and fresh, culture-ripened fresh cheeses develop much of their flavor through the use of cultures added to the milk before coagulation. The enzyme rennet is the general coagulant here, rather than simple acids as used in the direct-acidification fresh cheeses. As a result, there is more flavor developed than in the simple direct-acidification cheeses. You'll learn the use of both direct and water-bath heating methods, how to fill cheese molds, how to drain molded curds, and how to dry salt and air-dry the shaped curds.

Cabécou

CABÉCOU

MAKES Four 1½- to 2-ounce disks
MILK Pasteurized goat's milk
ALTERNATIVE MILK Raw goat's milk (see note page 52)
START TO FINISH About 2 weeks: 30 minutes to make the cheese; 18 hours to ripen;
2 days to drain; 2 days to dry; 1 week to age

The name of this classic French cheese means "little goat" in the dialect of Languedoc, where it originates. It typically is formed into petite disks and ripened for ten to fifteen days. This short ripening time keeps the cheese soft and mild. After fifteen days of ripening, cabécou may develop a little blue mold on the surface, sharpening the flavor, while some cabécou is ripened up to six weeks for a more pungent cheese with a firm texture suitable for grating. This marinated version of cabécou was made popular in the United States by American goat cheese maker Laura Chenel and is considered one of her company's signature cheeses. The recipe was contributed by Jacquelyn Buchanan, culinary director of Laura Chenel's chèvre and their cheese maker. You can use the marinating oil as a dipping oil once the cheese is finished.

2 quarts pasteurized goat's milk
¼ teaspoon MA 011 or C20G powdered mesophilic
    starter culture
1 drop liquid rennet diluted in 5 tablespoons cool
    nonchlorinated water
2 teaspoons kosher salt (preferably Diamond Crystal
    brand)
1 tablespoon herbes de Provence (optional)
2 teaspoons whole mixed peppercorns
4 bay leaves
About 4 cups fruity extra-virgin olive oil

1. Read through the recipe and review any terms and techniques you aren't familiar with (see chapter 1). Assemble your equipment, supplies, and ingredients, including a dairy or kitchen thermometer; clean and sterilize your equipment as needed and lay it out on clean kitchen towels.

2. Assemble a water bath using a nonreactive 4-quart stockpot set inside a larger pot. Pour water into the larger pot to come halfway up the side of the smaller pot. Remove the smaller pot and place the pot of water over low heat. When the water reaches 85°F, put the smaller pot back in the water to warm slightly, then pour the milk into the smaller pot. Gently mix the milk with a whisk using an

up-and-down motion for 20 strokes to evenly distribute the heat (see page 17). Cover and slowly warm the milk to 75°F over the course of about 10 minutes, lowering the heat, adding cool water to the water bath, or removing from the heat if the temperature is rising too quickly.

3. When the milk is at temperature, remove it from the heat. Sprinkle the starter over the milk and let it rehydrate for 5 minutes. Using a whisk, stir the starter into the milk to incorporate, using an up-and-down motion for 20 strokes. Add the diluted rennet to the milk, whisking with an up-and-down motion for 20 strokes to incorporate.

4. Cover and allow the milk to set at 72°F for 18 hours, until it coagulates. During maturation, do not touch or move the milk. The curds will form a solid mass during this period.

5. Set 4 crottin molds on a draining rack set over a tray and, using a ladle or skimmer, scoop the curds into the molds. When the molds are full, cover the rack with a kitchen towel or lid and let drain at room temperature.

6. After 2 days of draining, the cheeses will have sunk down to about 1 inch in height. Unmold them; they should

(continued)

be firm enough to maintain their shape. Salt the cheeses on both sides and dry them in the lower portion of the refrigerator for 2 days on mesh cheese mats, turning once a day. Keep them uncovered, as they need to air-dry until the surface is dry to the touch.

7. Place each disk of cheese in a sterilized glass jar. Divide the herbes de Provence, peppercorns, and bay leaves among the jars and cover the cheeses with olive oil. Close the lids tightly. The olive oil will preserve the cheese, add its own flavor, and carry the flavor of the herbs. Please note that the olive oil will solidify in the refrigerator but will return to liquid at room temperature. Age for 1 week to let the flavor develop; use within 3 weeks.

NOTE
If using raw goat's milk, pasteurize at 160°F for 1 minute (see page 10 for method). Cool, covered, for 20 minutes (do not remove the cover or you will recontaminate the milk). Bring the milk back to 75°F before adding the culture and rennet.

VARIATION
Substitute truffle-infused oil or walnut oil for the olive oil.

Profile: Laura Chenel's Chèvre

Laura Chenel is considered the pioneer of goat cheese making in the United States. Established in the late 1970s, Laura Chenel was the first US creamery to make goat cheese. Her first love was for the goats, and after her experiments to make chèvre at home did not succeed, she went to France to study with the farmstead goat cheese authority Jean-Claude Le Jaouen. When she returned to Sonoma County, she was skilled enough to start making chèvre—and not only did she start, but Laura Chenel's Chèvre has never since ceased production. She began selling to a few innovative chefs, such as John Ash in Sonoma County, and in 1979 she took her chèvre to Alice Waters at Chez Panisse. Production grew from there, and today the label is a national brand.

It is largely due to Laura's efforts that the American taste for goat cheese—especially soft and creamy chèvre—developed. Laura took her company full circle: first inspired by the work of the most respected French cheese making authority, she later sold Laura Chenel's Chèvre to a highly respected French company, the Rians Group. She is no longer involved in the company, though her cheese making heirs, her staff, still work alongside the cheese makers and management from Rians. The creative team is guided by culinary director Jacquelyn Buchanan, a talented chef and culinary visionary.

REAL CREAM CHEESE

MAKES 1½ pounds
MILKS Pasteurized whole, reduced fat (2 percent), or low-fat (1 percent) cow's milk, pasteurized heavy cream
ALTERNATIVE MILKS Raw cow's milk; pasteurized or raw goat's milk
START TO FINISH 18½ to 20½ hours: 30 minutes to make the cheese; 12 hours to ripen; 6 to 8 hours to drain

Cream cheese originated in the United States, though not in Philadelphia as the popular brand name suggests. It is typically made with a blend of whole cow's milk and cream, though reduced fat and nonfat versions are made as well. Much of what is marketed as cream cheese is factory made and mixed with stabilizers to create a firm cheese with an extended shelf life. This recipe is for *real* cream cheese, made from cultured milk that's allowed to ripen for twelve hours or longer, until a firm curd mass is formed. This process develops fabulous flavor and a wonderful creamy texture.

1 quart pasteurized whole cow's milk

1 quart pasteurized heavy cream

¼ teaspoon MA 4001 powdered mesophilic starter

2 drops calcium chloride diluted in 2 tablespoons cool nonchlorinated water

3 drops liquid rennet diluted in 2 tablespoons nonchlorinated water

1 teaspoon kosher salt (preferably Diamond Crystal brand)

1. Read through the recipe and review any terms and techniques you aren't familiar with (see chapter 1). Assemble your equipment, supplies, and ingredients, including a dairy or kitchen thermometer; clean and sterilize your equipment as needed and lay it out on clean kitchen towels.

2. In a nonreactive, heavy 6-quart stockpot, heat the milk and cream over medium heat to 75°F, stirring occasionally to prevent scorching. This should take about 15 minutes. Turn off the heat.

3. Sprinkle the starter over the milk and let it rehydrate for 5 minutes. Whisk the starter into the milk to incorporate, using an up-and-down motion for 20 strokes. Add the diluted calcium chloride and incorporate in the same way, and then the diluted rennet. Cover, remove from the water bath, and let sit at room temperature for 12 hours, or until solid curds form and liquid whey floats on top. The whey will be almost clear and light green in color.

4. Place a nonreactive strainer over a nonreactive bowl or bucket large enough to capture the whey. Line it with clean, damp butter muslin and gently ladle the curds into it. Tie the ends of the muslin to fashion a draining sack (see page 20) and let drain for 6 to 8 hours, or until firm to the touch. Discard the whey or reserve it for another use.

5. Transfer the curds to a bowl, add the salt, and stir or knead to combine. Form into a brick and wrap with plastic wrap or store in a covered container. Refrigerate for up to 2 weeks.

CRÈME FRAÎCHE COTTAGE CHEESE

MAKES 1½ pounds
MILKS Pasteurized whole, reduced fat (2 percent), or low-fat (1 percent) cow's milk, cultured crème fraîche
ALTERNATIVE MILKS Raw cow's milk; pasteurized or raw goat's milk
START TO FINISH 7 to 8 hours: 1½ hours to make the cheese; 5 to 6 hours to ripen; 15 minutes to drain

Cottage cheese has been produced in Europe for many years using a range of milks. Traditionally, this fresh cheese is made by natural lactic acid coagulation rather than with rennet. Because this recipe is made with pasteurized milk, small amounts of mesophilic culture and rennet are used to enhance bacterial development and aid coagulation. Many of us know cottage cheese as the mass-produced variety, which has little flavor. This rich cottage cheese is anything but flavorless, made with whole cow's milk with cultured crème fraîche folded in after the curds are set. Commercial crème fraîche can be used successfully if it's a high-quality artisan brand such as Bellwether or Kendall Farms. You can use low-fat milk instead of whole milk or fold in Greek yogurt rather than crème fraîche. Play with combinations that satisfy your palate and desired fat intake.

---

1 gallon pasteurized whole cow's milk

3/8 teaspoon Aroma B powdered mesophilic starter culture

1/4 teaspoon calcium chloride diluted in 1/4 cup cool nonchlorinated water (omit if using raw milk)

1/4 teaspoon liquid rennet diluted in 1/4 cup cool nonchlorinated water

1 teaspoon kosher salt (preferably Diamond Crystal brand) or cheese salt

1 to 1 1/2 cups crème fraîche, homemade (page 44) or store-bought

1. Read through the recipe and review any terms and techniques you aren't familiar with (see chapter 1). Assemble your equipment, supplies, and ingredients, including a dairy or kitchen thermometer; clean and sterilize your equipment as needed and lay it out on clean kitchen towels.

2. Assemble a water bath using a 6-quart stockpot set inside a larger pot. Pour water into the larger pot to come two-thirds of the way up the side of the smaller pot. Remove the smaller pot and place the pot of water over low heat. When the water reaches 80°F, put the smaller pot back in the water to warm slightly, then pour the milk into the smaller pot. Cover the pot and slowly warm the milk to

70°F over the course of about 15 minutes, lowering the heat, adding cool water to the water bath, or removing from the heat if the temperature is rising too quickly.

3. When the milk is at temperature, sprinkle the starter over the milk and let it rehydrate for 5 minutes. Whisk the starter into the milk to incorporate, using an up-and-down motion for 20 strokes. Add the diluted calcium chloride and incorporate in the same way, and then the diluted rennet. Cover, remove from the water bath, and let sit at room temperature for 5 to 6 hours. The milk protein will coagulate into solid curds, and the liquid whey will be almost clear and light green in color.

4. Check the curds for a clean break (see page 18), using a sanitized long-blade curd cutting knife or 10-inch cake decorating spatula. If the cut edge is clean and there's some accumulation of light-colored whey in the cut area, the curds are ready. If the cut edge is soft and the curds are mushy, the curds are not ready; allow them to sit longer before testing again. When ready, cut the curds into ¾-inch pieces (see page 18) and gently stir using a rubber spatula for 5 minutes to firm up the curds slightly.

(continued)

5.   Return the pot to the water bath over low heat and slowly bring the temperature of the curds to 115°F, raising the temperature about 5°F every 5 minutes. This will take about 40 minutes. During this time, gently stir the curds two or three times to expel more whey and firm them up slightly. When the curds are near temperature, half-fill a large bowl with cold water and ice and line a colander or strainer with clean, damp butter muslin. When the curds are at temperature, they should be firm and bean-sized.

Ladle the curds into the cloth-lined colander and immediately set the colander in the ice water bath. This will set up the curds and stop them from ripening any further.

6.   Let the curds drain completely in the colander, about 15 minutes, then toss with the salt until evenly combined. Gently fold in enough crème fraîche to coat the curds. The cheese may be refrigerated for up to 10 days.

CRESCENZA

MAKES 2 pounds
MILK Pasteurized whole cow's milk
START TO FINISH 11 hours: 2 hours to make the cheese; 6 hours to drain; 2 hours to brine; 1 hour to dry

Crescenza is a soft, creamy cow's milk cheese made seasonally in the Po Valley region of Italy. It is eaten fresh, usually not more than a week old. Square in shape, it has a texture similar to that of a young, mild Taleggio and a rind that's barely begun to form. Traditionally, raw milk would be allowed to ripen naturally overnight. My version uses pasteurized milk with a starter culture and is ripened for a short period of time.

2 gallons pasteurized whole cow's milk
¼ teaspoon Aroma B powdered mesophilic starter culture
¼ teaspoon calcium chloride diluted in ¼ cup cool nonchlorinated water
¼ teaspoon liquid rennet diluted in ¼ cup cool nonchlorinated water
Kosher salt (preferably Diamond Crystal brand) or cheese salt
Nonchlorinated water, chilled to 55°F

1. Read through the recipe and review any terms and techniques you aren't familiar with (see chapter 1). Assemble your equipment, supplies, and ingredients, including a dairy or kitchen thermometer; clean and sterilize your equipment as needed and lay it out on clean kitchen towels.

2. In a nonreactive, heavy 10-quart stockpot, heat the milk over low heat to 90°F. This should take about 20 minutes. Turn off the heat.

3. Sprinkle the starter over the milk and let it rehydrate for 5 minutes. Whisk the starter into the milk to incorporate, using an up-and-down motion for 20 strokes. Cover and, maintaining the temperature at 90°F, allow the milk to ripen for 30 minutes. (Refer to page 17 for tips on maintaining milk or curds at a steady temperature over a period of time.) Add the diluted calcium chloride and incorporate in the same way, then add the diluted rennet. Cover and let sit at room temperature for 45 minutes, or until the curds are firm and there is a clean break between curds and whey (see page 18).

4. Cut the curds into 1-inch pieces (see page 18) and let rest for 10 minutes. Gently stir with a rubber spatula for 5 minutes to firm up the curds slightly. Allow the curds to settle to the bottom of the pot. Ladle off enough whey to expose the tops of the curds.

5. Place a Taleggio mold on a draining rack set over a tray and line the mold with clean, damp butter muslin. Gently ladle the soft curds into the mold, cover the curds with the tails of the muslin, and let drain for 3 hours at room temperature. Lift the cloth sack from the mold, unwrap the cheese, flip it over, and return it to the cloth. Place the sack back in the mold and let drain for another 3 hours, then remove the cheese from the cloth.

6. In a food-grade container with a lid, make enough brine to cover the unwrapped cheese by combining 1 part salt with 5 parts of the chilled water. Place the cheese in the brine for 2 hours at room temperature, flipping the cheese after 1 hour to ensure even salt absorption.

7. Remove the cheese from the brine, pat dry, and place on the draining rack to further drain and air-dry for 1 hour at room temperature, or until the surface is dry to the touch.

8. Wrap thoroughly in plastic wrap or vacuum-seal and refrigerate until ready to use. This cheese is best when consumed within 1 week of wrapping, though if vacuum-sealed it can keep for up to 1 month.

BASIC CHÈVRE

MAKES 1 pound
MILK Pasteurized goat's milk
START TO FINISH 18 to 24 hours: 30 minutes to make the cheese;
12 hours to ripen; 6 to 12 hours to drain

Chèvre is the common name for spreadable goat cheese. This fresh cheese is easy to make and, in its log shape, it is the most recognizable goat cheese in the United States. It often has dried herbs or other flavorful additives blended into the cheese or used to coat the log. This version uses a premixed blend of culture and rennet from New England Cheesemaking Supply designed specifically for making chèvre. This is the simplest method, perfect for any novice cheese maker.

---

1 gallon pasteurized goat's milk
1/2 teaspoon C20G powdered mesophilic starter
culture
1/2 teaspoon fine sea salt

1. Read through the recipe and review any terms and techniques you aren't familiar with (see chapter 1). Assemble your equipment, supplies, and ingredients, including a dairy or kitchen thermometer; clean and sterilize your equipment as needed and lay it out on clean kitchen towels.

2. In a nonreactive, heavy 6-quart stockpot, heat the milk over low heat to 86°F. This should take 18 to 20 minutes. Turn off the heat.

3. When the milk is at temperature, sprinkle the starter over the milk and let it rehydrate for 5 minutes. Whisk the starter into the milk to incorporate, using an up-and-down motion for 20 strokes. Cover and, maintaining the temperature between 72°F and 78°F, allow the milk to ripen for 12 hours. (Refer to page 17 for tips on maintaining milk or curds at a steady temperature over a period of time.)

4. The curds are ready when they have formed one large mass in the pot with the consistency of thick yogurt, surrounded by clear whey. Place a nonreactive strainer over a nonreactive bowl or bucket large enough to capture the whey. Line it with a single layer of clean, damp butter muslin and gently ladle the curds into it. Let drain for 5 minutes, then gently toss the curds with the salt. At this point you can cover the curds with the tails of the muslin and leave to drain over the bowl, or you can spoon the curds into 2 chèvre molds set on a draining rack set over a tray. Let drain at room temperature for 6 hours for creamy cheese, or 12 hours if you wish to shape the cheese. If you are using the molds, flip the cheeses once during the draining process.

5. Remove the cheese from the cheesecloth or molds and place in a covered container. Use right away, or store refrigerated for up to 1 week.

Leaf-Wrapped Cheeses

Typically, soft-ripened lactic-acid or young bloomy-rind goat or mixed milk cheeses are the ones that get trussed up in leaves. However, sheep's milk, cow's milk blue, or even pressed cheeses can be aged in plain or macerated leaves. The major cheese making regions of Europe have been wrapping local cheeses in local leaves for hundreds of years, from chestnut to fig, grape to kale, and even fern fronds, nettle leaves, straw, and hay. Today's cheese makers have also adopted hoja santa leaves, banana leaves, and even seaweed. Sometimes the bundles are also rubbed with olive oil and herbs are tucked inside for added flavor, or the leaves are soaked in alcohol (macerated) before being wrapped around the cheese. These aged cheeses are uncloaked just before serving, often presented on the leaf that dressed them.

Leaves protect a fragile fresh cheese or its newly forming rind from air, light, and unwanted bacteria, yet many are porous enough to let the cheeses breathe. And leaves contribute desirable earthy, mushroomy, and vegetal flavors to the finished cheese.

Here's how to prepare and store leaves for wrapping cheeses. For large leaves such as grape, fig, cabbage, or kale, collect the leaves just before they fall from the tree or vine or, in the case of vegetable leaves, pick them at their prime. Remove the tough center stem or end to make the leaf more pliable. Drop the leaves into a shallow skillet of simmering lightly salted water just to wilt them, then remove and shock them in an ice bath. Let them drain on paper towels and air-dry. Either stack the blanched leaves flat, store in resealable bags, and freeze until ready to use, or store them in a macerating alcohol. Thaw, let drain, and pat the leaves dry before wrapping the cheese. Small leaves that are used fresh, such as nettles, young grape, persimmon, hoja santa, bay, and lemon, are simply steamed to soften and patted dry before using.

Toasted Grape Leaf–Wrapped Chèvre

This is a very simple wrapped cheese to create, so it's a good way to get comfortable with the process of leaf-wrapping cheese. The combination of tangy chèvre with toasted, wine-soaked grape leaves creates the perfect aging environment for the young cheese. If desired, you could also add a little smokiness by cold smoking the chèvre, the macerated grape leaves, or the wrapped parcels themselves—ideally using grape vine pieces or chips as a smoking wood (see page 27). When you're ready to serve these, unwrap each cheese and present it on the leaf it was ripened in.

You will need four 2-ounce rounds of Basic Chèvre (page 58); 4 large fresh grape leaves, stemmed, blanched, and patted dry; $1/2$ cup Sauvignon Blanc; $1^1/_2$ teaspoons flake sea salt; 1 teaspoon herbes de Provence; and four 2-foot-long strands of raffia.

Over an open flame on your kitchen stove or an outdoor grill, lightly toast the grape leaves by passing them over the flame a few times—just enough to release their aroma and give a little charred flavor to the leaves. Do this to both sides of each leaf. Place the grape leaves in the wine in a resealable bag overnight; lay flat and refrigerate. Drain the leaves before using.

Lay the rounds of chèvre on a draining rack and lightly salt on both sides. Sprinkle one side of each round with a light dusting of herbs de Provence. Stack the macerated leaves with the leaves open flat. Place 1 seasoned round of chèvre in the center of the top leaf, herb side up. Carefully wrap the leaf around the cheese to encase it. Secure with a length of raffia by tying as you would a gift package, finishing with a bow. Place the parcels in a ripening box at 50°F to 55°F for 2 weeks (see page 26). Consume at 2 weeks, or vacuum-seal or wrap tightly in plastic wrap and store refrigerated for another 1 to 2 months.

O'BANON

MAKES Four 3¼-ounce cheeses
MILK Pasteurized goat's milk
START TO FINISH 2 weeks to 2 months: 1 hour to make the cheese; 8 hours to ripen;
14 to 20 hours to drain; 2 weeks to 2 months to age

Fashioned after the leaf-wrapped Provençal cheese Banon, O'Banon is an award-winning goat cheese made by Judy Schad and her crew at Capriole in Greenville, Indiana—this recipe is an adaptation of that cheese, developed with Judy for home cheese making. Judy has made O'Banon since the creamery opened for business in 1988. Like its smaller relative, O'Banon is made of goat's milk and wrapped in alcohol-soaked chestnut leaves. But Judy's farmstead cheese is an American original, rooted in farm-raised goat's milk and rural Indiana traditions. Rather than being flavored by eau-de-vie as Banon is, O'Banon's chestnut leaves are macerated in good old Kentucky bourbon before being wrapped around fresh chèvre rounds. The rounds are tied securely with raffia and set to air-dry overnight before being refrigerated. The tannins in the leaves and the bourbon give this creamy, dense cheese a delightful kick. O'Banon is terrific at two weeks and even better when allowed to ripen in its leafy cocoon for up to two months.

1 cup bourbon
½ cup nonchlorinated water
4 prepared chestnut or maple leaves (see page 59)
1 gallon pasteurized goat's milk
¼ teaspoon MA 011 powdered mesophilic starter culture
⅛ teaspoon calcium chloride diluted in ¼ cup cool nonchlorinated water
¼ teaspoon liquid rennet diluted in ¼ cup cool nonchlorinated water
2 teaspoons kosher salt (preferably Diamond Crystal brand) or cheese salt

1. Read through the recipe and review any terms and techniques you aren't familiar with (see chapter 1). Assemble your equipment, supplies, and ingredients, including a dairy or kitchen thermometer; clean and sterilize your equipment as needed and lay it out on clean kitchen towels.

2. Twenty-four hours before you make the cheese, combine the bourbon with the water and chill to 55°F. Place the leaves in a resealable bag with the bourbon and water and lay flat in the refrigerator. Drain when ready to use.

3. In a nonreactive heavy 6-quart stockpot, heat the milk over low heat to 86°F. This should take about 15 minutes. Turn off the heat.

4. When the milk is at temperature, sprinkle the starter over the milk and let it rehydrate for 5 minutes. Whisk the starter into the milk to incorporate, using an up-and-down motion for 20 strokes. Add the diluted calcium chloride and gently whisk in, then add the rennet in the same way. Cover and maintain 72°F, allowing the milk to ripen for 8 hours, or until the curds have formed a solid mass with the consistency of thick yogurt and clear whey is floating around the sides of the pot. (Refer to page 17 for tips on maintaining milk or curds at a steady temperature over a period of time.) Check the curds for a clean break, using a sanitized long-blade curd cutting knife or 10-inch cake decorating spatula (see page 18). If the cut edge is clean and there's some accumulation of light-colored whey in the cut area, the curds are ready. If the cut edge is soft and the curds are mushy, the curds are not ready; allow them to sit longer before testing again.

5. Place a nonreactive strainer over a nonreactive bowl or bucket large enough to capture the whey. Line it with clean, damp butter muslin. When the curds are ready, gently cut them into ½-inch-thick slices using a ladle or skimmer and gently place them into the strainer to drain for 20 minutes (see page 18). Sprinkle 1 teaspoon of the salt over the curds and gently but thoroughly toss with clean hands to combine. Let the curds drain for another 20 minutes.

6. Place four 2¾-inch crottin molds on a draining rack set over a tray. Gently ladle the curds into the molds and let drain for 12 to 18 hours at room temperature, until the cheeses are firm. After 8 hours, or when the molded curds are firm enough to handle, flip the cheeses over and replace in the molds to finish draining. At this point the cheese will have compressed to slightly over 1 inch in thickness.

7. Remove the firmed cheeses from their molds and sprinkle a pinch of salt over the top and bottom of each cheese. Set the cheeses on a rack and air-dry at 58°F to 60°F with good air circulation for 8 hours (see page 25).

8. Remove the macerated leaves from their liquid and lay them flat on a cutting board. Place 1 round of goat cheese in the center of each leaf and wrap the leaf around the cheese to enclose, then tie securely with a 2-foot length of raffia (you will need 4 lengths of raffia in all).

9. Place the parcels 1 inch apart on a mat in a ripening box with the lid ajar and ripen at 50°F to 55°F and 80 percent humidity for 2 weeks (see page 26). The cheese will be ready to eat at this point, or it can be aged in the ripening box for 6 more weeks. Vacuum-seal or wrap tightly in plastic wrap and store in the refrigerator for up to 2 months.

Profile: Judy Schad and Capriole Farmstead Goat Cheeses

Capriole Goat Cheese and its ingenious proprietor, Judy Schad, are synonymous with American artisan farmstead cheese making. Judy, like many cheese makers, started making goat cheese in her home kitchen with milk from her farm's dairy goats—a benefit of raising goats as part of her children's 4-H projects. Judy has been selling her award-winning farmstead goat cheeses since 1988. Early on, Judy banded together with other women who were raising and showing dairy goats, among them Jennifer Bice, Mary Keehn, and Laura Chenel. This group soon became the genesis of a goat sisterhood. It didn't take long for these creative women to start experimenting with making French-style goat cheeses, which were virtually unheard of in America at that time. These visionary cheese makers helped bring goat cheeses to their current stature in America.

FROMAGE BLANC

MAKES 1½ pounds
MILK Pasteurized reduced fat (2 percent) cow's milk
ALTERNATIVE MILKS Pasteurized whole, low-fat (1 percent), or nonfat cow's milk;
raw cow's milk; pasteurized or raw goat's milk
START TO FINISH 16 to 18 hours: 30 minutes to make the cheese; 12 hours to ripen; 4 to 6 hours to drain

Literally translated, *fromage blanc* means "white cheese" in French. This unripened, spreadable cheese is similar in texture and consistency to cream cheese. In France, it is traditionally made with nonfat milk, though some cheese makers add cream to give it a richer flavor. This version is made with reduced fat (2 percent) milk, but you may use combinations of milks with different fat levels or add cream if you choose. Note that if you make it with only nonfat milk, the yield will decrease and the cheese will have a drier texture. As with cream cheese, fromage blanc can have flavors added to it, such as herbs or spices. It makes a lovely substitute for ricotta in cooking.

1 gallon pasteurized reduced fat (2 percent) cow's milk

¼ teaspoon MA 4001 powdered mesophilic starter culture

4 drops calcium chloride diluted in 2 tablespoons cool nonchlorinated water (omit if using raw milk)

4 drops liquid rennet diluted in 2 tablespoons cool nonchlorinated water

1 teaspoon kosher salt (preferably Diamond Crystal brand) or cheese salt

1. Read through the recipe and review any terms and techniques you aren't familiar with (see chapter 1). Assemble your equipment, supplies, and ingredients, including a dairy or kitchen thermometer; clean and sterilize your equipment as needed and lay it out on clean kitchen towels.

2. Assemble a water bath using a 6-quart stockpot set inside a larger pot. Pour water into the larger pot to come two-thirds of the way up the side of the smaller pot. Remove the smaller pot and place the pot of water over low heat. When the water reaches 85°F, put the smaller pot back in the water to warm slightly, then pour the milk into the smaller pot. Cover the pot and slowly warm the milk to 75°F over the course of about 15 minutes, lowering the heat, adding cool water to the water bath, or removing from the heat if the temperature is rising too quickly. Turn off the heat.

3. When the milk is at temperature, sprinkle the starter over the milk and let it rehydrate for 5 minutes. Whisk the starter into the milk to incorporate, using an up-and-down motion for 20 strokes. Add the diluted calcium chloride and incorporate in the same way, then add the diluted rennet in the same way. Cover and let set at room temperature for 12 hours, or until the curds are solid and the whey is almost clear and yellowish in color and is floating on top.

4. Place a nonreactive strainer over a nonreactive bowl or bucket large enough to capture the whey. Line it with clean, damp butter muslin and gently ladle the curds into it. Make a draining sack (see page 20) or leave the curds to drain in the colander for 4 to 6 hours, or until the desired consistency is achieved. Discard the whey or reserve it for another use.

5. Transfer the curds to a bowl and sprinkle with the salt, then whisk to combine. Use right away, or store refrigerated for up to 2 weeks.

QUESO FRESCO

MAKES 2 pounds
MILK Pasteurized whole cow's milk
ALTERNATIVE MILKS Raw cow's milk; pasteurized or raw goat's milk
START TO FINISH About 8½ hours: 2½ hours to make the cheese; 6 hours to press

Widely popular in Latin cuisines, queso fresco ("fresh cheese" in Spanish) is in the same family as queso blanco (page 38). Instead of using vinegar as the coagulant, here we are using rennet along with mesophilic culture to develop a more complex flavor than its blanco relative. Additionally, this cheese is pressed and allowed to age slightly over two weeks or longer.

....

2 gallons pasteurized whole cow's milk

¼ teaspoon Meso II powdered mesophilic starter culture

¼ teaspoon calcium chloride diluted in ¼ cup cool nonchlorinated water (omit if using raw milk)

¼ teaspoon liquid rennet diluted in ¼ cup cool nonchlorinated water

1½ teaspoons kosher salt (preferably Diamond Crystal brand) or cheese salt

1.   Read through the recipe and review any terms and techniques you aren't familiar with (see chapter 1). Assemble your equipment, supplies, and ingredients, including a dairy or kitchen thermometer, a 5-inch tomme mold with a follower, and a cheese press or 8-pound weight such as a gallon jug filled with water. Clean and sterilize your equipment as needed and lay it out on clean kitchen towels.

2.   In a nonreactive, heavy 10-quart stockpot, heat the milk over medium heat to 90°F, stirring occasionally with a rubber spatula to prevent scorching. This should take about 20 minutes. Turn off the heat.

3.   When the milk is at temperature, sprinkle the starter over the milk and let it rehydrate for 5 minutes. Whisk the starter into the milk to incorporate, using an up-and-down motion for 20 strokes. Cover and maintain the temperature at 90°F for 30 minutes to ripen the milk. (Refer to page 17 for tips on maintaining milk or curds at a steady temperature over a period of time.) Add the diluted calcium chloride and gently incorporate with a whisk using an up-and-down

motion for 1 minute. Add the diluted rennet and incorporate in the same way. Cover and maintain the 90°F temperature for 45 minutes more, or until the curds give a clean break when cut with a knife (see page 18).

4.   Cut the curds into ¼-inch pieces (see page 18) and let them set for 10 minutes. Return the uncovered pot to low heat and gradually increase the temperature to 95°F over 20 minutes, gently stirring the curds a few times to keep them from matting. Remove the pot from the heat and let the curds settle for 5 minutes, then ladle off enough whey to expose the curds.

5.   Place a nonreactive strainer over a nonreactive bowl or bucket large enough to capture the whey. Line it with clean, damp butter muslin and gently ladle the curds into it. Let drain for 5 minutes. Distribute the salt over the curds and gently toss to incorporate, being careful not to break up the curds in the process.

6.   Lift the cloth full of curds from the strainer and place it into the 5-inch tomme mold. Using your hands, distribute the curds evenly in the mold. Cover the curds with the tails of the cloth and set the follower in place, then place in a press at 8 pounds of pressure for 6 hours at room temperature. You may also use a 1-gallon container full of water for the weight.

7.   Remove the cheese from the mold and the cloth and use right away, or store refrigerated in a covered container for up to 2 weeks.

QUARK

MAKES 1½ pounds
MILKS Pasteurized whole cow's milk, pasteurized reduced fat (2 percent) cow's milk
START TO FINISH 18 to 29 hours: 30 minutes to make the cheese; 12½ to 18½ hours to ripen; 6 to 10 hours to drain

The word *quark* means "curd" in German, and this soft cultured cheese is a favorite in Germany and across central Europe. The consistency of sour cream or yogurt, quark is often flavored with dried fruits. It is traditionally made fat free, though blends of higher-fat milks and cream can be used. In keeping with American tastes, this is a lower-fat version. American cheese makers such as Vermont Butter & Cheese and Marin French produce award-winning versions of quark.

2 quarts pasteurized whole cow's milk

2 quarts pasteurized reduced fat (2 percent) cow's milk

¼ teaspoon Aroma B powdered mesophilic starter culture

¼ teaspoon calcium chloride diluted in ¼ cup cool nonchlorinated water

¼ teaspoon liquid rennet diluted in ¼ cup cool nonchlorinated water

1½ teaspoons kosher salt (preferably Diamond Crystal brand) or cheese salt

1. Read through the recipe and review any terms and techniques you aren't familiar with (see chapter 1). Assemble your equipment, supplies, and ingredients, including a dairy or kitchen thermometer; clean and sterilize your equipment as needed and lay it out on clean kitchen towels.

2. In a nonreactive 6-quart stockpot slowly heat both milks over low heat to 72°F. This should take about 15 minutes. Turn off the heat.

3. When the milk is at temperature, sprinkle the starter over the milk and let it rehydrate for 5 minutes. Whisk the starter into the milk to incorporate, using an up-and-down motion for 20 strokes. Cover and, maintaining the temperature at 72°F, allow the milk to ripen for 30 minutes. (Refer to page 17 for tips on maintaining milk or curds at a steady temperature over a period of time.) Add the diluted calcium chloride and gently stir with a whisk using an up-and-down motion for 1 minute. Add the diluted rennet and incorporate in the same way.

4. Cover and let sit at room temperature for 12 to 18 hours, until the whey is floating on top and the curds give a clean break when cut with a knife (see page 18). If the cut edge is clean and there's some accumulation of light-colored whey in the cut area, the curds are ready. If the cut edge is soft and the curds are mushy, the curds are not ready; allow them to sit 10 minutes longer before testing again.

5. Slowly return the curds and whey to 72°F over low heat. Cut the curds into ½-inch pieces (see page 18), remove from the heat, and gently stir for 5 minutes. Let the curds rest and sink to the bottom of the pot, maintaining temperature. Ladle off whey until the curds are exposed, then ladle the curds into a colander lined with clean, damp butter muslin. Let the curds drain for 6 to 10 hours, or until the desired moisture level is achieved; longer draining will result in drier quark.

6. Transfer the curds to a bowl and toss with the salt, gently folding it in using a rubber spatula. Let drain for another 5 minutes if excess whey exists. Use right away, or store refrigerated in a covered container for up to 2 weeks.

Salt-Rubbed and Brined Cheeses

After working through the fresh cheeses and cultured dairy products, you have the skills to tackle cheeses soaked or stored in concentrated brine or rubbed with salt while fresh—practices that result in a distinctive brininess or tang and a firm texture. Many popular varieties of salt-rubbed or brined cheeses we know today are still made in the traditional way, including cotija, feta, Halloumi, Manchego, ricotta salata, and São Jorge. Haystack Mountain's goat feta and Matos's St. George are two modern American examples. Some of these cheeses are very young, ripened for only a week or two, while others age for several months. If allowed to age until very dry, they can also be used as grating cheeses.

These simple cheeses are made using direct acidification or mesophilic starter cultures. Some styles are hung to drain off their whey, while others are pressed before brining or salt-rubbing.

COTIJA

MAKES 1¾ pounds
MILK Pasteurized whole cow's milk
ALTERNATIVE MILKS Pasteurized goat's milk; sheep's milk
START TO FINISH 16 days to 6 weeks: about 3 hours to make the cheese;
8½ hours to press; 24 hours to brine; 2 to 6 weeks to mature

Cotija is a very popular Mexican cheese that's dry, crumbly, and salty. Pressed in round or rectangular shapes, it is used in a manner similar to Parmesan, as a grating or finishing cheese. Cotija is most frequently used young, though if left to age, the saltiness will dissipate and mellow.

---

2 gallons pasteurized whole cow's milk

¼ teaspoon Meso II powdered mesophilic starter culture

¼ teaspoon Thermo B powdered thermophilic starter culture

¼ teaspoon calcium chloride diluted in ¼ cup cool nonchlorinated water

¼ teaspoon liquid rennet diluted in ¼ cup cool nonchlorinated water

Kosher salt (preferably Diamond Crystal brand) or cheese salt

1. Read through the recipe and review any terms and techniques you aren't familiar with (see chapter 1). Assemble your equipment, supplies, and ingredients, including a dairy or kitchen thermometer, a 5-inch tomme mold with a follower, and a cheese press or 15-pound weight. Clean and sterilize your equipment as needed and lay it out on clean kitchen towels.

2. In a nonreactive 10-quart stockpot over low heat, slowly heat the milk to 100°F, stirring occasionally to prevent scorching. This should take about 25 minutes. Turn off the heat.

(continued)

3. When the milk is at temperature, sprinkle the starters over the milk and let it rehydrate for 5 minutes. Whisk the starters into the milk to incorporate, using an up-and-down motion for 20 strokes. Cover and, maintaining the temperature at 100°F, let the milk ripen for 30 minutes. (Refer to page 17 for tips on maintaining milk or curds at a steady temperature over a period of time.) Add the diluted calcium chloride to the milk and incorporate using the same up-and-down technique, then add the diluted rennet in the same way. Cover and maintain the temperature at 100°F for 1½ hours, or until the curds give a clean break when cut (see page 18).

4. Continuing to maintain the curds at 100°F, cut them into ½-inch pieces (see page 18) and let sit for 10 minutes. Slowly raise the temperature to 105°F over 10 minutes, gently stirring around the edge of the pot with a rubber spatula and moving the curds continuously to firm up the surface and prevent them from matting. The curds will expel whey and shrink to the size of lentils. Let the curds rest for 10 minutes, still maintaining 105°F.

5. Place a nonreactive strainer over a nonreactive bowl or bucket large enough to capture the whey. Line it with clean, damp butter muslin and gently ladle the curds into it. Let drain for 15 minutes, or until the whey stops dripping. Distribute 1½ teaspoons of salt over the curds and use your hands to gently toss the curds to incorporate, being careful not to break up the curds in the process.

6. Place the 5-inch tomme mold on a draining rack set over a baking sheet. Line the mold with damp cheesecloth or butter muslin. Gently transfer the drained curds to the lined cheese mold, cover with the tails of the cloth, and set the follower on top of the curds. Press at 15 pounds for 30 minutes. Remove the cheese from the mold and peel away the cloth, flip the cheese over, and redress. Press again at the same pressure for 8 hours or overnight.

7. Two or more hours before you'll need it, make the brine by combining 1½ cups of salt and 1 quart of water in a non-corrosive bucket or a container with a lid; chill to 50°F to 55°F. Remove the cheese from the mold and unwrap it, then place it in the brine. Let it soak at 50°F to 55°F for 24 hours, flipping it over after 12 hours to evenly distribute the brine.

8. Remove the cheese from the brine and pat dry. Air-dry for 6 hours, then place on a cheese mat in a ripening box (see page 26). Age at 55°F at 80 to 85 percent humidity, turning daily. Remove any unwanted mold with cheesecloth dampened in a vinegar-salt solution (see page 25) and wipe down the box to maintain humidity. After 2 weeks, wrap the cheese in cheese paper and store in your refrigerator for up to 4 more weeks. Alternately, vacuum-seal the cheese and refrigerate for up to 2 months.

RICOTTA SALATA

MAKES 12 ounces
MILKS Raw or pasteurized whole cow's milk, heavy cream
ALTERNATIVE MILK Pasteurized or raw goat's milk
START TO FINISH 3 to 9 weeks: 1½ hours to make the fresh ricotta; 1 day to press and dry;
7 days to salt cure; 2 weeks to 2 months to age

Ricotta salata is a dry, salted ricotta that is often shaved into slivers and used as a garnishing cheese. It can be eaten young (two to four weeks after making) or used as a grating cheese when it is more mature (five weeks to two months after making). The younger the cheese the saltier it will be; by two months the cheese will have bloomed into a lovely, mellow-flavored treat.

1 gallon pasteurized whole cow's milk
½ cup heavy cream
1 teaspoon citric acid powder
Kosher salt (preferably Diamond Crystal brand)
　　or cheese salt

1. Follow the whole milk ricotta recipe on page 39 through the first draining in the colander (step 4).

2. Add 1 tablespoon kosher salt or cheese salt to the curds and toss with your hands to distribute. Line a ricotta mold with clean, damp cheesecloth and place on a draining rack set over a tray. Press the cheese into the mold, cover with the tails of the cheesecloth, and weight it down with a slightly less than 2-pound weight, such as a pint jar full of water. Press for 1 hour, then unmold the cheese, unwrap it, flip it over, redress it in the same cheesecloth, and return it to the mold. Press it at the same weight for 12 hours or overnight.

3. Unmold and unwrap the cheese, then lightly rub the surface with kosher or cheese salt. Redress the cheese with clean cheesecloth, return it to the mold, set it on a drying rack, and refrigerate for 12 hours.

4. Take the cheese out of the cheesecloth, flip it over, and rub all over with more salt, then return the undressed cheese to the mold. Continue this process of flipping and salting once a day for 7 days to pull out moisture and assist in the curing process. After 3 days, remove the cheese from the mold and keep aging it on the rack. If any unwanted mold appears, wipe it off with cheesecloth dampened in a vinegar-salt solution (see page 25).

5. After 1 week, brush any excess salt from the surface and age the cheese in the refrigerator until the desired texture is achieved. Use right away, or wrap in cheese paper and store in the refrigerator for at least 2 weeks and up to 2 months.

FETA

MAKES 1 pound
MILK Pasteurized or raw goat's milk
ALTERNATIVE MILKS Cow's milk; sheep's milk
START TO FINISH 5 to 26 days: 2½ hours to make the cheese; 4 hours to drain;
5 days to cure dry salted; 21 days to cure in brine (optional)

Though feta is often associated with Greece as its place of origin, many Balkan countries also make it. Known for its crumbly texture, feta is traditionally made with sheep's or goat's milk, and its unique salty flavor is created by brining. This home-crafted formula is made with goat's milk and cured with salt, though I've also offered a brine option. I like to salt cure for twenty-four to thirty-six hours to expel more of the whey, then place the feta in a light brine to finish curing. For a stronger flavor, add lipase powder to the milk before ripening.

---

1 gallon pasteurized goat's milk

¼ teaspoon mild lipase powder diluted in ¼ cup cool nonchlorinated water 20 minutes before using (optional)

¼ teaspoon Aroma B powdered mesophilic starter culture

¼ teaspoon liquid calcium chloride diluted in ¼ cup cool nonchlorinated water (omit if using raw milk)

½ teaspoon liquid rennet diluted in ¼ cup cool nonchlorinated water

2 to 4 tablespoons flake sea salt or kosher salt (preferably Diamond Crystal brand)

Kosher salt (preferably Diamond Crystal brand) or cheese salt for brining (optional)

1. Read through the recipe and review any terms and techniques you aren't familiar with (see chapter 1). Assemble your equipment, supplies, and ingredients, including a dairy or kitchen thermometer; clean and sterilize your equipment as needed and lay it out on clean kitchen towels.

2. In a nonreactive, heavy 6-quart stockpot, combine the milk and the diluted lipase, if using, gently whisking the lipase into the milk using an up-and-down motion for 20 strokes. Place over low heat and slowly heat the milk to 86°F. This should take 18 to 20 minutes. Turn off the heat.

3. When the milk is at temperature, sprinkle the starter over the milk and let it rehydrate for 2 minutes. Whisk the starter into the milk to incorporate, using an up-and-down motion for 20 strokes. Cover and, maintaining the temperature at 86°F, let the milk ripen for 1 hour. (Refer to page 17 for tips on maintaining milk or curds at a steady temperature over a period of time.)

4. Add the diluted calcium chloride to the ripened milk and gently stir with a whisk using an up-and-down motion for 1 minute. Add the diluted rennet and incorporate in the same way. Cover and maintain at 86°F for 1 hour, or until the curds form a solid mass with light yellow whey floating on top and show a clean break (see page 18). If there is no clean break after 1 hour, test again in 15 minutes.

5. Cut the curds into ½-inch pieces (see page 18). Still maintaining a temperature of 86°F, allow them to sit undisturbed for 10 minutes. Using a rubber spatula, gently stir the curds for 20 minutes to release more whey and keep the curds from matting. The curds will look more pillowlike at the end of this process. If you want a firmer curd, raise the temperature to 90°F for this step. Let the curds rest for 5 minutes, undisturbed, still at temperature. The curds will settle to the bottom of the pot.

6. Line a colander with clean, damp cheesecloth or butter muslin and, using a slotted spoon, transfer the curds to the colander. Tie the corners of the cloth together to create a draining sack (see page 20), then let drain for 4 hours, or until the whey has stopped dripping. The curds should form a solid mass and feel firm; if not, let them dry for another hour. If you desire a more uniform shape, after 1 hour of draining in the colander, transfer the sack to a square cheese mold or plastic mesh tomato basket set over a draining rack. Line the mold with the cloth of the sack, spread the cheese out into the corners of the mold, and finish draining. Remove the cheese from the cloth and flip it over every hour in this draining process to help even out the texture and firm up the cheese.

7. When it is drained, transfer the cheese to a bowl. Cut it into 1-inch-thick slices and then into 1-inch cubes. Sprinkle the chunks with flake sea salt, making sure all the surfaces are covered. Loosely cover the bowl with a lid or plastic wrap and allow to age in the salt for 5 days in the refrigerator. Check daily and pour off any expelled whey. The feta can be used at this point or stored in a brine. Or, for a saltier flavor, dry salt and refrigerate for 24 to 36 hours, then transfer to a light brine (see page 24) to finish for another 21 days. If the finished cheese is too salty for your taste, soak the cheese in nonchlorinated water for 1 hour, then let drain before using. Feta can be stored for a few months in a brine.

HALLOUMI

MAKES 12 ounces
MILK Pasteurized or raw whole cow's milk
ALTERNATIVE MILKS A blend of cow's and goat's milk; sheep's milk
START TO FINISH From 5½ days to 2 months: 1½ hours to make the cheese; 6 hours to press;
1 hour to cook; 45 minutes to dry; 5 days to 2 months to brine

Originating in Cypress, this cheese is traditionally made from sheep's milk or a combination of sheep's and goat's milk with only rennet added for coagulation. This simple version is made with cow's milk with a small amount of lipase powder added to emulate the rich flavor of the original. (If you use other milks—goat's milk plus cow's milk, or sheep's milk—omit the lipase.) For a variation, you can add dried mint to the drained curds as a nod to the traditional regional flavors. As a bonus, the whey from cooking the pressed curds will be lightly flavored with mint and is absolutely delicious; use it within a few hours to cook rice or as soup stock.

1 gallon pasteurized whole cow's milk
¼ teaspoon mild lipase powder dissolved in ¼ cup cool nonchlorinated water 20 minutes before using (optional)
½ teaspoon calcium chloride diluted in ¼ cup cool nonchlorinated water (omit if using raw milk)
½ teaspoon liquid rennet diluted in ¼ cup cool nonchlorinated water
½ teaspoon dried mint (optional)
Kosher salt (preferably Diamond Crystal brand) or cheese salt for brining

1. Read through the recipe and review any terms and techniques you aren't familiar with (see chapter 1). Assemble your equipment, supplies, and ingredients, including a dairy or kitchen thermometer; you will also need a 5-inch tomme mold with a follower and a cheese press or an 8-pound weight (a gallon container filled with water will do). Clean and sterilize your equipment as needed and lay it out on clean kitchen towels.

2. In a nonreactive, heavy 6-quart stockpot, slowly heat the milk over low heat to 90°F. This should take about 20 minutes. Turn off the heat.

3. If using lipase, gently whisk it into the milk using an up-and-down motion for 1 minute, then let rest for 5 minutes.

Add the diluted calcium chloride and gently stir with a whisk using an up-and-down motion for 1 minute. Add the diluted rennet and incorporate in the same way. Cover and, maintaining the temperature at 90°F, let the milk ripen for 30 to 45 minutes, or until the curds give a clean break when cut with a knife (see page 18). Still maintaining 90°F, cut the curds into ¾-inch pieces (see page 18) and let sit for 5 minutes.

4. Over low heat, slowly bring the curds to 104°F over a 15-minute period. The curds will break up slightly. Maintaining the 104°F temperature, gently and continuously stir with a rubber spatula for 20 minutes. The curds will shrink and firm up slightly, taking on an individual shape. Let the curds rest for 5 minutes, maintaining temperature. They will sink to the bottom and the whey will rise to the top. Ladle off enough whey to expose the top of the curds.

5. Place a nonreactive strainer over a nonreactive bowl or bucket large enough to capture the whey. Line it with clean, damp butter muslin and gently ladle the curds into it. Toss the dried mint with the curds if using, and let drain for 15 minutes, or until the whey stops dripping. Reserve the whey for later use in the recipe, storing it in the refrigerator to prevent souring.

6. Place the 5-inch tomme mold on a draining rack set over a tray. Line the mold with clean, damp cheesecloth, then gently transfer the drained curds to the mold. Cover the top of the curds with the excess cheesecloth and set the follower on top. Place the mold in a cheese press or place an 8-pound weight on top of the follower and press at 8 pounds of pressure for 3 hours.

7. Remove the cheese from the mold, peel away the cheesecloth, flip the cheese over, and redress with the cheesecloth. Press again at 8 pounds for another 3 hours.

8. Remove the pressed curds from the mold and cut off the rounded edges to create a 4-inch square. Reserve the trimmings to use as a crumbled cheese topping. If the pressed curds are 2 inches thick or more, halve the slab horizontally.

9. Using a cheese making pot, slowly heat the reserved whey to 190°F over 30 minutes. Place the square or squares of curds in the hot whey and cook for 30 to 35 minutes, or until the cheese shrinks slightly and floats on the top of the whey. Be sure to maintain the temperature throughout cooking and do not let the whey boil.

10. Using a mesh skimmer, remove the cheese from the whey and place it on a draining rack to cool. Air-dry, flipping at least once, until the surfaces are dry to the touch, about 45 minutes.

11. Meanwhile, make a medium-heavy brine (see page 24) by combining the salt with 1 gallon of 50°F to 55°F water. Place the dried cheese in a noncorrosive container and cover with the cool brine. Store covered in the refrigerator for 5 days or up to 2 months. Save the unused brine in a labeled container at 50°F to 55°F for another brining.

CHAPTER 3
Intermediate Cheese Making

Stretched-Curd and Semisoft, Firm, and Hard Cheeses

Farmhouse Chive Cheddar at 3 months (page 122)

In contrast to the recipes in chapter 2, those in this and the following chapter assume a working familiarity with the basic terms and techniques of cheese making. The cheeses in this chapter will use techniques not found in chapter 2, including cooking curds, stretching curds, working with more complex flavor- and aroma-enhancing cultures, cheddaring, and waxing. If you are still something of a novice, be sure to read through a new recipe carefully

and review any unfamiliar terms and techniques—they're all explained in detail in chapter 1, particularly in the "Processes and Techniques" section (pages 16–33).

If you are an experienced cheese maker, you know this, but bear with me—it's important! Before you begin, read through the recipe and assemble your equipment and supplies. Sterilize any item that will come in contact with the milk, other ingredients, the curds, or the aging cheese—or at least clean it very well in very hot water. Always use only nonchlorinated water and noniodized salt in your cheeses and brines. Avoid homogenized milk whenever possible, and never use ultra-pasteurized milks and creams or those with any additives or thickeners.

Stretched-Curd Cheeses

Stretched-curd cheeses (also known as pasta filata cheeses) are a category of semisoft, hand-shaped cheeses made primarily from cow's, goat's, water buffalo's, and sheep's milk and including both fresh and aged types from a variety of traditions. The notable cornerstones mozzarella, burrata, Provolone, Scamorza, and Caciocavallo come from Italy, though Mexico (queso Oaxaca), Greece (Kasseri), and the Middle East (string cheese) produce tasty members of this family. The fresh varieties, like mozzarella, are the best melters due to their high moisture content. These cheeses' texture is smooth, stretchy, and pleasantly chewy, and their flavor is milky and mild. Lipase is added to some varieties when a more robust flavor is desired. In the cheese making process, the curds are formed and brought to the proper acidity for elasticity, then melted in very hot water or whey, stretched and worked to create the desired silky texture, shaped, and plunged into a cold bath to firm up. The fresh cheeses are then transferred to a brine for a period of time before vacuum-sealing or packing in water. Some, such as Scamorza, Provolone, and some styles of string cheese, are smoked with aromatic woods and hung or waxed to age. Depending on the desired finished flavor, stretched-curd cheeses are aged in the range of one day for fresh cheeses; two to four months for aged cheeses; and six to twelve months for grating-quality cheeses. In every beginning cheese making class I've taught, after students have made a few fresh cheeses, they ask to

Stretching curds into ribbons for Queso Oaxaca (page 79)

make mozzarella—soft, pliable, and fun. What I try to tell my students is that you may not nail it the first time; it takes practice to become successful at the stretching and shaping of the curds.

One way to practice is to stretch and shape ready-made curds you've purchased from a reliable cheese retailer. One pound should be enough to play with. Follow the directions in any of the recipes given here to shape and complete a stretched-curd cheese. Though technically you won't be "making" the cheese yet, this practice will help prepare you for success in making a stretched-curd cheese entirely from scratch. It may take two or three times of going through the process before you are completely successful, but once you are, there's no stopping you.

Note that in order to make mozzarella and other stretched-curd cheeses that are stretchable, monitoring pH is essential, as the curd is best stretched in the pH range of 4.9 to 5.2. A pH meter is a very useful tool for making these cheeses, and I will call for its use in a number of the recipes here. You can use pH test strips when you first start to make stretched-curd cheeses. They are available from most cheese making suppliers; though they are a little fiddlier and less precise than the meter, they are less of an investment for a beginner curd stretcher. If you take this route, make sure you get strips that have a range higher than 5 pH.

TRADITIONAL MOZZARELLA

MAKES 1 pound

MILK Pasteurized whole cow's or goat's milk

START TO FINISH 7 to 16 hours: 5½ to 6½ hours to make and cook the curds;
about 1 hour to melt, stretch, and shape the curds; 20 minutes to 8 hours to brine

Mozzarella is, of course, the best-known cheese of the stretched-curd family. The word *mozzarella* is from the Italian *mozzare*, which means "to tear," referencing the tearing of the stretched mozzarella to form balls and other shapes. Mozzarella is traditionally made with water buffalo's milk; however, almost all of the mozzarella made in North America is made with cow's milk. Freshly made mozzarella is moist and creamy, and very unlike processed mozzarella, which can be chewy and flavorless. This home-crafted formula is made with cow's milk and cured in a whey-based brine. This recipe is time intensive yet rewarding; once you master it you will be able to branch out into any of the other stretched-curd cheeses with confidence. If you prefer to make a simpler mozzarella, try Junket Mozzarella (page 80). Note that for this recipe you will need heat-resistant neoprene or rubber gloves and a pH meter or pH strips.

---

1 gallon pasteurized whole cow's or goat's milk

¼ teaspoon Thermo B powdered thermophilic starter culture

¼ teaspoon calcium chloride diluted in ¼ cup cool nonchlorinated water

¾ teaspoon liquid rennet diluted in ¼ cup cool nonchlorinated water

Kosher salt (preferably Diamond Crystal brand) or cheese salt for brining

1.   In a nonreactive 6-quart stockpot, slowly heat the milk to 95°F over low heat; this should take about 20 minutes. Turn off the heat.

2.   Sprinkle the starter over the milk and let it rehydrate for 5 minutes. Mix well using a whisk in an up-and-down motion for 20 strokes. Cover and maintain 90°F to 95°F, letting the milk ripen for 45 minutes. Add the diluted calcium chloride and gently whisk in. Let rest for 10 minutes. Add the diluted rennet and gently whisk in. Cover and let sit, maintaining 90°F to 95°F for 1 hour, or until the curds give a clean break.

3.   Cut the curds into ½-inch pieces and let sit undisturbed for 30 minutes, maintaining at 90°F to 95°F. During this time the curds will firm up and release more whey. Over low heat, slowly raise the temperature to 105°F over 30 minutes, gently stirring from time to time and frequently checking the temperature and adjusting the heat as needed. If you raise the temperature too quickly, the curds won't coagulate or bind properly. Once 105°F is reached, remove from the heat and, using a rubber spatula, gently stir for 10 minutes around the edges of the pot and under the curds to move them around. Maintaining temperature, let the curds rest for another 15 minutes; they will sink to the bottom.

4.   Line a colander with damp butter muslin, set it over another pot, and scoop the curds into it with a slotted spoon. Let drain for 15 minutes, or until the curds stop dripping whey. Reserve the whey.

5.   Gently return the drained curds to the original pot and place it in a 102°F to 105°F water bath. Hold the water bath temperature for 2 hours. The curds will melt into each other, binding into a slab; turn the slab two times during this period, using a spatula.

(continued)

6. When 2 hours have elapsed, begin testing the curds' pH using a pH meter or pH strips. Check the pH every 30 minutes during this period; once it drops below 5.6, check it every 15 minutes, as it will fall rapidly after this point. Once the pH drops into the 4.9 to 5.2 range, the curds are ready to stretch.

7. Transfer the curds to a warm strainer, let drain for a couple of minutes, then transfer to a sterilized cutting board. Cut the curds into approximately 1-inch cubes and put them in a clean stainless steel bowl large enough to hold them with plenty of room to spare (the curds will be covered with hot liquid). In a clean pot, heat 4 quarts of water or of the reserved whey to 170°F to 180°F. Pour this over the curds to cover them completely.

8. Wearing heat-resistant gloves, work the submerged cubes of curd into one large ball, kneading and shaping it in the hot water. Once the curds are shaped into a firm ball, lift it out of the water and, working quickly, pull and stretch it into a long rope about 18 inches long. If the curd rope cools and becomes brittle, dip it into the hot water to make it warm and pliable again. Loop the rope back on itself, and then pull and stretch it again two or three times, just until the curd is shiny and smooth. (The process is something like stretching taffy.) Be careful not to overwork the curd, or you'll toughen the cheese.

9. The curd is now ready for shaping. To shape into a ball, pinch off the amount you want to shape, stretching the surface of the ball to become tight and shiny; tuck the ends into the underside as though forming a ball of pizza dough. Turn the ball over in your hand and press the underside edges up into the center of the ball, into the palm of your hand. Immediately submerge the ball in a bowl of ice water to chill and firm up for 10 minutes.

10. While the cheese is chilling, prepare a light brine (see page 24). You can use the reserved whey for the brine, supplementing water as needed to equal 3 quarts, dissolving 9 ounces of kosher salt into it, and chilling it to 50°F to 55°F. This results in a less salty finished cheese. For a saltier finished cheese, make 3 quarts of saturated brine (see page 24) and chill to 50°F to 55°F. Place the chilled cheese in the brine solution. If using the saturated brine, soak the cheese for 20 minutes, flipping it over a few times. If using the weaker whey brine, you can leave the cheese in the brine, refrigerated, for up to 8 hours, flipping the cheese over a few times. Either way, remove from the brine and use immediately, or place in a plastic food storage container, cover with water, and store refrigerated for up to 1 week.

Burrata

MAKES 4 large pouches or 8 small pouches

Burrata is a soft stretched-curd pouch filled with pieces of mozzarella, a mascarpone-butter mixture, or ricotta. When made with mozzarella curds, the pouches are formed by stretching the melted curds into a slab or cup, filling it, then closing. Burrata is best served when freshly made and slightly warm. When the closed pouch is cut into, the filling oozes out.

1. Prepare Traditonal Mozzarella (page 75) up to the point of stretching and shaping into a single smooth ball and chilling in ice water.

2. Prepare the filling of your choice:

    MOZZARELLA FILLING: mozzarella scraps broken into small pieces and mixed with a small amount of cream to moisten

    MASCARPONE FILLING: $3/4$ cup mascarpone mixed well with $1^1/2$ ounces soft unsalted butter and $1/4$ teaspoon salt, chilled until firm, then formed into 4 balls of filling and set aside on parchment paper and chilled until ready to use

    RICOTTA FILLING: 1 cup ricotta (to be traditional, you can make your own whey ricotta while making the mozzarella for this recipe, page 41)

3. Divide the mozzarella into four 4-ounce portions, place the pieces in a bowl, and cover them with 170°F to 180°F water. When the mozzarella is heated through and pliable, about 5 minutes, pull the pieces out of the water and quickly stretch them into approximately 4-inch squares, either cupped in the palm of your hand or pressed into shape on a cutting board. If you like, as you form the squares you can drape them inside a 4-ounce stainless steel ladle to shape into pouches; dip the ladle in the hot water if needed to keep the mozzarella elastic.

4. Once a piece of mozzarella is stretched, fill it with $1^1/2$ ounces or so of filling and quickly pull 2 opposite flaps up and over the filling to completely enclose. Bring the other 2 flaps together and pinch closed, then dip the pouch into the hot water briefly to seal. Smooth the surface of the ball with the palm of your hand and place in an ice bath to cool for 2 to 3 minutes. Form and fill the other pouches. If you like, you can tie a chive around the closure before chilling.

5. Burrata are best if served immediately so that the filling is still soft. Otherwise, place in a container, cover with water, and refrigerate for up to 3 days. Bring to room temperature before serving.

ARTISAN CHEESE MAKING AT HOME

Queso Oaxaca

Queso Oaxaca is often referred to as Mexican mozzarella. It is made using mozzarella curds that are stretched out into thin flat ribbons and then shaped like a ball of yarn. I had the good fortune to taste the sublime version made by an extraordinary team of cheese makers at the Mozzarella Company in Dallas: warm ribbons of curd smothered in salt and lime juice. Divine!

To make queso Oaxaca in the style of the Mozzarella Company, make Traditional Mozzarella (page 75) through to melting the curds in the hot whey. Pinch off palm-size pieces of the kneaded submerged ball of curds, then pull and stretch the hot pieces into 1-inch-wide ribbons about 2 feet long. Lay the thin ribbons out flat on a work surface in one continuous back-and-forth rope of curds—like ribbon candy. Generously salt the warm ribbons with kosher salt and leave it for 5 minutes. Then squeeze the juice of 1 lime over the top and gently rub the salt and lime juice into the ribbons. Leave for 10 minutes, then wind the ribbons into yarnlike balls about the size of your fist, crisscrossing the strands as the ball is formed and tucking in the end. Set the ball on the work surface to drain while you form the rest of the curds into balls (you'll have 4 or 5 total). Make 2 quarts of light brine (see page 24), cooled to 50°F to 55°F. Immerse the balls in the brine for 15 minutes, then remove and let drain for 30 minutes before wrapping in plastic wrap and refrigerating overnight, or for up to 10 days.

Bocconcini

Bocconcini are rounded bite-size morsels of mozzarella. They are stored in either brine or whey, as mozzarella is, or marinated in olive oil with herbs and spices. To make bocconcini, follow the recipe for Traditional Mozzarella (page 75) to the point when you have cut the curds into cubes and heated the whey, but have not poured the hot whey over the cubes. Place a handful of cubed curds into a skimmer or slotted spoon and, wearing heat-resistant gloves, dip the utensil into the hot whey for several seconds, melting the curds until they're stretchable. Using a spoon or your fingers, and working quickly, knead the melted curds in the utensil, dipping it back into the hot whey as needed to keep the curds pliable. When the curds are kneaded into a firm ball, pull and stretch them into a small rope and fold them over onto themselves, repeating a few times until the ball of curds is smooth, pliable, and shiny. Don't overwork the curds, or you'll toughen the cheese.

Form the curds into a bite-size ball shape and place it in a bowl of ice water for 10 minutes to chill and firm up. Repeat with the rest of the curds until all are stretched and shaped into balls. Make a brine with the hot whey by dissolving 6 ounces of kosher salt in it and adding water to make 2 quarts of brine, then chill it to 50°F to 55°F. Place the chilled cheese in the whey brine for 2 hours. Use immediately for best flavor, or store in the salted whey, covered and refrigerated, for up to 1 week.

JUNKET MOZZARELLA

MAKES 1 pound
MILK Pasteurized but not homogenized whole cow's milk
START TO FINISH 4½ hours to 1 week: 1½ hours to make the curds;
1 hour to stretch the curds and form balls; 2 hours to 1 week to brine

This interesting—and very easy—method for making mozzarella is from Paula Lambert, the proprietor of the Mozzarella Company in Dallas. It uses ingredients you can find in your local supermarket: pasteurized whole cow's milk, distilled vinegar, and junket rennet tablets. Junket rennet tablets come in a box usually found in the pudding section of the supermarket, or they can be purchased online (see Resources); make sure you buy rennet tablets and not custard tablets, and that your milk is not homogenized. To simplify the curd making process, no pH reading is taken—the amount of vinegar called for has been carefully calculated to achieve the level of acidity needed to create stretchable curds. Note that for this recipe you will need heat-resistant neoprene or rubber gloves.

....

1 gallon pasteurized but not homogenized whole
    cow's milk
7 tablespoons distilled vinegar (5 percent acidity)
4 tablets junket rennet dissolved in ½ cup cool
    nonchlorinated water
1½ teaspoons plus ¼ cup kosher salt (preferably
    Diamond Crystal brand) or cheese salt

1. In a nonreactive 6-quart stockpot, slowly heat the milk to 88°F over low heat; this should take about 20 minutes. Stir in the vinegar using a whisk in an up-and-down motion to incorporate thoroughly. Add the dissolved rennet and gently whisk in for 1 minute.

2. Slowly raise the temperature to 90°F over 8 minutes. Remove from the heat, cover, and let sit, maintaining the temperature for 1 hour, until the curds form a solid mass of bonded small curds the consistency of soft tofu. A few small curds may be floating in the clear, yellow whey. Check for a clean break, and if there isn't a clean break, check again in 15 minutes.

3. Cut the curds into ½-inch pieces and let sit undisturbed for 10 minutes, maintaining them at 90°F. Over low heat, raise the temperature to 108°F over 15 minutes, gently stirring every 5 minutes and frequently checking the temperature and adjusting the heat as needed. If you raise the temperature too quickly, the curds won't coagulate and bind properly. Once 108°F is reached, remove from the heat and, using a rubber spatula, gently stir for 10 minutes around the edges of the pot and under the curds to move them around and expel more whey. Let the curds rest for another 15 minutes. At this point the curds will be slightly below the surface of the whey. Gently press one of the curds between two fingers. It should feel springy and stretchable; if it doesn't, leave the curds for 10 minutes and then test again.

4. Line a colander with damp butter muslin, set it over another pot, and scoop the curds into it with a slotted spoon. Let drain for 15 minutes, or until the whey has stopped dripping and the curds are compacted together. Reserve the whey.

5. Add the 1½ teaspoons of salt to the whey and stir to dissolve. Slowly heat the whey over medium-low heat to 175°F to 180°F; this should take about 30 minutes.

6. Meanwhile, wrap the muslin over the curds and place the packet on a cutting board. Flatten the curds slightly and let sit for 20 minutes. Open the muslin and cut the slab of curds into ½-inch strips or chunks.

7. Place a handful of curd strips or chunks in a skimmer or slotted spoon and, wearing heat-resistant gloves, dip the utensil into the hot whey for several seconds, melting the curds until stretchable. Using a spoon or your fingers, and working quickly, knead the melted curds in the utensil, dipping it back into the hot whey as needed to keep the curds pliable. When the curds are kneaded into a firm ball, pull and stretch them into a small rope and fold them over onto themselves, repeating a few times until the ball of curds is smooth, pliable, and shiny. Don't overwork the curds, or you'll toughen the cheese. Shape the curds into a ball and place it in a bowl of ice water for 10 minutes to chill and firm up. Repeat the melting, kneading, stretching, shaping, and chilling with the remaining curd strips.

8. Make a light brine by dissolving the ¼ cup of kosher salt in the hot whey, then chill it to 50°F to 55°F. Place the chilled cheese in the brine for 2 hours. Use immediately for best flavor, or store in the salted whey, covered and refrigerated, for up to 1 week.

Profile: Mozzarella Company

Paula Lambert's Mozzarella Company in Dallas, Texas, is legendary in the artisan cheese world. Inspired by a time living in Perugia, Italy, Paula returned home to Texas to pursue a business making handmade pasta. After learning that another pasta company was launching in Dallas, she opted to shift her vision to a different passion: beautiful, hand-crafted Italian-style cheeses, especially the company's namesake. Paula opened the Mozzarella Company in 1982. Many pounds of curds and scores of awards later, all of the Mozzarella Company cheeses are still hand stretched and shaped by Paula's amazing family of cheese makers, many of whom have been with her for more than twenty years. The Mozzarella Company's repertoire of cheeses expands in concert with Paula's wide travels and keen curiosity, even as the company continues to produce some of the finest-quality fresh and aged cheeses available in the United States.

BRAIDED STRING CHEESE

MAKES 1 pound

MILK Pasteurized low-fat (1 percent) or reduced fat (2 percent) cow's milk

START TO FINISH 6½ to 10 hours: 4 hours to make and cook the curds;
2 hours to melt and stretch the curds and form braids; 15 minutes to 4 hours to brine

String cheese is a mild cheese made from low-moisture curds that are stretched repeatedly to become stringy. It is a traditional cheese of Syria and Armenia, where it's typically shaped into a braid, though it's also a popular snack cheese with kids in the States. This recipe has many similarities to the Traditional Mozzarella recipe on page 75. Note you will need a pH meter or pH strips for testing acidity and heatproof neoprene or rubber gloves for handling the hot curds.

....

1 gallon pasteurized low-fat (1 percent) or reduced fat (2 percent) cow's milk

¼ teaspoon Thermo B powdered thermophilic starter culture

¼ teaspoon calcium chloride diluted in ¼ cup cool nonchlorinated water

¾ teaspoon liquid rennet diluted in ¼ cup cool nonchlorinated water

Kosher salt (preferably Diamond Crystal brand) for brining

1. In a nonreactive 6-quart stockpot, slowly heat the milk to 95°F; this should take about 25 minutes. Turn off the heat.

2. Sprinkle the starter over the milk and let it rehydrate for 5 minutes. Mix well using a whisk in an up-and-down motion. Cover and maintain 90°F to 95°F, letting the milk ripen for 45 minutes. Add the diluted calcium chloride and gently whisk in. Let rest for 10 minutes. Add the diluted rennet and gently whisk in. Cover and let sit, maintaining 90°F to 95°F for 1 hour, or until the curds give a clean break.

3. Cut the curds into ½-inch pieces and let sit undisturbed for 30 minutes, maintaining a 90°F to 95°F temperature. During this time the curds will firm up and release more whey. Over low heat, slowly raise the temperature to 105°F over 30 minutes, gently stirring and frequently checking the temperature and adjusting the heat as needed. If you raise the temperature too quickly, the curds won't coagulate

and bind properly. Once 105°F is reached, remove from the heat and, using a rubber spatula, gently stir for 10 minutes around the edges of the pot and under the curds to move them around. Maintaining temperature, let the curds rest for another 15 minutes; they will sink to the bottom.

4. Using a skimmer or slotted spoon, transfer the curds to a colander or strainer that will fit over the same pot, reserving 5 inches of whey in the pot. Place the colander of curds over the pot. Over low heat, heat the whey in the pot to 102°F to 105°F over the course of 10 minutes. Cover the curds in the colander with the pot lid while the whey is heating; more whey will drain into the pot below. When the whey is at temperature, remove from the heat and hold at 102°F to 105°F for 2 hours. The curds will melt into each other, binding into a slab; turn the slab two times during this period, using a spatula.

5. When 2 hours have elapsed, begin testing the pH of the curds with a pH meter or pH strips every 30 minutes. Once the pH drops below 5.6, begin checking every 15 minutes. Once the pH drops into the 4.9 to 5.2 range, the curds are ready to stretch.

6. Transfer the curds to a cutting board. Cut the curds into approximately ½-inch cubes and put them in a clean stainless steel bowl large enough to hold them with plenty of room to spare (the curds will be covered with hot liquid). In a clean pot, heat 4 quarts of water or of the reserved whey

to 170°F to 180°F. Pour this over the curds to cover them completely.

7. Wearing heat-resistant gloves, work the submerged cubes of curd into one large ball, kneading and shaping it in the hot water. Once the curds are shaped into a firm ball, lift it out of the water and, working quickly, pull and stretch it into an 8-inch-long rope. If the curd cools and becomes brittle, dip it into the hot water to make it warm and pliable again.

8. Working lengthwise along the rope, pull off 1-inch sections and, working quickly, pull and stretch the lengths into 1-foot-long, 1-inch-thick ropes, then fold them over onto themselves two or three times, stretching each time. The more the strips are stretched, the stringier the cheese will be. Place the stretched lengths on a cutting board.

9. Using kitchen scissors or a knife, cut the lengths into 6- to 8-inch-long pieces. In groups of 3, twist them together to look like a braid. Once they are formed, immediately place the pieces in a bowl of ice water for 5 minutes to chill and firm up.

10. Make a light brine (see page 24) by dissolving 6 ounces of kosher salt into all of the whey, adding water as needed to make 2 quarts and chilling it to 50°F to 55°F. This light brine results in a less salty finished cheese. For a saltier finished cheese, make 2 quarts of saturated brine (see page 24) and chill it to 50°F to 55°F. Place the chilled cheese in the brine solution. If using the saturated brine, soak the cheese for 10 to 15 minutes; if using the weaker whey brine, you can leave the cheese in the brine, refrigerated, for up to 4 hours. Flip the cheese over a few times whether using the saturated brine or the whey brine. Remove from the brine and use immediately, or wrap in plastic wrap and store refrigerated for up to 5 days, or vacuum-seal and refrigerate for up to 1 month.

Bread Cheese

Similar to Finland's juustoleipa and comparable in texture to string cheese, this firm, cooked cheese is shaped into a square, then toasted in a broiler or wood-fired oven, giving it the look of bread, hence the name. I love cooking in cast iron, so this version uses a 10-inch cast-iron grill pan in which the cheese is cooked and can be presented. You can also use other shapes of pans that are cast iron and have a ribbed-bottom surface. The cheese is cooked to melt and develop a thin golden crust from the fat that's brought to the surface as the slab of curds heats up. It is served with bread as a snack or warmed for breakfast.

To make bread cheese, make Braided String Cheese (page 82) up to the point where the cut curds are melting in the bowl of hot water. Wearing heat-resistant gloves, work the melted curds into a slab big enough to fill your pan. Fold the slab over onto itself lengthwise, then stretch it out again to the size of the pan. Repeat two more times, discarding any whey that is expelled in the stretching. Preheat the griddle pan over medium-high heat. Place the slab into the heated pan and cook to melt slightly and form a golden crust on the bottom of the cheese.  Using a spatula, flip it over and brown the other side for about 5 minutes. Remove from the heat and let the cheese cool slightly in the pan. Remove from the pan and cut into slices and serve while still warm. Bread cheese can be vacuum-sealed or wrapped tightly in foil and refrigerated for up to 3 months. To serve, reheat it briefly in a 350°F oven or under the broiler.

VARIATION

If you are in a hurry to make this cheese, you can use ready-made low-moisture mozzarella or string cheese. Cut it into small cubes and fill the cast-iron skillet with them—don't preheat the skillet. Proceed with the cooking process as above.

KASSERI

MAKES Two 1-pound cheeses
MILKS Pasteurized whole cow's milk, pasteurized goat's milk, pasteurized half-and-half
START TO FINISH 2 to 6 months: 6½ hours to make the cheese; 6 to 7 hours to press;
2½ days to drain; 2 to 6 months to age

Kasseri is a firm Greek cheese that's often compared to Provolone, another pressed cheese in this family. Its curds are pressed twice: once in slab form, after which they are milled and cut into pieces, and then in a mold for final shaping before aging. It is traditionally made from a combination of goat's and sheep's milks and aged for at least three months and sometimes up to a year. Kasseri made in the United States is often made with cow's milk, sometimes partially skimmed. This recipe is made with a blend of cow's and goat's milks and half-and-half, with a small amount of mild lipase to add a rich flavor reminiscent of sheep's milk. Remember to avoid using ultra-pasteurized milks or creams or those with any additives or thickeners. Note that for this recipe you will need heat-resistant neoprene or rubber gloves.

5 quarts pasteurized whole cow's milk

2 quarts pasteurized goat's milk

1 quart pasteurized half-and-half

¼ teaspoon Thermo B powdered thermophilic starter culture

⅛ teaspoon mild lipase powder dissolved in ¼ cup cool nonchlorinated water 20 minutes before using

½ teaspoon calcium chloride diluted in ¼ cup cool nonchlorinated water (omit if using all raw milk)

½ teaspoon liquid rennet diluted in ¼ cup cool nonchlorinated water

Kosher salt (preferably Diamond Crystal brand) or cheese salt

1. Combine the milks and half-and-half in a 10-quart stockpot set in a 108°F water bath over low heat. Bring the milk to 98°F over 12 minutes. Turn off the heat.

2. Sprinkle the starter over the milk and let it rehydrate for 5 minutes. Mix well using a whisk in an up-and-down motion. Cover and maintain 98°F, letting the milk ripen for 45 minutes. Add the dissolved lipase and gently whisk in. Let sit for 10 minutes. Add the diluted calcium chloride and gently whisk in for 1 minute. Let sit for 5 minutes. Add the diluted rennet and gently whisk in for 1 minute. Cover and let sit, maintaining 98°F for 45 minutes, or until the curds give a clean break.

3. Using a whisk, gently cut the curds into bean-size pieces and let sit undisturbed for 10 minutes, maintaining 98°F. This helps firm up the curds. Over low heat, slowly raise the temperature of the water bath so that the milk comes to 104°F over 30 minutes. Gently stir from time to time and frequently check the temperature and adjust the heat as needed. If you raise the temperature too quickly, the curds won't coagulate and bind properly. Once 104°F is reached, remove from the heat and, using a rubber spatula, gently stir for 10 minutes around the edges of the pot and under the curds to move them around. Maintaining temperature,

let the curds rest for another 15 minutes; they will sink to the bottom.

4.   Line a colander with damp butter muslin, set it over another pot, and scoop the curds into it with a slotted spoon. Let the curds drain for 15 to 20 minutes, or until they have stopped dripping.

5.   Lift the cloth and curds out of the colander and place on a cutting board. Using your hands, compress the curds into a flat, rectangular shape and wrap the cloth around it to secure. Place the bundle of curds on a draining rack set over a tray, cover the bundle with another tray, and place a 3-pound weight on top. Press and let drain at room temperature for 6 to 7 hours or overnight at 50°F to 55°F.

6.   Heat 3 quarts of water to 175°F. Open the bundle of curds and cut the slab into 1-inch slices. Place the slices in the pot of 175°F water. Let sit for 30 seconds or so to heat through, then, wearing heat-resistant gloves, check the curds for readiness by skimming a slice of curd out and pressing and kneading it with your fingers. Hold one end of the piece and let it stretch from its own weight, then pull on it to stretch it into a string. If this stretching happens easily, the curds are ready to be shaped. If the stretching does not happen easily, keep the curds in the hot water until they are easily stretchable.

7.   Still wearing heat-resistant gloves, work the submerged slices of curd into a large ball, kneading and stretching until the ball is smooth. Lift the ball out of the water and, working quickly, press it into two 5-inch square or rectangular cheese molds. If the curds cool and become brittle while you are working them, dip the mass into the hot water to make it warm and pliable again.

8.   Place the molds on a draining rack set over a pan and let the curds drain for 2 hours at room temperature, flipping the cheeses two or three times by taking them out of the molds, turning them over, and replacing them in the molds. Cover the draining pan and mold with a lid or kitchen towel to keep the cheeses warm and let drain for 12 hours at room temperature. This process will release more whey, which should be drained off periodically.

9.   Remove the cheeses from their molds and place them on a cheese mat on a draining rack set over a pan. Rub the tops of the cheeses with salt and let them drain for 2 hours at room temperature. Flip the cheeses over and rub the unsalted tops. Let them drain for 24 hours at room temperature. Repeat the process one more time: salting, draining for 2 hours, salting, and draining for 24 hours.

10.   Gently rinse the salt off the cheeses with cool water. Pat the cheeses dry with a paper towel, then place them on a cheese mat in a ripening box at 65°F and 85 percent relative humidity. Turn the cheeses daily for 1 week, wiping off any unwanted mold with cheesecloth dampened in a vinegar-salt solution (see page 25) and wiping down the sides of the box. Flip the cheeses twice weekly thereafter. Age for 2 to 4 months. When aged to your taste, wrap the cheeses in foil and refrigerate for up to 2 more months.

PROVOLONE

MAKES 1 pound
MILK Pasteurized whole cow's or goat's milk
START TO FINISH 3 weeks to 12 months: 5½ to 6½ hours to make and cook the curds;
1 hour to melt, stretch, and form the curds; 2 to 24 hours to brine; 3 weeks to 12 months to hang and dry

Though it originated in southern Italy, Provolone is also made in several regions in the northern part of the country, where it enjoys DOC status (an Italian quality assurance label requiring that a food product be produced in a specific region). Sometimes smoked, this cheese is notable for its myriad shapes, ranging from sausage, pear, and melon shapes to shapes like long-necked bottles and jugs. The cheeses are almost always tied with twine in some way, which is done so the cheese may hang to dry or age. This formula is similar to mozzarella, with a few adjustments in temperatures and other nuances. Like mozzarella, this Provolone is cured in a whey-based brine; it is then hung to ripen. Note you'll need a pH meter or pH strips and heat-resistant neoprene or rubber gloves to handle the hot curds.

1 gallon pasteurized whole cow's or goat's milk

¼ teaspoon Thermo B powdered thermophilic starter culture

¼ teaspoon sharp lipase powder dissolved in ¼ cup cool nonchlorinated water 20 minutes before using

¼ teaspoon calcium chloride diluted in ¼ cup cool nonchlorinated water

¾ teaspoon liquid rennet diluted in ¼ cup cool nonchlorinated water

Kosher salt (preferably Diamond Crystal brand) or cheese salt for brining

1. In a nonreactive 6-quart stockpot, slowly heat the milk to 97°F over low heat; this should take about 25 minutes. Turn off the heat.

2. Sprinkle the starter over the milk and let it rehydrate for 5 minutes. Mix well using a whisk in an up-and-down motion. Cover, let sit, and maintain 97°F, letting the milk ripen for 45 minutes. Add the diluted lipase and gently whisk in. Let rest for 10 minutes. Add the diluted calcium chloride and gently whisk in. Add the diluted rennet and gently whisk in. Cover and let sit, maintaining 97°F for 1 hour, or until the curds give a clean break.

3. Cut the curds into ½-inch pieces and let sit undisturbed for 30 minutes, maintaining 97°F. Over low heat, slowly raise the temperature to 108°F over 35 minutes. Gently stir from time to time and frequently check the temperature and adjust the heat as needed. If you raise the temperature too quickly, the curds won't coagulate and bind properly. Once 108°F is reached, remove from the heat and, using a rubber spatula, gently stir for 10 minutes around the edges of the pot and under the curds to move them around. Maintaining temperature, let the curds rest for another 15 minutes; they will sink to the bottom.

4. Using a skimmer or slotted spoon, transfer the curds to a colander or strainer set over another pot and let them drain for 10 minutes, or until the whey stops dripping. Pour the whey from the original pot into the new pot and set it aside. Gently return the drained curds to the original pot and set it in a 112°F to 115°F water bath to bring the curds to 102°F to 105°F. Hold the temperature of the curds at 102°F to 105°F for 2 hours. The curds will melt into each other, binding into a slab; turn the slab two times during this period, using a spatula.

5. When 2 hours have elapsed, begin testing the pH of the curds with a pH meter or pH strips every 30 minutes. Once the pH drops below 5.6, begin checking every 15 minutes. Once the pH drops into the 4.9 to 5.2 range, the curds are ready to stretch.

6. Transfer the curds to a strainer, let drain for 10 minutes, then place on a cutting board. Cut the curds into 1-inch cubes and put them in a stainless steel bowl large enough to hold them with plenty of room to spare (the curds will be covered with hot liquid). In a clean pot, heat 4 quarts of water or of the reserved whey to 170°F to 180°F and pour it over the curds to cover completely.

7. Wearing heat-resistant gloves, work the submerged cubes of curd into one large ball, kneading and shaping it in the hot water. Once the curds are shaped into a firm ball, lift it out of the water and, working quickly, pull and stretch it into a 1-foot-long rope. If the curd rope cools and becomes brittle, dip it into the hot water to make it warm and pliable again. Loop the rope back on itself, and then pull and stretch it again two or three times, or until the curd is shiny and smooth. (The process is something like stretching taffy.) Be careful not to overwork the curd, or you'll toughen the cheese.

8. Pinch off the amount of curd you want to shape. If shaping a ball, stretch the surface of the ball to become tight and shiny; tuck the ends into the underside as though forming a ball of pizza dough. Once the cheese is formed into the desired shape, immediately submerge it in a bowl of ice water for 10 minutes to chill and firm up. Remove the shaped cheese or cheeses from the water and set aside to air-dry while making the brine.

9. To make a light brine, use all of the reserved whey, adding water as needed to equal 2 quarts, dissolve 6 ounces of kosher salt into it, and chill it to 50°F to 55°F. This results in a less salty finished cheese. For a saltier finished cheese, make 2 quarts of saturated brine (see page 24), and chill to 50°F to 55°F. Place the chilled cheese in the brine solution. If using the saturated brine, soak the cheese for 2 hours, flipping it over a few times. If using the weaker whey brine, you can leave the cheese in the brine, refrigerated, for up to 24 hours, flipping it over a few times. Remove from the brine and pat dry. Tie a length of twine around each cheese to hang.

10. Hang the cheeses for 3 weeks at 50°F to 55°F and at 80 to 85 percent humidity. Use immediately, or place in your refrigerator (at 40°F) for 2 to 3 months for a mild Provolone, or 3 to 12 months for a sharp Provolone. If you choose to smoke the Provolone, see page 27 for instructions.

Smoked Scamorza

Scamorza is a stretched-curd cheese originating in Southern Italy and traditionally made with cow's, sheep's, or water buffalo's milk and aged for only 2 to 3 days. It is a bit drier than mozzarella due to its 2 days of air-drying. Scamorza can be found in a number of different shapes, most often gourdlike or with a knob on top where the string is tied for the cheese to be

hung and aged. The sizes range from 6 ounces to over 1 pound. Often smoked over local woods, the cheese's exterior can range from light tan to dark brown. The smoking produces a nutty flavor that slightly permeates the cheese, making it very aromatic and flavorful. The cheese is typically eaten while young—within 1 week. However, the cheese can be waxed after smoking to preserve it for futher aging.

Here, I'm presenting a smoked version of Scamorza using mozzarella curds. Follow the recipe for Traditional Mozzarella on page 75 through the point when the curds have been kneaded and stretched until shiny and smooth. The smoking procedure can be found on page 27. You'll need a large bowl for an ice bath, light or saturated brine (see page 24), 2-foot-long strands of raffia to tie around the neck of each shaped cheese, and wax for coating.

Pinch off the amount of cheese you want to shape. One of the traditional shapes looks like a small hourglass or peppermill, with a small knob at the top and a larger bulbous bottom. The top is shaped from one-third of the ball, with the bottom being the larger portion.

While the curds are malleable, place the ball of hot stretched curds into the palm of your hand. Using your thumb and forefinger, gently squeeze the ball to form a 1½-inch-diameter neck about one-third down from the top, rotating while shaping. Then put the cheese into an ice bath for 1 hour to firm up the shape. Drain, then wrap the neck with raffia, leaving a tail to hang the cheese, as is traditional.

Make a light brine: You can use all of the reserved whey for the brine, adding water to it as needed to equal 2 quarts, then dissolve 6 ounces of kosher salt into it, and chill it to 50°F to 55°F. This results in a less salty finished cheese. For a saltier finished cheese, make 2 quarts of saturated brine (see page 24) and chill it to 50°F to 55°F. Place the cheese in the light brine for 1 hour, or in the saturated brine for 20 minutes. Remove the cheese from the brine and air-dry for 2 days. You can stop at this point, or carry on to smoke the cheese as described on page 27. Wax coat the cheese by holding the tail of raffia and dipping the cheese into a deep pot of wax to fully cover it. Hang to air-dry and set up the wax. The cheese can be further preserved by vacuum-sealing, then refrigerating. It is ready to eat when waxed, or it can be aged.

Semisoft, Firm, and Hard Cheeses

This large group of cheeses encompasses a broad range of styles, including some of the most recognizable classics grounded in old-world traditions. Depending on the aging techniques and timelines used, the semisoft cheeses are pliable, whereas the firm and hard cheeses have a dense consistency. These complex flavored cheeses are made with cow's, goat's, or sheep's milk or a combination of these using a variety of mesophilic and thermophilic cultures, as well as flavor-enhancing secondary cultures and enzymes. Semisoft cheeses have little or no rind and are not aged long: a few weeks to a few months. Traditional varieties include Bel Paese, Caerphilly, Colby, Fontina, Havarti, and Jarlsberg.

Firm or hard cheeses (including Beaufort, Cheddar, Gruyère, Gouda, Mimolette, Parmesan, Romano, and Alpine-style cheeses) typically develop a thin, slightly chewy natural rind and contain 50 percent moisture or less. Firm cheeses may be aged for a few months or longer. Depending on style and size, hard cheeses may be aged for several months to a year or more. This extended aging creates the salty and sweet complexity of flavors identified with this group of cheeses. For firm and hard cheeses, I generally recommend pressing them in a 2-gallon capacity cheese press for the best textural results. However, suggested cheese molds and weights are listed in the recipes.

DILL HAVARTI

MAKES 2 pounds
MILK Pasteurized whole cow's milk
START TO FINISH 18 hours to 1 month: 2½ hours to make the cheese; 18 hours to press and ripen;
8 hours to brine; 12 hours to dry (optional); 1 month or longer to age (optional)

This recipe is from Mt. Mansfield Creamery in Morrisville, Vermont, and was one of the first cheeses made by co-owner and resident cheese maker Stan Biasini, a former chef. His aged raw-milk version of this dill Havarti is called Forerunner. (The home-version recipe for another of Mt. Mansfield's cheeses, their Alpine-Style Tomme, can be found on page 100.)

2 gallons pasteurized whole cow's milk
1/2 teaspoon MM 100 powdered mesophilic starter culture
1/2 teaspoon calcium chloride diluted in 1/4 cup cool nonchlorinated water

1/2 teaspoon liquid rennet diluted in 1/4 cup cool nonchlorinated water
4 teaspoons kosher salt (preferably Diamond Crystal brand) or cheese salt
1 teaspoon dried dill

(continued)

1. In a nonreactive 10-quart stockpot, heat the milk over low heat to 70°F; this should take about 12 minutes. Turn off the heat.

2. Sprinkle the starter over the milk and let it rehydrate for 5 minutes. Mix well using a whisk in an up-and-down motion for 1 minute. Cover and maintain 70°F, letting the milk ripen for 45 minutes. Add the calcium chloride and gently whisk in for 1 minute. Slowly raise the heat to 86°F over 7 to 8 minutes, then add the rennet and gently whisk in for 1 minute. Cover and let sit, maintaining 86°F for 30 to 45 minutes, or until the curds give a clean break.

3. Still maintaining 86°F, cut the curds into ½-inch pieces and let sit for 5 minutes. Gently stir the curds for 10 minutes, then let sit for 5 minutes. Ladle out about one-third of the whey (this should be about 2½ quarts) and add 3 cups of 130°F water. When the temperature of the curds and whey reaches 92°F to 94°F, add another 3 cups of 130°F water. Gently stir for 5 minutes, then add another 2 cups of 130°F water. Add the salt and stir to dissolve. Check the temperature and add 130°F water as needed to bring the curds and whey to about 97°F. Continue stirring until the curds feel springy in your hand when squeezed, about 20 minutes. Ladle off enough whey to expose the curds. Gently stir in the dill.

4. Line an 8-inch tomme mold (with follower) with damp butter muslin and place it on a draining rack. Gently ladle the curds into the mold and press them in with your hands. Pull the cloth tight and smooth, removing any wrinkles. Fold the cloth tails over the curds, set the follower on top, and press at 8 pounds for 30 minutes.

5. Remove the cheese from the mold, peel away the cloth, flip the cheese over, and redress with the same cloth. Press again at 8 pounds, redressing every 30 minutes for up to 3 hours, or until the whey stops draining.

6. Leave the cheese in the mold without pressure for about 3 more hours before putting in the refrigerator for 12 hours or overnight. Remove the cheese from the mold. It is now ready to eat, or it can be aged for more intense flavor.

7. Make 2 quarts of saturated brine in a noncorrosive container with a lid (see page 24), and chill it to 50°F to 55°F. Submerge the cheese in the brine and soak at 50°F to 55°F for 8 hours or overnight.

8. Remove the cheese from the brine and pat dry. Air-dry at room temperature on a rack for 12 hours, then age at 55°F and 85 percent humidity on a cheese mat set in a ripening box, flipping daily. Age for 1 month, or longer if desired, removing any unwanted mold with cheesecloth dampened in a vinegar-salt solution (see page 25).

EDAM BOULE

MAKES Two 1-pound boules
MILK Pasteurized reduced fat (2 percent) cow's milk
START TO FINISH 2 to 6 months: 3½ hours to make the cheese; 1½ to 2½ days to dry;
12 hours to brine; 2 to 6 months to age

Edam is a pressed cow's milk cheese from the small Dutch town of the same name. The cheese is spherical in shape with a flattened bottom. Most are wax coated, though some have a simple thin natural rind. Rather than being pressed in a mold, this version is rolled and shaped in its draining sack, becoming more rustic in shape—similar to the ball-shaped Mimolette jeune boule, with a slightly flattened bottom and pinched top. It is then waxed to age. In keeping with the Mimolette influence, a fair amount of annatto is added to the curds to create a bright orange paste that deepens in color as the cheese ages beneath the waxed exterior.

2 gallons pasteurized reduced fat (2 percent)
    cow's milk
½ teaspoon Meso II or MM 100 powdered mesophilic
    starter culture
1 teaspoon liquid annatto coloring diluted in ⅓ cup
    cool nonchlorinated water
½ teaspoon calcium chloride diluted in ¼ cup cool
    nonchlorinated water
½ teaspoon liquid rennet diluted in ¼ cup cool
    nonchlorinated water
Kosher salt (preferably Diamond Crystal brand) or
    cheese salt

1. In a nonreactive 10-quart stockpot, heat the milk over low heat to 88°F; this should take about 15 minutes. Turn off the heat.

2. Sprinkle the starter over the milk and let it rehydrate for 5 minutes. Mix well using a whisk in an up-and-down motion. Cover and maintain 88°F, letting the milk ripen for 30 minutes. Add the annatto and gently whisk in for 1 minute. Add the calcium chloride and gently whisk in for 1 minute, then add the rennet in the same way. Cover and let sit, maintaining 88°F for 30 to 45 minutes, or until the curds give a clean break.

3. Cut the curds into ½-inch pieces and let sit for 5 minutes. Over low heat, slowly raise the temperature to 92°F over 15 minutes. Gently and frequently stir to keep the curds from matting together. The curds will release more whey, firm up slightly, and shrink to the size of small peanuts. Once 92°F is reached, remove from the heat, maintain the temperature, and let the curds rest undisturbed for 30 minutes; they will sink to the bottom. Ladle out enough whey to expose the curds and reserve the whey. Stir the curds continuously for 20 minutes, or until they are matted and cling together when pressed in your hand. Add just enough warm water (about 2 cups) to bring to 99°F, then maintain the temperature for 20 minutes. The curds will settle again.

4. Place a strainer over a bowl or bucket large enough to catch the whey. Line it with damp butter muslin and ladle the curds into it. Let the curds drain for 5 minutes, then toss with 1 tablespoon of salt. Divide the curds into 2 portions, placing each portion on damp muslin and tying the corners of the muslin to create tight sacks around the curds. Shape the curds into balls within the muslin and hang to let drain for 30 minutes, or until the whey stops dripping.

(continued)

5. Place the reserved whey in the cheese pot and heat over medium heat to 122°F. Turn off the heat. Take the boules of curds out of the cloth and submerge them in the warm whey for 20 minutes, maintaining the temperature. Turn the boules a few times to ensure even heating. Redress the boules in their cloth sacks, then hang to let drain and air-dry at room temperature for 6 hours.

6. Make 2 quarts of medium brine (see page 24) in a noncorrosive container with a lid and cool to 50°F to 55°F.

Remove the cheeses from the cloth. Place in the brine, cover, and soak overnight at 50°F to 55°F.

7. Remove the cheeses from the brine and pat dry. Air-dry at room temperature on a cheese mat for 1 to 2 days, or until the surface is dry to the touch.

8. Wax the cheese using liquid wax and then cheese wax (see page 28). Ripen at 50°F to 55°F and 85 percent humidity for 2 to 3 months, flipping the cheese daily for even ripening. Age 6 months for optimum flavor, maintaining 50°F to 55°F and 85 percent humidity.

FONTINA

MAKES One 1½-pound cheese or two 12-ounce cheeses
MILK Pasteurized whole cow's milk
START TO FINISH 2 to 6 months or longer: 2½ hours to make the cheese; 8 hours to press;
12 hours to brine; 1 to 2 days to dry; 2 to 6 months or longer to age

Though Fontina is made in a number of countries, true Fontina hails from Fontina Val d'Aosta in northern Italy. It is a natural rind cow's milk cheese without a wax coating. When made in the style of Fontina Val d'Aosta, the cheese is pressed, then dry rubbed or brined, then washed, brushed, and oiled as part of the ripening process. The young version, identified as Fontinella, is aged for two months and is quite delightful. If you make two smaller cheeses, you can try one at the younger age and one more mature.

2 gallons pasteurized whole cow's milk

½ teaspoon Meso II or MM 100 powdered mesophilic starter culture

¼ teaspoon mild lipase powder diluted in ¼ cup cool nonchlorinated water 20 minutes before using

½ teaspoon calcium chloride diluted in ¼ cup cool nonchlorinated water

½ teaspoon liquid rennet diluted in ¼ cup cool nonchlorinated water

Kosher salt (preferably Diamond Crystal brand) or cheese salt for brining

1. In a nonreactive 10-quart stockpot, heat the milk over low heat to 88°F; this should take about 20 minutes. Turn off the heat.

2. Sprinkle the starter over the milk and let it rehydrate for 5 minutes. Mix well using a whisk in an up-and-down motion for 20 strokes. Cover and maintain 88°F, letting the milk ripen for 30 minutes. Add the lipase and gently whisk in for 1 minute. Add the calcium chloride and gently whisk in for 1 minute, then add the rennet in the same way. Cover

and let sit, maintaining 88°F for 45 to 50 minutes, or until the curds give a clean break.

3. Still maintaining 88°F, cut the curds into pea-size pieces and stir for 10 minutes. Maintaining temperature, let the curds rest undisturbed for 30 minutes; they will sink to the bottom of the pot.

4. Heat 1 quart of water to 145°F and maintain that temperature. Ladle off enough whey to expose the curds. Ladle in enough hot water to bring the temperature to 102°F. Stir the curds continuously for 10 minutes, or until they are matted and cling together when pressed in your hand. The curds will be half their original size at this point. Again, ladle off enough whey to expose the curds.

5. Line an 8-inch tomme mold (with follower) or 2 fresh cheese molds with damp butter muslin and place on a draining rack. Pack the drained curds into the mold or molds. Pull the cloth up tight and smooth around the curds, cover with the tails of damp muslin (and the follower if using the tomme mold), and press at 5 pounds for 15 minutes. Remove the cheese from the mold, unwrap the cloth, flip the cheese over, and redress, then press at 10 to 20 pounds for 8 hours.

6. Make 2 quarts of medium-heavy brine (see page 24) in a noncorrosive container with a lid and cool to 50°F to 55°F. Remove the cheese from the mold or molds and cloth. Place in the brine and soak at 50°F to 55°F, covered, for 12 hours, flipping a few times during that time.

7. Remove the cheese from the brine and pat dry. Air-dry at room temperature on a cheese mat for 1 to 2 days, or until the surface is dry to the touch.

8. Place on a rack in a ripening box and ripen at 55°F to 60°F and 90 to 95 percent humidity for at least 2 months, flipping the cheese daily for even ripening. After 3 days, wipe the cheese with a simple brine solution (see page 24), then repeat every 2 days for 1 month. Continue to wipe and flip twice a week for the duration of the ripening time: from 2 months to 6 months or longer, maintaining 55°F to 60°F and 90 to 95 percent humidity.

GOUDA

MAKES 1½ pounds
MILK Pasteurized whole cow's milk
ALTERNATIVE MILKS Blend of pasteurized cow's and pasteurized goat's milk; all pasteurized sheep's milk
START TO FINISH 1 to 6 months: 2½ hours to make the cheese; 6 to 8 hours to press; 8 hours to brine;
1 to 2 days to dry; 1 to 6 months to age

Dating back to the thirteenth century, wax-coated Gouda is one of the most well-known cow's milk cheeses and the one most often produced in Holland. Some amazing hand-crafted Gouda-style cheeses are also made in Ireland, Wales, and the United States. Gouda appeals to many palates with its mild flavor and smooth, elastic paste (the result of cooking the curds). The color of the wax indicates specific qualities in the cheese: red is plain Gouda, green indicates herbs have been added, yellow means cumin has been added, and black is used for aged Gouda. The cheese's nutty flavor intensifies with age.

2 gallons pasteurized whole cow's milk

¼ teaspoon Meso II powdered mesophilic starter culture

½ teaspoon calcium chloride diluted in ¼ cup cool nonchlorinated water

½ teaspoon liquid rennet diluted in ¼ cup cool nonchlorinated water

Kosher salt (preferably Diamond Crystal brand) or cheese salt for brining

1. Heat the milk in a 10-quart stockpot set in a 96°F water bath over low heat. Bring the milk to 86°F over 15 minutes. Turn off the heat.

2. Sprinkle the starter over the milk and let it rehydrate for 5 minutes. Mix well using a whisk in an up-and-down motion. Cover and maintain 86°F, allowing the milk to ripen for 45 minutes. Add the calcium chloride and gently whisk in for 1 minute, then add the rennet and gently whisk in for 1 minute. Cover and let sit, maintaining 86°F for 30 to 45 minutes, or until the curds give a clean break.

3. Still maintaining 86°F, cut the curds into ½-inch pieces and let sit for 5 minutes. Stir for 5 minutes, then let sit for 5 more minutes.

4. Heat 2 quarts of water to 140°F and maintain that temperature. When the curds sink to the bottom of the pot, ladle off 2 cups of whey, then add enough 140°F water to bring the curds to 92°F (start with 2 cups). Gently stir for 10 minutes, then let the curds settle again.

5. Ladle off enough whey to expose the top of the curds, then add enough 110°F water to bring the curds to 98°F (start with 2 cups). Holding the curds at that temperature, gently stir for 20 minutes, or until the curds have shrunk to the size of small beans. Let the curds settle for 10 minutes; they will knit together in the bottom of the pot.

6. Line an 8-inch tomme mold (with follower) with damp butter muslin and place it on a draining rack. Warm a colander with hot water. Drain off the whey and transfer the knitted curds to the warm colander. Let drain for 5 minutes. Using your hands, break off 1-inch chunks of curd and distribute into the cloth-lined mold, filling the mold with all of the curds. Press the curds into the mold with your hands as you go. Pull the cloth up tight and smooth around the curds, cover with the tails of the cloth and the follower, and press at 10 pounds for 30 minutes. Remove the cheese from the mold, unwrap the cloth, flip the cheese over, and redress, then press at 15 pounds for 6 to 8 hours.

7. Make 2 quarts of medium-heavy brine (see page 24) in a noncorrosive container with a lid and cool to 50°F to 55°F. Remove the cheese from the mold and cloth. Place in the brine and soak at 50°F to 55°F for 8 hours or overnight.

8. Remove the cheese from the brine and pat dry. Place on a rack and air-dry at room temperature for 1 to 2 days, or until the surface is dry to the touch.

9. Place on a mat in a ripening box, cover loosely, and age at 50°F to 55°F and 85 percent humidity for 1 week, turning daily. Remove any unwanted mold with cheesecloth dampened in a vinegar-salt solution (see page 25).

10. Coat the cheese with wax (see page 28) and age at 55°F for 1 month and up to 6 months.

JACK CHEESE

MAKES 2 pounds
MILK Pasteurized whole cow's milk
START TO FINISH 2 to 6 weeks: 2½ hours to make the cheese;
6 to 8 hours to press; 24 hours to dry; 2 to 6 weeks to age

Jack cheese is an American original. History says this cheese was first made in Monterey, California, by David Jack, whose cheese was probably influenced by those brought through Mexico to California in the 1700s by Franciscan monks. My version takes its inspiration from the cheeses produced in the region that's close to my heart, specifically Sonoma Cheese's Sonoma Jack and Vella's Original High Moisture Monterey Jack. These benchmark Jack cheeses are perfectly moist, having been ripened to a relatively young age, and they have a characteristic creamy yet firm paste and no developed rind. This same cheese can be aged longer, then rubbed with oil or coated, as in the Cocoa-Rubbed Dry Jack Cheese on page 127. My thanks to Lou Biaggi for his contributions to this recipe.

---

2 gallons pasteurized whole cow's milk

½ teaspoon MA 4001 powdered mesophilic starter culture

½ teaspoon calcium chloride diluted in ¼ cup cool nonchlorinated water

½ teaspoon liquid rennet diluted in ¼ cup cool nonchlorinated water

2 tablespoons kosher salt (preferably Diamond Crystal brand) or cheese salt

1. In a nonreactive 10-quart stockpot, heat the milk over low to 86°F; this should take about 15 minutes. Turn off the heat.

2. Sprinkle the starter over the milk and let it rehydrate for 5 minutes. Mix well using a whisk in an up-and-down motion. Cover and maintain 86°F, allowing the milk to ripen for 1 hour. Add the calcium chloride and gently whisk in for 1 minute. Add the rennet and gently whisk in for 1 minute. Cover and let sit, maintaining 86°F for 30 to 45 minutes, or until the curds give a clean break.

3. Still maintaining 86°F, cut the curds into ¾-inch pieces and let sit for 5 minutes. Over low heat, slowly bring the curds to 102°F over 40 minutes, stirring continuously to keep the curds from matting together. They will release whey, firm up slightly, and shrink to the size of dried beans. Maintain 102°F and let the curds rest undisturbed for 30 minutes; they will sink to the bottom. Ladle out enough whey to expose the curds. Stir continuously for 15 to 20 minutes, or until the curds are matted and cling together when pressed in your hand.

4. Place a colander over a bowl or bucket large enough to capture the whey. Line it with damp butter muslin and ladle the curds into it. Let drain for 5 minutes. then sprinkle in 1 tablespoon of the salt and mix thoroughly with your hands.

5. Draw the ends of the cloth together and twist to form a ball to help squeeze out the excess moisture. Roll the ball on a flat surface to release more whey. Tie off the top of the cloth sack, press with your hands to flatten slightly, and place on a cutting board sitting on top of a draining rack. Put a second cutting board on top of the flattened sack, place an 8-pound weight (such as a 1-gallon container filled with water) directly over the cheese, and press into a wheel at 75°F to 85°F for 6 hours for moist Jack or 8 hours for firmer Jack.

6. Remove the cheese from the sack and pat dry. Rub the entire surface with the remaining 1 tablespoon of salt and place the cheese back on the draining rack to air-dry. Dry at room temperature for 24 hours, or until the surface is dry to the touch, flipping once.

7. Place the cheese on a mat in a ripening box and ripen at 50°F to 55°F and 80 to 85 percent humidity for 2 to 6 weeks, flipping daily. When the desired ripeness is reached, vacuum-seal or wrap well in plastic wrap and refrigerate until ready to eat. Once opened, this cheese will dry out and harden over time, creating a wonderful grating cheese.

Creating Your Own Cheeses

By this point in your cheese making journey you've made a variety of really enjoyable tasty cheeses (and a few not so good), and you've identified one or two styles that really speak to you. So it's time to seek out inspiration. Maybe you've just discovered a fabulous farmstead cheese at your local farmers' market or cheese shop—one that knocks your socks off.

Now that you're a dedicated, determined hobbyist cheese maker, equipped with enough knowledge and expertise to create a cheese or two of your own, go for it! On my website you will find detailed worksheets and guidelines for doing just that (www.artisancheese makingathome.com).

JUST JACK

MAKES 1 pound
MILKS Pasteurized whole cow's milk, pasteurized heavy cream
START TO FINISH 2 or more months: 5 hours to make the cheese; about 10 hours to press;
24 hours to dry; 2 months or longer to age

This recipe for amazing Jack cheese, which is anything but *just*, hails from Brad Sinko, the cheese maker at the award-winning Beecher's Handmade Cheese in Seattle, Washington. Brad makes his Just Jack by pressing it lightly, then rubbing it with lard or butter, cheesecloth bandaging it as one would a cheddar, and aging it for two months or longer.

....

1 gallon pasteurized whole cow's milk

1 cup pasteurized heavy cream

1/2 teaspoon Meso III powdered mesophilic starter culture

1/2 teaspoon calcium chloride diluted in 1/4 cup cool nonchlorinated water

1/2 teaspoon liquid rennet diluted in 1/4 cup cool nonchlorinated water

1 tablespoon kosher salt (preferably Diamond Crystal brand) or cheese salt

2 ounces butter or lard at room temperature

1. In a nonreactive 6-quart stockpot, heat the milk and cream over low heat to 89°F; this should take about 20 minutes. Turn off the heat.

2. Sprinkle the starter over the milk and let it rehydrate for 5 minutes. Mix well using a whisk in an up-and-down motion. Cover and maintain 89°F, letting the milk ripen for 45 minutes. Add the calcium chloride and gently whisk in for 1 minute. Add the rennet and gently whisk in for 1 minute. Cover and let sit, maintaining 89°F for 35 minutes, or until the curds give a clean break.

3. Maintaining 86°F to 89°F, cut the curds into ½-inch pieces and let rest for 10 minutes. Over low heat, slowly bring the curds to 101°F over 35 minutes, stirring frequently to keep the curds from matting. They will release whey, firm up slightly, and shrink to the size of dried beans. Ladle off enough whey to expose the curds and continue to stir for 45 to 60 minutes, keeping the temperature between 98°F and 100°F. Ladle out most of the whey and add enough 50°F water to bring the curd temperature down to 79°F. Let rest at that temperature for 4 minutes.

4. Place a colander over a bowl or bucket large enough to capture the whey. Line it with damp cheesecloth and ladle the curds into it. Keep the curds broken up for 30 minutes by gently using your hands to keep the curds from knitting together, then sprinkle in the salt. Using your hands, toss the curds and salt together for 5 minutes.

5. Line a 5-inch tomme mold (with follower) with damp cheesecloth and place it on a draining rack. Ladle the curds into the mold, let drain for 10 minutes, then pull the cloth tight and smooth. Fold the cloth tails over the curds, place the follower on top, and press at 1 pound for at least 15 minutes. Remove from the mold, unwrap the cheesecloth, flip the cheese over, and redress, then press at 4 pounds for at least 10 hours. Remove the cheese from the mold and let it air-dry at 50°F to 55°F and 80 to 85 percent humidity for 24 hours. This will set up the surface for rind development.

6. Rub the cheese with the butter or lard, then bandage with cheesecloth (see page 28) and age at 55°F and at 65 to 75 percent humidity for at least 2 months, flipping it every other day. When the desired ripeness is reached, vacuum-seal or wrap well in plastic wrap and refrigerate until ready to eat. Opened, the cheese will dry out and harden over time, creating a wonderful grating cheese.

Profile: Beecher's Handmade Cheese

The owner of Seattle's Beecher's Handmade Cheese, Kurt Beecher Dammeier, has a keen eye for both business and great-tasting cheese. In 2003 Kurt opened what he thought would be a small-scale cheese business in the well-trafficked Pike Place Market. Being a smart man, he knew he needed a qualified, passionate cheese maker to ensure the venture would be successful, so he recruited Brad Sinko, who had worked at his family's creamery in Oregon. You'll still find Brad at the flagship store, creating products like Beecher's Flagship cheddars and Just Jack, which continue to garner recognition and awards. Kurt recently opened his second cheese making facility in the Flatiron District of Manhattan.

ALPINE-STYLE TOMME

MAKES 2 pounds
MILK Pasteurized whole cow's milk
START TO FINISH 2 to 4 months: less than 4 hours to make the cheese; 3 hours to press; 8 hours to dry;
5 days to dry salt or 8 hours to brine; 2 to 4 months to age

"Alpine style" refers to firm, pressed cow's milk cheeses made seasonally in the French, Austrian, Swiss, and Italian Alps—Comté, Gruyère, Emmental, Beaufort, and Fontina, to name a few. *Tomme*, in today's cheese making, refers to cheeses that are made in an old-world style, with rustic, textured rinds. Typically molded into wheels eight inches in diameter and five inches high, tommes are pressed and brined or dry salted to create a firm natural rind, then the cheese is aged. This tomme recipe is shared by cheese maker Stan Biasini of Mt. Mansfield Creamery in Morrisville, Vermont, where he makes very special small-batch raw-milk tommes.

2 gallons pasteurized whole cow's milk

1/4 teaspoon Meso II powdered mesophilic starter culture

1/4 teaspoon Thermo C powdered thermophilic starter culture

1/2 teaspoon calcium chloride diluted in 1/4 cup cool nonchlorinated water

1/2 teaspoon liquid rennet diluted in 1/4 cup cool nonchlorinated water

1 tablespoon kosher salt (preferably Diamond Crystal brand) or cheese salt, plus more for brining

1. In a nonreactive 10-quart stockpot, heat the milk over low heat to 70°F; this should take about 10 minutes. Turn off the heat.

2. Sprinkle the starter cultures over the milk and let rehydrate for 5 minutes. Mix well using a whisk in an up-and-down motion. Over low heat, slowly raise the temperature to 90°F. Add the calcium chloride and gently whisk in, then add the rennet in the same way. Cover and maintain 90°F, letting the milk ripen for 45 minutes, or until the curds give a clean break.

3. Still maintaining 90°F, cut the curds to the size of small peas. Let the curds rest for 5 minutes, then gently stir for 10 minutes. You may cut the curds again if they are not uniform in size. Slowly raise the temperature 1°F every 2 minutes, stirring continuously, until the curds have reached 95°F. Continuing to stir, raise the temperature a little faster—1°F every minute—until the temperature is 100°F. Holding this temperature, let the curds rest for about 5 minutes.

4. Ladle off the whey to about 1 inch above the curds. Place a strainer over a bowl or bucket large enough to capture the whey. Line it with damp butter muslin and ladle the curds into it. Let drain for 10 minutes, or until the curds stop dripping whey.

5. Set an 8-inch tomme mold (with follower) on a draining rack. Place the sack of drained curds into the mold. Fold the cloth tails over the curds, set the follower on top, and press at 10 pounds for 15 minutes. Remove the cheese from the mold, unwrap the cloth, flip the cheese over, and redress. Press at 20 pounds for 15 minutes, then redress again. Continue pressing at 20 pounds for a total of 3 hours, redressing every 30 minutes.

6. Remove the cheese from the mold and let air-dry at room temperature for 8 hours or overnight. Rub the surface of the cheese with about 1 tablespoon of salt, set it on a draining rack, and cover with a damp kitchen towel. Refrigerate for 5 days, redampening the towel every few days to keep the rind from drying out, and flipping the cheese daily. Or instead of dry salting, you can make a near-saturated brine (see page 24) and submerge the cheese in it for 8 hours, then pat dry and refrigerate.

7. Age at 50°F and 80 to 85 percent humidity for 2 to 4 months. If mold becomes noticeable, brush the cheese with a dedicated nailbrush or wipe with cheesecloth dampened in salt water. If the mold is persistent, you may run the cheese under trickling cold water, then let the rind air-dry, using a small fan to circulate the air, before storing again. (Too much washing of the rind may age the cheese too fast; it is better to dry-brush the rind every 5 to 7 days to remove unwanted mold.)

GRUYÈRE

MAKES 1¾ pounds
MILK Pasteurized whole cow's milk
START TO FINISH 2 months or longer: 3 hours to make the cheese; 12 hours to press;
12 hours to brine; 8 hours to dry; 2 months or longer to age

Gruyère is actually an entire family of cow's milk cheeses, including the Alpine and Pyrenees Italian Asiago and Montasio, and the French Beaufort and Comté. The Swiss version is the one formally named Gruyère. This cheese is the classic fondue cheese, with a nutty flavor that gets sweeter as it ages. Cheeses made in the Gruyère style are also hand-crafted in the United States. These firm, pressed cheeses, some of which have small holes, or eyes, are intended to be ripened over long periods of time—anywhere from 2 months to 2 years or more.

....

2 gallons pasteurized whole cow's milk

½ teaspoon Thermo C powdered thermophilic starter culture

½ teaspoon calcium chloride diluted in ¼ cup cool nonchlorinated water

½ teaspoon liquid rennet diluted in ¼ cup cool nonchlorinated water

Kosher salt (preferably Diamond Crystal brand) or cheese salt for brining

1. Heat the milk in a nonreactive 10-quart stockpot set in a 100°F water bath over low heat. Bring the milk to 90°F over 20 minutes. Turn off the heat.

2. Sprinkle the starter over the milk and let it rehydrate for 5 minutes. Mix well using a whisk in an up-and-down motion for 20 strokes. Cover and maintain 90°F, letting the milk ripen for 30 minutes. Add the calcium chloride and gently whisk in for 1 minute. Add the rennet and gently whisk in for 1 minute. Cover and let sit, maintaining 90°F for 30 to 40 minutes, or until the curds give a clean break.

3. Cut the curds into ¼-inch pieces and let sit undisturbed for 5 minutes. Over low heat, raise the temperature slowly to 122°F over 1 hour. Remove from the heat and gently stir for 15 minutes. The curds will release whey, firm up slightly, and shrink to the size of peanuts. Let the curds rest for 20 minutes. Ladle off enough whey to expose the curds.

4. Line an 8-inch tomme mold (with follower) with damp cheesecloth and place on a draining rack. Gently ladle the curds into the mold and let drain for 5 minutes. Gently press with your hand to compact the curds. Pull the cheesecloth tight and smooth. Fold the cloth tails over the curds, place the follower on top, and press at 8 pounds for 1 hour. Remove the cheese from the mold, unwrap the cheesecloth, flip the cheese over, and redress, then press at 10 pounds for 12 hours.

5. Meanwhile, make 2 quarts of a near-saturated brine solution (see page 24) in a noncorrosive container and chill to 50°F to 55°F. Remove the cheese from the mold and cloth and place it in the brine at 50°F to 55°F to soak for 12 hours, flipping it over once. Remove from the brine and pat dry. Place on a drying rack, cover loosely with cheesecloth, and air-dry at room temperature for 8 hours, or until the surface is dry to the touch. Flip the cheese over at least one time during the drying process.

6. Place the cheese in a ripening box, cover loosely, and ripen at 54°F and 90 percent humidity, flipping daily for 1 week. Rub with a simple brine solution (see page 24) twice a week for 3 more weeks. The salt solution will decrease the amount of mold that grows on the surface. Age for 2 months or longer. Wrap and store in the refrigerator.

VARIATION

For an aged Gruyère that allows for desirable mold growth, do not rub the cheese with brine but rather use the dry-brushing process (see page 101) once a week for the duration of the aging.

Tea-Smoked Gruyère

This tea-smoking method also works for crottin, Brie, and Fontina. In a bowl, combine 1/2 cup of brown sugar, 1/2 cup of white rice, 1/4 cup of black or oolong tea leaves, and 2 whole star anise pods. Line the bottom of a wok with foil, fitting it tightly along the interior. Put the tea mixture in the wok.

Bring the cheese to room temperature, pat it dry, and place it in a bamboo steamer basket or on a rack large enough to hold the cheese at least 2 inches above the tea mixture. Place a pan or pie tin of ice water slightly smaller in diameter than the smoking rack or steamer between the smoldering smoke source and the cheese. The water pan will act as a barrier to the heat and keep the cheese cool enough to absorb the smoke properly without melting. Prop up the water pan with wads of foil if needed.

Heat the wok over medium heat until the tea mixture begins to smoke. Cover the wok, reduce the heat to low, and smoke the cheese for 10 to 12 minutes. Turn off the heat and continue to smoke for another 6 to 8 minutes. Remove the cheese from the wok and set it aside to cool, then wrap and chill before serving. Discard the smoking ingredients. The smoked cheese can be stored in the refrigerator for up to 1 month.

JARLSBERG

MAKES 1¾ pounds
MILKS Pasteurized whole and low-fat (1 percent) cow's milk
START TO FINISH 2 to 6 months: 3½ hours to make the cheese; 8½ hours to press;
12 hours to brine; 2 days to dry; 2 to 6 months to age

Jarlsberg is the Norwegian cow's milk member of the Swiss Emmental family of cheeses. Known as Alpine cheeses, these have the characteristic large eyes (holes) and sweet taste created by propionic bacteria in the milk. *Propionibacterium shermanii* produces the characteristic flavor compounds and also carbon dioxide, bubbles of which create the eyes. A low-salt environment allows these bacteria to work properly. Patterned after the Swiss Emmental, Jarlsberg is a pressed natural-rind cheese that is ripened for 6 months to 1 year. The development of Jarlsberg's large eyes takes place when the cheese is ripened first in a cooler environment (50°F) for a specified period of time, then held in a warmer environment (65°F) for the remainder of ripening.

7 quarts pasteurized whole cow's milk

1 quart pasteurized low-fat (1 percent) milk

½ teaspoon Thermo C powdered thermophilic starter culture

⅛ teaspoon propionic bacteria powder

½ teaspoon calcium chloride diluted in ¼ cup cool nonchlorinated water

½ teaspoon liquid rennet diluted in ¼ cup cool nonchlorinated water

Kosher salt (preferably Diamond Crystal brand) or cheese salt for brining

1. Heat the milks in a nonreactive 10-quart stockpot set in a 102°F water bath over low heat. Bring the milk to 92°F over 15 minutes. Turn off the heat.

2. Sprinkle the starter and bacteria powder over the milk and let rehydrate for 5 minutes. Mix well using a whisk in an up-and-down motion. Cover and maintain the temperature, allowing the milk to ripen for 45 minutes. Add the calcium chloride and gently whisk in for 1 minute. Add the rennet and gently whisk in for 1 minute. Cover and let sit, maintaining the temperature at 92°F for 40 to 45 minutes, or until the curds give a clean break.

3. Cut the curds into ¼-inch pieces and stir for 20 minutes, then let rest for 5 minutes. Meanwhile, heat 3 cups of water to 140°F. Ladle out enough whey to expose the tops of the curds. Add enough 140°F water (about 1 to 2 cups) to bring the temperature to 100°F. Over low heat, slowly raise the temperature to 108°F over 30 minutes, gently stirring the curds. When the curds reach 108°F, stop stirring and allow them to settle. Hold at this temperature for 20 minutes.

4. Place a strainer over a bowl or bucket large enough to capture the whey. Line it with damp cheesecloth and gently ladle the curds into it. Let drain for 5 minutes, then transfer the curds, cloth and all, to an 8-inch tomme mold. Pull the cheesecloth up around the curds, tight and smooth. Fold the cloth tails over the curds and set the follower on top. Press at 10 pounds for 30 minutes. Remove the cheese from the mold, unwrap the cheesecloth, flip the cheese over, redress, then press at 15 pounds for 8 hours or overnight.

5. Meanwhile, make a near-saturated brine solution (see page 24) in a noncorrosive container with lid and chill at 50°F to 55°F.

6. Remove the cheese from the mold and cloth. Place it in the brine, cover, and soak at 50°F to 55°F for 12 hours, flipping over once. Remove from the brine and pat dry. Place on a drying rack, cover loosely with cheesecloth, and air-dry at room temperature for 2 days, or until the surface is dry to the touch. Flip the cheese over at least two times during this time to even out the drying.

7. Coat with 2 to 3 layers of cheese wax (see page 28).

8. Place the waxed cheese in an open ripening box or on a shelf to ripen at 50°F and 85 percent humidity for 2 weeks, flipping daily. After 2 weeks, continue the ripening at the warmer temperature of 65°F and 80 percent humidity for 4 to 6 weeks. The cheese may be consumed at this point or moved to the refrigerator to age for another 3 to 4 months.

SAFFRON-INFUSED MANCHEGO

MAKES 2 pounds
MILK Pasteurized whole cow's milk
ALTERNATIVE MILK Pasteurized sheep's milk
START TO FINISH 11 days to 3 months: 3 to 4 hours to make the cheese; 9 hours to press;
6 to 8 hours to brine; 10 days to 3 months to age

Manchego originated in Spain, where it was traditionally made from sheep's milk, though much of today's Manchego is made from cow's milk. Its rich, mellow flavor makes it one of the most popular Spanish cheeses in the United States. This version has saffron added to the milk for its floral flavor and golden color. In home-crafting this style of cheese, the pressed cheese is brined, then air-dried to age to the desired ripeness. The cheese can be rubbed with olive oil. Manchego is wonderful at five days (Manchego fresco), aged three months or longer (Manchego viejo), or aged in olive oil for more than a year (Manchego en aceite). For a plain Manchego, simply omit the saffron.

⅛ teaspoon saffron threads

2 gallons pasteurized whole cow's milk

¼ teaspoon MM 100 powdered mesophilic starter culture

¼ teaspoon Thermo B powdered thermophilic starter culture

¼ teaspoon mild lipase powder diluted in ¼ cup cool nonchlorinated water (optional)

¼ teaspoon calcium chloride diluted in ¼ cool nonchlorinated water

½ teaspoon liquid rennet diluted in ¼ cup cool nonchlorinated water

½ teaspoon sweet paprika

⅓ cup olive oil

1.   In a nonreactive 10-quart stockpot, stir the saffron into the milk, then heat over low heat to 86°F; this should take about 15 minutes. Turn off the heat.

2.   Sprinkle the starter cultures over the milk and let rehydrate for 5 minutes. Mix well using a whisk in an up-and-down motion. Cover and maintin 86°F, allowing the milk to ripen for 45 minutes. Add the lipase, if using (it lends a stronger flavor and aroma), gently whisking it in. Add the calcium chloride and gently whisk in, then add the rennet and gently whisk in for 1 minute. Cover and let sit, maintaining 86°F for 30 to 45 minutes, or until the curds give a clean break.

3.   Still maintaining 86°F, cut the curds into ½-inch pieces and let sit for 5 minutes. Cut the curds into rice-size pieces by gently stirring them with a stainless steel whisk. Switching to a rubber spatula, slowly stir around the edges of the pot, keeping the curds moving for about 30 minutes to release the whey and firm up the curds.

4. Over low heat, bring the curds to 104°F over 30 minutes, gently stirring with a rubber spatula to prevent the curds from matting into one mass. The whey will be a light greenish yellow color and only slightly cloudy. Turn off the heat when the temperature reaches 104°F and let the curds rest for 5 minutes. The curds will sink to the bottom. Ladle off enough whey to expose the curds.

5. Place a strainer over a bowl or bucket large enough to capture the whey. Line it with damp butter muslin and gently ladle the curds into it. Let drain for 15 minutes, or until the whey stops dripping.

6. Gently transfer the sack of drained curds to an 8-inch tomme mold. Pull the cloth up tight and smooth around the curds, cover with the tails of cloth, and place the follower on top. Press at 15 pounds for 15 minutes. Remove the cheese from the mold, unwrap the cloth, flip the cheese over, and redress. Press again at 15 pounds for 15 minutes. Repeat this process one more time, then flip and redress the cheese and press at 30 pounds for 8 hours or overnight.

7. Make 3 quarts of medium-saturated brine (see page 24) in a noncorrosive container with a lid and chill to 50°F to 55°F. Remove the cheese from the mold and cloth. Place it in the brine and soak at 50°F to 55°F for 6 to 8 hours. Remove the cheese from the brine and pat dry.

8. Place the cheese on a drying mat in an uncovered ripening box and age at 55°F and 80 to 85 percent humidity for 10 days to 3 months, flipping daily. Remove any unwanted mold with cheesecloth dampened in a vinegar-salt solution (see page 25). When the cheese has reached the desired ripeness, combine the paprika and olive oil and rub the cheese with this mixture. Wrap and store in the refrigerator.

PARMESAN

MAKES 1¾ pounds

MILK Pasteurized reduced fat (2 percent) cow's milk

START TO FINISH 7 months or more: 2½ hours to make the cheese; 13½ hours to press;
12 hours to brine; 2 to 3 days to dry; 7 months or more to age

Parmesan is probably the best-known and most imitated cheese in the world. The real deal is one of the world's greatest cheeses: flaky, brittle, nutty, crunchy, and sharp. However, the identifier "parmesan" has become a generic term for many mediocre cheeses made outside of Italy. To be called Parmigiano-Reggiano, the cheese must come from only two designated areas of Italy, Emilia-Romagna and Lombardy, where it is made with skimmed milk, then pressed, brined, and aged for one to two years or more. In the United States, there are a few extraordinary examples of aged artisan cheeses inspired by Parmigiano-Reggiano. If you can be patient and allow your Parmesan to age to one year, you will be amazed at how delicious it is.

2 gallons pasteurized reduced fat (2 percent) cow's milk

¼ teaspoon Thermo B powdered thermophilic starter culture

½ teaspoon calcium chloride diluted in ¼ cup cool nonchlorinated water

½ teaspoon liquid rennet diluted in ¼ cup cool nonchlorinated water

Kosher salt (preferably Diamond Crystal brand) or cheese salt for brining

Olive oil for rubbing

1. Heat the milk in a nonreactive 10-quart stockpot set in a 104°F water bath over low heat. Bring the milk to 94°F over 20 minutes. Turn off the heat.

2. Sprinkle the starter over the milk and let it rehydrate for 5 minutes. Mix well using a whisk in an up-and-down motion. Cover and maintain the temperature, letting the milk ripen for 45 minutes. Add the calcium chloride and gently whisk in for 1 minute. Add the rennet and gently whisk in for 1 minute. Cover and let sit, maintaining 94°F for 45 minutes, or until the curds give a clean break.

3. Using a whisk, cut the curds into pea-size pieces and let sit undisturbed for 10 minutes. Over low heat, slowly raise the temperature to 124°F over 1 hour, continuously stirring the curds to firm them up. Once 105°F has been reached, stop stirring and allow the curds to settle and mat together. Cover and maintain 124°F for 10 minutes.

4. Line a colander with damp butter muslin and ladle the curds into it. Let drain for 5 minutes, then transfer the curds, cloth and all, to a 5-inch tomme mold and let drain for 10 minutes. Pull up the cloth and smooth out any wrinkles, fold the tails of the cloth over the curds, and put the follower on top. Press at 10 pounds for 30 minutes. Remove the cheese from the mold, flip it over, and redress, then press again at 10 pounds for 1 hour. Once again remove from the mold, flip, and redress the cheese, then press at 20 pounds for 12 hours.

5. Make 3 quarts of near-saturated brine (see page 24) and chill to 50°F to 55°F. Remove the cheese from the mold and cloth and place in the brine to soak at 50°F to 55°F for 12 hours, flipping it over once during that time.

6. Remove the cheese from the brine and pat dry. Place on a drying rack, cover with cheesecloth, and air-dry at room temperature for 2 to 3 days, or until the surface is dry to the touch, flipping each day.

7. Place on a mat in a ripening box and ripen at 50°F to 55°F and 85 percent humidity, flipping daily, for 2 weeks. Flip twice a week for the next month, then once a week for the duration of ripening. Remove any unwanted mold with cheesecloth dampened in a vinegar-salt solution (see page 25).

8. After 3 months of ripening, rub the surface with olive oil. Return the cheese to the ripening box and age for a total of 7 months, or until the desired ripeness is reached, flipping once a week and rubbing with olive oil once a month. Wrap and store in the refrigerator.

ROMANO

MAKES 2 pounds
MILKS Pasteurized whole cow's milk, pasteurized goat's milk
START TO FINISH 5 months or more: 3½ hours to make the cheese; 13½ hours to press;
12 hours to brine; 2 days to dry; 5 months or more to age

Hailing from central Italy near Rome, Romano is a hard, salty cheese used mostly for grating. The most notable Romano is Pecorino Romano, which is made with sheep's milk, though goat's milk Caprino Romano is also widely acclaimed. This recipe calls for a blend of cow's and goat's milks, though you can make an all goat's milk version if you prefer a sharper, tangier taste. Capalase lipase (goat lipase) powder is optional here for an even sharper taste. If you are using goat's milk exclusively, add ⅛ teaspoon more rennet. By nature of being a hard, pressed cheese, Romano takes at least five months of ripening to acquire the desired flavor and texture. If you can be patient, let it age for a full year for a more pronounced flavor.

....

1 gallon pasteurized whole cow's milk
1 gallon pasteurized goat's milk
¼ teaspoon Thermo B powdered thermophilic starter culture
⅛ teaspoon Capalase lipase powder dissolved in ¼ cup cool nonchlorinated water before using (optional)
½ teaspoon calcium chloride diluted in ¼ cup cool nonchlorinated water
½ teaspoon liquid rennet diluted in ¼ cup cool nonchlorinated water
Kosher salt (preferably Diamond Crystal brand) or cheese salt for brining
Olive oil for rubbing

1. Heat the milks in a nonreactive 10-quart stockpot set in a 100°F water bath over low heat. Bring the milk to 90°F over 20 minutes. Turn off the heat.

2. Sprinkle the starter over the milk and let it rehydrate for 5 minutes. Mix well using a whisk in an up-and-down motion. Cover and maintain 90°F, letting the milk ripen for 30 minutes. Add the lipase, if using, and gently whisk in. Add the calcium chloride and gently whisk in for 1 minute. Add the rennet and gently whisk in for 1 minute. Cover and let sit, maintaining 90°F for 1 hour, or until the curds give a clean break.

3. Cut the curds into ¼-inch pieces and let sit undisturbed for 5 minutes. Over low heat, slowly raise the temperature to 117°F over 40 to 50 minutes, continuously stirring the curds to firm them up. Once 117°F has been reached, stop stirring and allow the curds to settle. Cover and maintain 117°F for 30 minutes.

4. Line a colander with damp butter muslin and ladle the curds into it. Let drain for 5 minutes, then transfer the curds, cloth and all, to an 8-inch tomme mold. Pull up the cloth and smooth out any wrinkles, fold the tails of the cloth over the curds, and put the follower on top. Press at 10 pounds for 30 minutes. Remove the cheese from the mold, flip it over, and redress, then press again at 10 pounds for 1 hour. Once again remove, flip, and redress the cheese, then press at 20 pounds for 12 hours.

5. Make 2 quarts of near-saturated brine (see page 24) and chill to 50°F to 55°F. Remove the cheese from the mold and cloth and place in the brine to soak at 50°F to 55°F for 12 hours, flipping it over once during that time.

6. Remove the cheese from the brine and pat dry. Place on a drying rack, cover with cheesecloth, and air-dry at room temperature for 2 days, or until the surface is dry to the touch, flipping each day.

7. Place the cheese on a cheese mat in a ripening box and ripen at 50°F to 55°F and 85 percent humidity, flipping daily for 2 weeks. Flip twice a week for the next month, then once a week for the duration of ripening. Remove any unwanted mold with cheesecloth dampened in a vinegar-salt solution (see page 25).

8. After 2 months of ripening, rub the surface with olive oil. Return the cheese to the ripening box and age for a total of 5 months, or until the desired ripeness is reached, flipping once a week and rubbing with olive oil once a month. Wrap and store in the refrigerator.

ASIAGO PEPATO

MAKES Two 1-pound wheels
MILKS Pasteurized whole and reduced fat (2 percent) cow's milk
START TO FINISH 3 weeks for Asiago Pressato or 2 months to 1 year for aged Asiago:
about 4 hours to make the cheese; 16 hours to press; 12 hours to brine; 8 hours to dry; 3 weeks to 1 year to age

Asiago is a firm pressed cheese from the Veneto region of Italy made with either all cow's milk or a blend of cow's and goat's milks. This version has peppercorns in the center, adding a nice bite to the finished cheese. Asiago has a natural rind developed by first brining the cheese, then air-drying it to set up the rind, and finally aging the cheese to the desired flavor. When aged for three weeks, the cheese is known as Asiago Pressato; when aged longer (up to one or two years), it has a hard, gratable texture and is called stravecchio. This recipe makes two smaller wheels rather than one larger cheese, allowing you to enjoy one in its young, Pressato stage while you age the other further. This gives you the chance to make the Asiago once and savor it twice!

6 quarts pasteurized whole cow's milk

2 quarts pasteurized reduced fat (2 percent) cow's milk

1/2 teaspoon Thermo B powdered thermophilic starter culture

1/2 teaspoon calcium chloride diluted in 1/4 cup cool nonchlorinated water

1/2 teaspoon liquid rennet diluted in 1/4 cup cool nonchlorinated water

1 1/2 teaspoons black or green peppercorns (omit if making plain Asiago)

Kosher salt (preferably Diamond Crystal brand) or cheese salt for brining

1. In a nonreactive 10-quart stockpot, heat the milks over low heat to 92°F; this should take about 20 minutes. Turn off the heat.

2. Sprinkle the starter over the milk and let it rehydrate for 5 minutes. Mix well using a whisk in an up-and-down motion. Cover and maintain 92°F, allowing the milk to ripen for 45 minutes. Add the calcium chloride and gently whisk in for 1 minute. Add the rennet and gently whisk in for 1 minute. Cover and let sit, maintaining 92°F for 1 hour, or until the curds give a clean break.

3. Cut the curds into 1/2-inch pieces and let sit undisturbed for 5 minutes. Over low heat, slowly raise the temperature to 104°F over 40 minutes. Remove from the heat and stir for 15 minutes to release whey and shrink the curds to the size of peanuts. Over low heat, slowly raise the temperature to 118°F, stirring the curds to firm them up. Once 118°F has been reached, stop stirring and allow the curds to settle. Cover and maintain 118°F for 20 minutes.

4. Ladle off enough whey to expose the curds. Line two 4⅝-inch-wide Italian draining baskets with damp cheesecloth and place them on a draining rack. Fill each mold with one-fourth of the curds and let drain for 5 minutes. Cover with the tails of the cheesecloth and gently press with your hand to compact the curds. Unwrap and sprinkle half of the peppercorns over each mold of compacted curds. Divide the remaining curds between the molds to cover the peppercorns and pack down using your hand.

5. Pull the cheesecloth up around the curds and fold it over to cover the tops. Place a follower on top of each draining basket and press at 8 pounds for 1 hour. Remove, flip, and redress the cheese, then press at 8 pounds for another 8 hours.

6. Make 3 quarts of saturated brine (see page 24) and chill to 50°F to 55°F. Remove the cheeses from the molds and

Asiago Pepato at 4 weeks

cloth and place them in the brine to soak at 50°F to 55°F for 12 hours, flipping them over once.

7. Remove the cheeses from the brine and pat dry. Place on a drying rack, cover loosely with cheesecloth, and air-dry at room temperature for 8 hours, or until the surface is dry to the touch, flipping the cheeses at least one time during the drying process.

8. Place the cheeses on a mat in a ripening box with a lid. Cover loosely and ripen at 54°F and 85 percent humidity, flipping daily for 1 week. Brush with a simple brine (see page 24), cooled to 50°F to 55°F, twice a week for the first 3 weeks of aging. For an aged version, continue the brushing process once a week for at least 2 months and up to 1 year.

AMERICAN BRICK

MAKES 2 pounds
MILK Pasteurized whole cow's milk
START TO FINISH 4 months: 3 hours to make the cheese; 12 hours to press; 2 hours to brine;
24 hours to dry; 4 months to age

Brick is a relatively new American original cheese, having been created in the late 1800s in Wisconsin. It is a firm cheese originally formed in a special brick-shaped mold. The curds were pressed with five-pound bricks as weights, then washed with brine numerous times while ripening. The lore is that the name *brick* came from both the use of bricks as weights and the cheese's shape. You can replicate this shape and pressing method by creating a rectangular mold from a recycled food container (see page 7) and pressing with bricks. In this recipe the cheese is brined only once, then waxed and allowed to slowly ripen in cool storage.

2 gallons pasteurized whole cow's milk

½ teaspoon Meso II powdered mesophilic starter culture

½ teaspoon calcium chloride diluted in ¼ cup cool nonchlorinated water

½ teaspoon liquid rennet diluted in ¼ cup cool nonchlorinated water

Kosher salt (preferably Diamond Crystal brand) or cheese salt for brining

1. In a nonreactive 10-quart stockpot, heat the milk over low heat to 88°F; this should take about 20 minutes. Turn off the heat.

2. Sprinkle the starter over the milk and let it rehydrate for 5 minutes. Mix well using a whisk in an up-and-down motion. Cover and maintain 88°F, letting the milk ripen for 15 minutes. Add the calcium chloride and gently whisk in for 1 minute. Add the rennet and gently whisk in for 1 minute. Cover and let sit, maintaining 88°F for 30 to 45 minutes, or until the curds give a clean break.

3. Still maintaining 88°F, cut the curds into ½-inch pieces and let sit for 5 minutes. Over low heat, slowly bring the curds to 98°F over 45 minutes. Stir continuously to keep the curds from matting together; they will release whey, firm up slightly, and shrink to the size of peanuts.

4. Once the curds are at 98°F, turn off the heat, maintain the temperature, and let the curds rest undisturbed for 25 minutes; they will sink to the bottom.

5. Line a strainer with damp butter muslin and ladle the curds into it. Let drain for 5 minutes, then transfer the curds, cloth and all, to an 8-inch tomme mold. Pull up the cloth and smooth out any wrinkles, cover the curds with the tails of cloth, set the follower on top, and press at 5 pounds for 15 minutes. Remove the cheese, unwrap, flip, and redress, then press again at 10 pounds for 12 hours.

6. Make 4 quarts of near-saturated brine (see page 24) and chill to 50°F to 55°F. Remove the cheese from the mold and cloth and place it in the brine to soak at 50°F to 55°F for 2 hours.

7. Remove the cheese from the brine and pat dry. Air-dry on a cheese mat at room temperature for about 24 hours to dry and set up the rind. Rub off any mold spots that might develop with a solution of salt and distilled vinegar.

8. Wax the cheese (see page 28) and age at 50°F and 85 percent humidity for up to 4 months, flipping the cheese once a week for even ripening.

CAERPHILLY

MAKES 2 pounds
MILK Pasteurized whole cow's milk
START TO FINISH 2 to 6 months: 3 hours to make the cheese; 12½ hours to press; 8 hours to brine;
24 hours to dry; 2 to 6 months to age

Caerphilly (pronounced kar-FILL-ee) is a Welsh classic that was made exclusively in and around Cardiff until the mid-1800s. When the demand became too great for Welsh producers, English creameries in Somerset began making the cheese. In recent times the classic has been resurrected, and today there are a few farmstead producers making world-class Caerphilly, including Gorwydd by cheese maker Todd Trethowan, and the Caerphilly-inspired Landaff cheese from New Hampshire's Landaff Creamery. These cheeses are aged for only two to three months and are often affectionately likened to cheesecake, with their crumbly texture and lemony–sweet buttery flavor. In this recipe, ripening occurs through controlled mold development on the rind. In this case, mold is good!

2 gallons pasteurized whole cow's milk

¼ teaspoon MA 4001 powdered mesophilic starter culture

¼ teaspoon Aroma B powdered mesophilic starter culture

½ teaspoon calcium chloride diluted in ¼ cup cool nonchlorinated water

½ teaspoon liquid rennet diluted in ¼ cup cool nonchlorinated water

Kosher salt (preferably Diamond Crystal brand) or cheese salt for brining

1. In a nonreactive 10-quart stockpot, heat the milk over low heat to 90°F; this should take about 20 minutes. Turn off the heat.

2. Sprinkle the starter cultures over the milk and let rehydrate for 5 minutes. Mix well using a whisk in an up-and-down motion. Cover and maintain 90°F, letting the milk ripen for 1 hour. Add the calcium chloride and gently whisk in for 1 minute. Add the rennet and gently whisk in for 1 minute. Cover and let sit, maintaining 90°F for 45 to 55 minutes, or until the curds give a clean break.

3. Still maintaining 90°F, cut the curds into ½-inch pieces and let sit for 5 minutes. Over low heat, slowly bring the curds to 95°F over 20 minutes. Stir continuously to keep the curds from matting together; they will release whey, firm up slightly, and shrink to the size of peanuts.

4. Once the curds are at 95°F, turn off the heat, maintain the temperature, and let the curds rest undisturbed for 45 minutes; they will sink to the bottom.

5. Ladle enough whey from the pot to expose the tops of the curds. Line a strainer with damp butter muslin and ladle the curds into it. Let drain for 5 minutes.

6. Transfer the curds, cloth and all, to an 8-inch tomme mold. Pull up the cloth and smooth out any wrinkles, cover the curds with the tails of cloth, set the follower on top, and press at 8 pounds for 30 minutes. Remove the cheese from the mold, unwrap, flip, and redress, then press again at 10 pounds for 12 hours.

7. Make 4 quarts of medium-heavy brine (see page 24) and chill to 50°F to 55°F. Remove the cheese from the mold and cloth and place it in the brine to soak at 50°F to 55°F for 8 hours.

(continued)

8. Remove the cheese from the brine and pat dry. Air-dry on a cheese mat at room temperature for about 24 hours, or until the surface is dry to the touch. Rub off any mold spots that might develop with a solution of salt and distilled vinegar.

9. Place the cheese on a mat in a ripening box and ripen at 50°F to 55°F and 85 percent humidity, flipping daily. After 10 to 14 days a whitish gray mold will appear. Once this occurs, flip the cheese twice a week until a crust is formed. Brush the surface twice a week at the same time as you flip the cheese to encourage mold growth. Brush with a wad of dry cheesecloth or a dedicated soft nailbrush dampened in simple brine (see page 24) with the excess moisture removed. After 3 weeks from the beginning of ripening, the cheese will begin to soften under the crust. Consume at 2 months for a sharp flavor, or ripen longer—up to 6 months—for a more pungent flavor.

COLBY

MAKES 2 pounds
MILK Pasteurized whole cow's milk
START TO FINISH 6 weeks to 2 months: 3½ hours to make the cheese; 13 hours to press; 8 hours to brine;
24 hours to dry; 6 weeks to 2 months to age

Like brick, Colby is an American classic. Colby is similar to classic cheddar but is made using the washed-curd method, which produces a softer texture and milder flavor. Its orange color is the result of annatto being added to the milk. The deep color develops as the cheese ripens. Colby is a good candidate for a smoked cheese.

2 gallons pasteurized whole cow's milk

¹/₂ teaspoon Meso II powdered mesophilic starter culture

¹/₄ teaspoon liquid annatto diluted in ¹/₄ cup cool nonchlorinated water

¹/₂ teaspoon calcium chloride diluted in ¹/₄ cup cool nonchlorinated water

¹/₂ teaspoon liquid rennet diluted in ¹/₄ cup cool nonchlorinated water

Kosher salt (preferably Diamond Crystal brand) or cheese salt for brining

1. In a nonreactive 10-quart stockpot, heat the milk over low heat to 86°F; this should take about 15 minutes. Turn off the heat.

2. Sprinkle the starter over the milk and let it rehydrate for 5 minutes. Mix well using a whisk in an up-and-down motion. Cover and maintain 86°F, letting the milk ripen for 1 hour. Add the annatto and gently whisk in for 1 minute. Add the calcium chloride and gently whisk in for 1 minute, and then incorporate the rennet in the same way. Cover and let sit, maintaining 86°F for 30 to 45 minutes, or until the curds give a clean break.

3. Still maintaining 86°F, cut the curds into ½-inch pieces and let sit for 5 minutes. Over low heat, slowly bring the curds to 104°F over 50 minutes. Stir continuously to keep the curds from matting together; they will release whey, firm up slightly, and shrink to the size of peanuts.

4. Once the curds are at 104°F, turn off the heat, maintain the temperature, and let the curds rest undisturbed for 15 minutes; they will sink to the bottom.

5. Into a measuring cup, ladle out enough whey to expose the curds. Replace the whey with the same amount of 104°F water. Gently stir for 2 minutes, then cover and let the curds rest for 10 minutes.

6. Line a strainer with damp butter muslin and ladle the curds into it. Let drain for 5 minutes.

7. Line a 5-inch tomme mold with damp cheesecloth and gently transfer the drained curds to the mold. Pull up the cloth and smooth out any wrinkles, cover the curds with the cloth tails, set the follower on top, and press at 5 pounds for 1 hour. Remove the cheese from the mold, unwrap, flip, and redress, then press again at 10 pounds for 12 hours.

8. Make 4 quarts of medium-heavy brine (see page 24) and chill to 50°F to 55°F. Remove the cheese from the mold and cloth and place it in the brine to soak at 50°F to 55°F for 8 hours.

9. Remove the cheese from the brine and pat dry. Air-dry at room temperature on a cheese mat for about 24 hours, or until the surface is dry to the touch. Rub off any mold spots that might develop with a solution of salt and distilled vinegar.

10. Wax the cheese (see page 28) and age at 50°F and 80 to 85 percent humidty for 6 weeks to 2 months, flipping the cheese once a week for even ripening.

BREW-CURDS CHEDDAR

MAKES 2 pounds
MILK Pasteurized whole cow's milk
START TO FINISH 4 to 6 weeks: about 5 hours to make the cheese; 13 hours to press;
1 to 2 days to dry; 4 to 6 weeks to age

This cheddar is really fun, allowing you to incorporating your favorite brew into the finished cheese. If you choose a light Belgian ale, the cheese will be lighter in color and mellower in flavor than if you use a dark ale or a stout. You can add annatto as well if you want an orange color.

....

2 gallons pasteurized whole cow's milk

1/2 teaspoon Meso II powdered mesophilic starter culture

1/4 teaspoon liquid annatto diluted in 1/4 cup cool nonchlorinated water (optional)

1/2 teaspoon calcium chloride diluted in 1/4 cup cool nonchlorinated water

1/2 teaspoon liquid rennet diluted in 1/4 cup cool nonchlorinated water

One 12-ounce bottle dark ale or stout at room temperature

1 tablespoon kosher salt (preferably Diamond Crystal brand) or cheese salt

1. Heat the milk in a nonreactive 10-quart stockpot set in a 98°F water bath over low heat. Bring the milk to 88°F over 10 minutes. Turn off the heat.

2. Sprinkle the starter over the milk and let it rehydrate for 5 minutes. Mix well using a whisk in an up-and-down motion. Cover and maintain 88°F, letting the milk ripen for 45 minutes. Add the annatto, if using, and gently whisk in for 1 minute. Add the calcium chloride and gently whisk in for 1 minute, and then incorporate the rennet in the same way. Cover and let sit, maintaining 88°F for 30 to 45 minutes, or until the curds give a clean break.

3. Still maintaining 88°F, cut the curds into 1/2-inch pieces and let sit for 5 minutes. Over low heat, slowly bring the curds to 102°F over 40 minutes. Stir continuously to keep the curds from matting together; they will release whey, firm up slightly, and shrink to the size of peanuts.

4. Once the curds are at 102°F, turn off the heat, maintain the temperature, and let the curds rest undisturbed for 30 minutes; they will sink to the bottom.

5. Place a strainer over a bowl or bucket large enough to capture the whey. Line it with damp butter muslin and ladle the curds into it. Let drain for 10 minutes, or until the whey stops dripping. Reserve one-third of the whey and return it to the pot.

6. Return the whey in the pot to 102°F. Place the curds in a colander, set the colander over the pot, and cover. Carefully maintaining the 102°F temperature of the whey, wait 10 minutes for the curds to melt into a slab. Flip the slab of curds, and repeat every 15 minutes for 1 hour. The curds should maintain a 95°F to 100°F temperature from the heated whey below and continue to expel whey into the pot. After 1 hour, the curds will look shiny and white, like poached chicken.

(continued)

Waxed Brew-Curds
Cheddar at 6 weeks

7. Transfer the warm slab of curds to a cutting board and cut into 2 by ½-inch strips, like French fries. Place the warm strips in a bowl and cover completely with the brew. Soak for 45 minutes. Drain and discard the brew. Sprinkle the salt over the curds and gently toss to mix.

8. Line an 8-inch tomme mold with damp cheesecloth. Pack the drained curds into the mold, cover with the cloth tails, set the follower on top, and press at 8 pounds for 1 hour. Remove the cheese from the mold, unwrap, flip, and redress, then press at 10 pounds for 12 hours.

9. Remove the cheese from the mold and cloth and pat dry. Air-dry on a cheese mat at room temperature for 1 to 2 days, or until the surface is dry to the touch.

10. Wax the cheese (see page 28) and ripen at 50°F to 55°F and 85 percent humidity for 4 to 6 weeks, flipping the cheese daily for even ripening.

VARIATION

For a natural-rind cheese rather than waxed, after air-drying wash the cheese with brew twice a week. Place the cheese on a mat in a ripening box and ripen at 50°F to 55°F and 85 percent humidity, flipping daily. After 10 to 14 days a whitish gray mold will appear. Continue flipping daily until a crust is formed. Brush the rind with a wad of dry cheesecloth or a dedicated soft nailbrush dampened in simple brine (see page 24) with the excess moisture removed twice a week to encourage mold growth. After 3 weeks the cheese will begin to soften under the crust. Continue the process for 6 to 8 weeks, storing at 50°F to 55°F. Consume after 2 to 3 months.

CHEDDAR-JALAPEÑO CHEESE CURDS

MAKES 1 pound
MILK Pasteurized whole cow's milk
START TO FINISH 16 to 28 hours: 4 hours to make the curds; 12 to 24 hours to dry

Here's the perfect snack food: squeaky curds. These were created for this book by Robyn Rosemon of the Beverage People. You can make them spicy like this version, or make them plain if you'd rather. You can even change up the flavors by tossing in dried herbs right after the curds drain.

1 gallon pasteurized whole cow's milk

⅛ teaspoon Meso II powdered mesophilic starter culture

½ teaspoon calcium chloride diluted in 2 tablespoons cool nonchlorinated water

½ teaspoon liquid rennet diluted in 2 tablespoons cool nonchlorinated water

1 tablespoon plus ½ teaspoon kosher salt (preferably Diamond Crystal brand) or cheese salt

1 (4-ounce) can diced jalapeños, drained

½ to 1 teaspoon red pepper flakes

1. Heat the milk in a nonreactive 6-quart stockpot set in a 98°F water bath over low heat. Bring the milk to 88°F over 12 minutes. Turn off the heat.

2. Sprinkle the starter over the milk and let it rehydrate for 5 minutes. Mix well using a whisk in an up-and-down motion. Cover and maintain 88°F, letting the milk ripen for 45 minutes. Add the calcium chloride and gently whisk in. Add the rennet and gently whisk in. Cover and let sit, maintaining 86°F to 88°F for 40 minutes, or until the curds give a clean break.

3. Cut the curds into ½-inch pieces and let them rest for 5 minutes. Over low heat, slowly bring the curds to 102°F over about 30 minutes, stirring to reduce the curds to the size of peanuts. Turn off the heat and maintain 102°F for 30 minutes, stirring every couple of minutes to prevent matting. Give the curds a texture test: squeeze a spoonful of curds in your fist; they should lump together. Now push them apart with your thumb; if they separate, you are ready to proceed. Let the curds settle for 15 minutes.

4. Place a strainer over a bowl or bucket large enough to capture the whey. Line it with damp butter muslin and ladle the curds into it. Let drain for 10 minutes, or until the whey stops dripping. Pour the whey back into the pot.

5. Return the whey in the pot to 102°F. Place the curds in a colander, set the colander over the pot, and cover. Carefully maintaining the 102°F temperature of the whey, wait 10 minutes for the curds to melt into a slab. Flip the slab of curds, and repeat every 15 minutes for 1 hour. The curds should maintain a 98°F to 100°F temperature from the heated whey below and continue to expel whey into the pot. After 1 hour, the curds will look shiny and white, like poached chicken.

6. Transfer the warm slab of curds to a cutting board and cut into 2 by ½-inch strips, like French fries. Place the warm strips in a bowl, add the 1 tablespoon of salt, and mix with your hands. Put the salted curds in a strainer over a bowl to dry, uncovered, for 12 to 24 hours at room temperature.

7. Place the curds in a large bowl. Gently mix in the ½ teaspoon of salt, the jalapeños, and the red pepper flakes. Store the curds in a resealable bag or vacuum-seal and refrigerate. They'll keep for 1 to 2 weeks in the refrigerator.

FARMHOUSE CHIVE CHEDDAR

MAKES 2 pounds
MILK Pasteurized whole cow's milk
ALTERNATIVE MILK Pasteurized whole goat's milk
START TO FINISH 1 to 2 months: 3 hours to make the cheese; 13 hours to press; 8 hours to brine;
24 hours to dry; 1 to 2 months to age

This farmhouse cheese is a beautiful, rustic cheddar made without using the traditional and slightly lengthier cheddaring process. Annatto and dried chives are added for color and flavor, and they create a lovely color complement to each other. If waxed and aged for only one month, the cheese will be creamy and moist. You can also use this method for making a simple farmhouse cheddar without chives or annatto. Goat's milk or mixed milk can be used as well (reduce the amount of rennet if using goat's milk; see page 9).

---

2 gallons pasteurized whole cow's milk

1/2 teaspoon Meso II powdered mesophilic starter culture

1/4 teaspoon liquid annatto diluted in 1/4 cup cool nonchlorinated water

1/2 teaspoon calcium chloride diluted in 1/4 cup cool nonchlorinated water

1/2 teaspoon liquid rennet diluted in 1/4 cup cool nonchlorinated water

Kosher salt (preferably Diamond Crystal brand) or cheese salt

2 teaspoons dried chives

1. Heat the milk in a nonreactive 10-quart stockpot set in a 96°F water bath over low heat. Bring the milk to 86°F over 10 minutes. Turn off the heat.

2. Sprinkle the starter over the milk and let it rehydrate for 5 minutes. Mix well using a whisk in an up-and-down motion. Cover and maintain 86°F, letting the milk ripen for 1 hour. Add the annatto and gently whisk in for 1 minute. Add the calcium chloride and gently whisk in for 1 minute, and then incorporate the rennet in the same way. Cover and let sit, maintaining 86°F for 30 to 45 minutes, or until the curds give a clean break.

3. Still maintaining 86°F, cut the curds into ½-inch pieces and let sit for 5 minutes. Over low heat, slowly bring the curds to 102°F over 40 minutes. Turn off the heat, maintain temperature, and gently stir the curds for 20 minutes, or until they start to firm up. The curds will be the size of peanuts. Still maintaining 86°F, let the curds rest undisturbed for 30 minutes; they will sink to the bottom. Ladle off enough whey to expose the top of the curds. Stir continuously for 15 to 20 minutes, or until the curds are matted and cling together when pressed in your hand.

4. Line a strainer with damp butter muslin and ladle the curds into it. Let drain for 5 minutes, then toss in 2 teaspoons of salt and the chives and mix thoroughly with your hands.

5. Line an 8-inch tomme mold with damp cheesecloth and gently transfer the drained curds to the lined mold. Pull up the cloth and smooth out any wrinkles, cover the curds with the cloth tails, set the follower on top, and press at 8 pounds for 1 hour. Remove the cheese from the mold, unwrap, flip, and redress, and press at 10 pounds for 12 hours.

6. Make 4 quarts of near-saturated brine (see page 24) and chill to 50°F to 55°F. Remove the cheese from the mold and cheesecloth and place in the brine to soak at 50°F to 55°F for 8 hours.

7. Remove the cheese from the brine and pat dry. Air-dry on a cheese mat at room temperature for about 24 hours,

Farmhouse Chive Cheddar
at 3 months

until the surface is dry to the touch. Rub off any mold spots that might develop with a solution of salt and distilled vinegar.

8. Wax the cheese (see page 28) and age at 50°F and 80 to 85 percent humidity for 1 to 2 months, flipping the cheese once a week for even ripening.

VARIATION

After air-drying, rub the cheese with butter or lard. Cloth bandage the cheese (see page 28) and store at 55°F to 60°F and 65 to 75 percent humidity, for 2 to 3 months, flipping weekly.

IRISH-STYLE CHEDDAR

MAKES 2 pounds
MILK Pasteurized whole cow's milk
START TO FINISH 2 to 3 months: 4 hours to make the cheese; 13 hours to press; 8 hours to soak;
1 to 2 days to dry; 2 to 3 months to age

What makes this cheddar Irish-style is its double hit of Irish whiskey. The milled curds are tossed with a splash of whiskey, then after pressing, the wheel is soaked in whiskey for eight hours before being air-dried, waxed, and aged.

2 gallons pasteurized whole cow's milk

1/2 teaspoon MA 4001 powdered mesophilic starter culture

1/2 teaspoon calcium chloride diluted in 1/4 cup cool nonchlorinated water

1/2 teaspoon liquid rennet diluted in 1/4 cup cool nonchlorinated water

2 cups Irish whiskey at room temperature

1 tablespoon kosher salt (preferably Diamond Crystal brand)

1. Heat the milk in a nonreactive 10-quart stockpot set in a 98°F water bath over low heat. Bring the milk to 88°F over 10 minutes. Turn off the heat.

2. Sprinkle the starter over the milk and let it rehydrate for 5 minutes. Mix well using a whisk in an up-and-down motion. Cover and maintain 88°F, letting the milk ripen for 45 minutes. Add the calcium chloride and gently whisk in for 1 minute. Add the rennet and gently whisk in for 1 minute. Cover and let sit, maintaining 88°F for 30 to 45 minutes, or until the curds give a clean break.

(continued)

3. Still maintaining 88°F, cut the curds into ½-inch pieces and let sit for 5 minutes. Over low heat, slowly bring the curds to 102°F over 40 minutes. Stir continuously to keep the curds from matting together; they will release whey, firm up slightly, and shrink to the size of peanuts.

4. Once the curds are at 102°F, turn off the heat, maintain the temperature, and let the curds rest undisturbed for 30 minutes; they will sink to the bottom.

5. Place a strainer over a bowl or bucket large enough to capture the whey. Line it with damp butter muslin and ladle the curds into it. Let drain for 15 minutes, or until the whey stops dripping. Pour the whey back into the pot.

6. Return the whey in the pot to 102°F. Place the curds in a colander, set the colander over the pot, and cover. Carefully maintaining the 102°F temperature of the whey, wait 10 minutes for the curds to melt into a slab. Flip the slab of curds, and repeat every 15 minutes for 1 hour. The curds should maintain a 95°F to 100°F temperature from the heated whey below and will continue to expel whey into the pot. After an hour, the curds will look shiny and white, like poached chicken.

7. Transfer the warm slab of curds to a cutting board and cut into 2 by ½-inch strips, like French fries. Place the warm strips in a bowl and add ¼ cup of the whiskey and the salt. Gently toss with your hands to combine.

8. Line an 8-inch tomme mold with damp cheesecloth. Pack the drained curds into the mold, cover with the cloth tails, set the follower on top, and press at 10 pounds for 1 hour. Remove the cheese from the mold, unwrap, flip, and redress, then press at 15 pounds for 12 hours.

9. Remove the cheese from the mold and cloth, place in a container, and cover with the remaining 1¾ cups of whiskey. Cover the container and place it in a 55°F environment for 8 hours, flipping the cheese once during that time.

Double-Milled Cheddar

In double-milled cheddars the natural, white cheddar curds are broken or cut up and pressed twice. The cheddar goes through its initial cheddaring process where the curds are broken up before molding and pressing. The curds are then pressed, brined, and aged to a specified desired maturity, and then are broken apart or cut into pieces (milled) a second time. At this point the milled curds are flavored by tossing with any number of sweet or savory ingredients or by soaking in alcohol before being molded and pressed again. Once double-milled, the cheddar is further aged to assure that the milled curds bind together to form a cheddar wheel.

To make flavored Double-Milled Cheddar: This flavoring process can be applied to good quality store-bought white or orange cheddars (the same procedure applies).

Cut or shred the curds into irregular cubes or pieces of about ⅜ inch to ½ inch. Place them in a bowl and add the flavoring, gently but thoroughly mixing with your hands. As a general guide I suggest adding one-third as much by weight of a chunky additive (caramelized onions or dried cranberries, for example) as you have cheese. For herbs or spices, the proportion should be 1 part herb or spice to 6 parts cheese. Fill a cloth-lined cheddar mold or cheese press with the flavored cheese and press following steps 8 to 10 for Brew-Curds Cheddar (page 120).

To make stout or whisky cheddar, for every one pound of cheese you will use 10 to 12 ounces of brew or spirits, or enough to cover the milled curds. Soak the curds for 4 to 6 hours, then drain and fill your mold or press. Follow steps 8 to 10 for Brew-Curds Cheddar (page 120) for pressing and finishing instructions.

Then wax and store at 50°F to 55°F and 75 percent humidity or vacuum-seal and refrigerate. Allow the new cheese to age for at least 2 weeks or up to a few months before consuming.

10. Drain the cheese and pat dry. Discard the soaking whiskey. Place the cheese on a cheese mat and air-dry at room temperature for 1 to 2 days, or until the surface is dry to the touch.

11. Wax the cheese (see page 28) and ripen at 50°F to 55°F and 85 percent humidity for 2 to 3 months, flipping the cheese daily during the first week and twice a week thereafter for even ripening.

COATED AND RUBBED CHEESES

Embellished cheeses are made in an eclectic array of shapes and sizes using a variety of milks. They are sheltered in fragrant layers of dried aromatic herbs and spices; smeared with vegetable dust or paste or wood ash; bathed in flavored oils; or kissed by sweet-smelling smoke. Not only do the aromatic coverings impart flavor to the cheese, but they also provide protection from air and unwanted bacteria.

There is a wide variety of notable traditional coated or rubbed cheeses, including Corsican Fleur du Maquis, coated with a mixture of herbs and pepper; Italian Bigio, rubbed in wood ash; and Spanish Majorero Pimentón, rubbed with red pepper pimentón. Striking modern American examples include Andante's Cadenza, coated with red wine pomace; Beehive Cheese Company's Barely Buzzed, coated with coffee and lavender; Capriole's Julianna, coated with herbs and spices; and Love Tree Farmstead's Big Holmes, coated with rosemary and mint. As you build your skills as a cheese maker, you can use these and other embellished cheeses as inspirations to create your own special cheeses and rubs.

Marinated cheeses are typically fresh or brined cheeses that are flavored by being packed in herb- or spice-infused olive oil, nut oil, smoked olive oil, or a vinaigrette mixture. Marinating has been a method of preserving cheeses for hundreds of years, protecting the cheese from air, unwanted bacteria, and insects. Flavoring is an additional benefit from packing cheese in seasoned surroundings, and peppercorns, bay leaves, rosemary, sun-dried tomato pieces, or citrus peel all make delicious additions. Fresh or young goat cheeses do best with this method of flavoring. Examples of marinated cheese in this book include Cabécou (page 51) and Fromage à la Huile (page 143).

Smoking also contributes excellent flavor to cheeses. See page 27 for general instructions. In this book, you'll find smoked variations for ricotta (page 40), Scamorza (page 88), Gruyère (page 103), Gorgonzola (page 187), chèvre (page 59), and Fromage à l'Huile (page 143).

Brin d'Amour

MAKES 1 pound
MILKS Pasteurized goat's milk, pasteurized whole cow's milk
START TO FINISH 1 to 2 months: 1 hour to make the cheese; 8 hours to ripen; about 6 to 10 hours to drain and ripen; 24 hours to dry; 1 to 2 months to age

Brin d'Amour is a famous soft, unpressed herb-encrusted cheese from Corsica. It's a beauty, rolled in dried herbs, then decorated with peppercorns, juniper berries, and, sometimes, small red peppers. This lavishly embellished lady is typically made with sheep's milk, though goat's milk is sometimes used. My version uses a combination of cow's and goat's milks and a blend of aromatic dried herbs and spices. Two options for shaping—in a cloth sack or in a cheese mold—are offered. At the early stages of ripening, the cheese will be a bit runny, but as it ages it will become firmer and drier. My favorite source for the herbs and spices used here is Whole Spice (see Resources).

(continued)

Brin d'Amour at 4 weeks

Brin d'Amour, continued

2 quarts pasteurized goat's milk

2 quarts pasteurized whole cow's milk

1/4 teaspoon MA 4001 powdered mesophilic starter culture

1/8 teaspoon calcium chloride diluted in 1/4 cup cool nonchlorinated water

1/4 teaspoon liquid rennet diluted in 1/4 cup cool nonchlorinated water

2 teaspoons fine sea salt

1 1/2 teaspoons dried thyme

1 1/2 teaspoons dried oregano

1 1/2 teaspoons dried savory

1 1/2 teaspoons herbes de Provence

3 tablespoons dried rosemary

1/4 teaspoon paprika

1/4 teaspoon whole coriander seeds

1/4 teaspoon whole mixed peppercorns

1/4 teaspoon whole juniper berries

2 teaspoons olive oil

1. In a nonreactive 6-quart stockpot, heat the milks over low heat to 86°F; this should take about 15 minutes. Turn off the heat.

2. Sprinkle the starter over the milk and let it rehydrate for 5 minutes. Mix well using a whisk in an up-and-down motion. Add the calcium chloride and gently whisk in, and then add the rennet in the same way. Cover and maintain 72°F, allowing the milk to ripen for 8 hours, or until the curds form one large mass the consistency of thick yogurt and clear whey is floating around the sides of the pot. Check the curds for a clean break. If the cut edge is clean, the curds are ready.

3. Place a strainer over a bowl or bucket large enough to capture the whey. Line it with damp butter muslin. Gently cut 1/2-inch-thick slices of the curds using a ladle or skimmer and gently ladle the slices into the strainer. Gently toss the curds with 1 teaspoon of the salt, then tie the muslin into a draining sack and hang to let drain at room temperature for 6 to 10 hours, until the whey stops dripping. The longer the curds drain, the drier the finished cheese will be. Alternatively, you can drain the curds by hanging for 45 minutes, then moving the sack to a 4-inch Camembert mold without a bottom, placed on a draining rack. Drain and ripen in the mold for 6 to 10 hours, flipping the curds once during the draining process and sprinkling the remaining 1 teaspoon salt over the surface of the cheese.

4. If not using the mold for the final shape, transfer the sack to a clean work surface and roll the curds into a ball, then flatten slightly with your hands. Open the sack and sprinkle the remaining 1 teaspoon salt over the cheese and lightly rub it into the surface. Set the cheese on a draining rack at room temperature for 8 hours to allow the salt to be absorbed into the cheese and excess moisture to be released. Continue to air-dry for a total of 24 hours, or until the surface is dry.

5. Combine the herbs and spices in a small bowl. Pat the cheese dry of any moisture, then rub thoroughly with the olive oil. Spread a layer of the herb mixture on a sheet of parchment or waxed paper and roll the cheese in the mixture to coat, then gently press the herbs so they stick to the surface of the cheese. Reserve the unused herbs.

6. Cover the cheese with plastic wrap and place in a ripening box at 50°F to 55°F and 80 to 85 percent humidity for 3 days. Remove the plastic wrap, coat with more herbs if needed, and place in a ripening box at 50°F to 55°F for 27 more days. The cheese will be ready to eat at this point or can be aged for another month.

Cocoa-Rubbed Dry Jack Cheese

MAKES 2 pounds
MILK Pasteurized whole cow's milk
START TO FINISH 2 to 10 or more months: $2^1/_2$ hours to make the cheese; 6 to 8 hours to press; 32 hours to dry; 8 hours to brine; 2 to 10 months or longer to age

This is my version of Vella's legendary Dry Jack, which I've kept as a staple in my kitchen for many years. This cheese begins its life as plain Jack cheese, then is aged to a certain degree of firmness, at which point it is rubbed with a cocoa-coffee-pepper mixture and allowed to age further. The oil-based coating protects the cheese from drying out too quickly and also imparts a signature flavor to the aged cheese, whether seven months old and sliceable or more aged and gratable. To assist in the release of moisture and the distribution of salt into the cheese, it is first rubbed with salt and air-dried a bit, then brined, dried again, and aged.

2 gallons pasteurized whole cow's milk
$^1/_2$ teaspoon MA 4001 powdered mesophilic starter culture
$^1/_2$ teaspoon calcium chloride diluted in $^1/_4$ cup cool nonchlorinated water
$^1/_2$ teaspoon liquid rennet diluted in $^1/_4$ cup cool nonchlorinated water
Kosher salt (preferably Diamond Crystal brand) or cheese salt

2 tablespoons cocoa powder
2 teaspoons instant espresso
$1^1/_2$ teaspoons finely ground black pepper
$4^1/_2$ teaspoons olive oil

1. In a nonreactive 10-quart stockpot, heat the milk over low heat to 86°F; this should take about 15 minutes. Turn off the heat.

2. Sprinkle the starter over the milk and let it rehydrate for 5 minutes. Mix well using a whisk in an up-and-down motion. Cover and maintain 86°F, allowing the milk to ripen for 1 hour. Add the calcium chloride and gently whisk in for 1 minute. Add the rennet and gently whisk in for 1 minute. Cover and let sit, maintaining 86°F for 30 to 45 minutes, or until the curds give a clean break.

3. Still maintaining 86°F, cut the curds into $^3/_4$-inch pieces and let sit for 5 minutes. Over low heat, slowly bring the curds to 102°F over 40 minutes, stirring continuously to keep the curds from matting together. The curds will release whey, firm up slightly, and shrink to the size of dried beans. Maintain 102°F and let the curds rest undisturbed for 30 minutes; they will sink to the bottom.

(continued)

4. Ladle out enough whey to expose the curds. Still holding the temperature, stir continuously for 15 to 20 minutes, or until the curds are matted and cling together when pressed in your hand.

5. Place a strainer over a bowl or bucket large enough to capture the whey. Line it with damp butter muslin and ladle the curds into it Let drain for 5 minutes, then sprinkle in 1 table-spoon of salt and gently and thoroughly mix with your hands.

6. Draw the ends of the cloth together and twist to form a ball to help squeeze out the excess moisture. Roll the ball on a flat surface to release more whey. Tie off the top of the cloth sack, press it with your hands to flatten slightly, and place it on a cutting board sitting on top of a draining rack. Place a second cutting board on top of the flattened sack and set an 8-pound weight directly over the cheese. Press at 75°F to 85°F for 6 hours for moist Jack or 8 hours for drier Jack.

7. Remove the cheese from the sack and pat dry. Rub with 1 tablespoon of salt and place on a draining rack to air-dry for 8 hours.

8. Make 3 quarts of saturated brine (see page 24) and chill to 50°F to 55°F. Place the cheese in the brine and soak at 50°F to 55°F for 8 hours, flipping it over once during that time. Remove from the brine, pat dry, and air-dry on a rack at room tempera-ture for 24 hours, or until the surface is dry to the touch. Flip once during this drying period.

9. Place the cheese on a cheese mat in a ripening box at 50°F to 55°F and 85 percent humidity for 1 week, flipping the cheese daily for even ripening.

10. Combine the cocoa, espresso, and pepper in a small bowl. Add the olive oil and stir to combine. Rub one-fourth of the cocoa mixture all over the cheese. Place the cheese on a rack so air circulates all around it, then continue to ripen at 50°F to 55°F overnight. Repeat the rubbing and air-drying process every day for 3 more days, then ripen the cheese at 60°F and 75 percent humidity for 2 months, flipping twice a week. Wrap in cheese paper and refrigerate until ready to eat—up to 10 months or, for a very rich, deep flavor, up to 2 years, if you can wait that long! Once opened, the cheese will dry out and harden as time goes on, creating a wonderful grating cheese.

Lavender Mist Chèvre

MAKES Six 4-ounce disks
MILK Pasteurized goat's milk
START TO FINISH 4 to 11 days: $1/2$ hour to make the cheese; 12 hours to ripen; 6 to 12 hours to drain; 4 hours to dry salt; 3 to 10 days to cure

This coated chèvre was inspired by a delightful cheese from Cypress Grove Chevre called Purple Haze, which is dusted with lavender buds and fennel pollen powder and eaten while young. You can adjust the herb ratio to your liking or use this method to create your own version of an herb-coated chèvre. My favorite source for these and other herbs and spices is Whole Spice (see Resources).

1 gallon pasteurized goat's milk

$1/4$ teaspoon MA 4001 powdered mesophilic starter culture

$1/8$ teaspoon calcium chloride diluted in $1/4$ cup cool nonchlorinated water

$1/8$ teaspoon liquid rennet diluted in $1/4$ cup cool nonchlorinated water

1 teaspoon fine sea salt

$1/2$ teaspoon fennel pollen powder

$1/4$ teaspoon ground lavender or lavender buds

1. In a nonreactive 6-quart stockpot, heat the milk over low heat to 86°F; this should take about 15 minutes. Turn off the heat.

2. Sprinkle the starter over the milk and let it rehydrate for 5 minutes. Mix well using a whisk in an up-and-down motion. Add the calcium chloride and gently whisk in, and then whisk in the rennet in the same way. Cover and maintain 72°F, allowing the milk to ripen for 12 hours, or until the curds have formed one large mass the consistency of thick yogurt and clear whey is floating around the sides of the pot.

3. Place a strainer over a bowl or bucket large enough to capture the whey. Line it with damp butter muslin and gently ladle the curds into the strainer. Add $1/2$ teaspoon of the salt and gently toss to combine. Tie the tails of the cloth to make a draining sack and hang to let drain at room temperature for 6 to 12 hours.

4. Remove the cheese from the cloth and shape it into six 4-ounce round disks. Sprinkle the remaining $1/2$ teaspoon salt over the surface of each cheese and lightly rub it into the surface. Set the cheeses on a drying rack at room temperature for 4 hours to allow them to absorb the salt and release excess moisture.

5. Combine the fennel pollen and lavender in a small bowl. Pat the cheeses dry, then place them on a sheet of parchment or waxed paper and dust all sides with the herb mixture. Place the cheeses on a rack and let sit at room temperature for 1 hour, then wrap each cheese in plastic wrap and refrigerate for at least 3 days to allow the flavors of the rub to infuse the cheese and up to 10 days.

Honey-Rubbed Montasio

MAKES 2 pounds
MILKS Pasteurized reduced fat (2 percent) cow's milk, pasteurized goat's milk
START TO FINISH 2¹/₂ months to 1 year: 4 hours to make the cheese; 8 to 12 hours to press; 12 hours to brine; 24 hours to dry; 2¹/₂ months to 1 year to age

Montasio is a rustic Alpine-style cheese from the Friuli–Venezia Giulia region of Italy. It is often made with a blend of milks, though I've tasted wonderful versions made only with goat's milk. Montasio can have a natural rind or a coating of blended herbs and spices. For this version I recommend using Thermo C, a culture that is used in many Alpine cheeses; the blend of this culture contains some *Lactobacillus helveticus* bacteria, resulting in a nutty flavor profile. My version follows the old-world practice of draining the curds in a sack and then rolling and pressing the wrapped curds overnight before brining. This recipe is also a nod to the Mozzarella Company's award-winning ancho-rubbed Montasio Festivo, and a chipotle rub is given as an option to the honey rub (see Variation). Note: If you're making an all-goat's milk version of this cheese, you'll need to add 3 drops more calcium chloride and 3 drops more rennet to help stabilize the milk and firm up the curds. If using all cow's milk, use ¹/₄ teaspoon calcium chloride and ¹/₄ teaspoon rennet.

1 gallon pasteurized reduced fat (2 percent) cow's milk
1 gallon pasteurized goat's milk
¹/₂ teaspoon Thermo C powdered thermophilic starter culture
¹/₂ teaspoon calcium chloride diluted in ¹/₄ cup cool nonchlorinated water
¹/₂ teaspoon liquid rennet diluted in ¹/₄ cup cool nonchlorinated water
3 teaspoons flake sea salt (or Himalayan sea salt)
Kosher salt (preferably Diamond Crystal brand) or cheese salt for brining
3 tablespoons honey

Honey-Rubbed Montasio at 2 months

1. In a nonreactive 10-quart pot, heat the milks over low heat to 90°F; this should take about 20 minutes. Turn off the heat.

2. Sprinkle the starter over the milk and let it rehydrate for 5 minutes. Mix well using a whisk in an up-and-down motion. Cover and maintain 90°F, allowing the milk to ripen for 45 minutes. Add the calcium chloride and gently whisk in for 1 minute. Add the rennet and gently whisk in for 1 minute. Cover and let sit, maintaining 90°F for 30 to 45 minutes, or until the curds give a clean break.

3. Cut the curds into ¹/₂-inch pieces and let sit undisturbed for 5 minutes. Over low heat, slowly bring the curds to 104°F over 40 minutes, stirring two or three times. Remove from the heat and stir for 15 minutes to release whey and shrink the curds to the size of peanuts. Over low heat, slowly bring the temperature to 112°F over 5 to 7 minutes, stirring the curds to firm them up. Once 112°F is reached, remove from the heat, maintain the temperature, and let the curds rest for 20 minutes; they will sink to the bottom.

4. Ladle off enough whey to expose the curds. Place a strainer over a bowl or bucket large enough to capture the whey. Line it with damp butter muslin and gently ladle the curds into it. Let

drain for 10 minutes, then sprinkle 1¹/₂ teaspoons of the sea salt over the curds and gently but thoroughly toss with your hands. Let drain for 5 more minutes.

5. Draw the ends of the muslin together to form a ball and twist to help squeeze out the excess moisture. Place the sack on a sanitized cutting board, roll it into a ball, and tie off the top to secure the curds in a round shape. Place both wrapped curds and cutting board on a draining rack and press down on the curds with your hands to flatten slightly. Smooth out the knot and ties as best you can to create a stable surface for a second cutting board to rest on. Place the second cutting board on top of the cheese, press down to even out the bundle, then cover the whole assembly completely with a kitchen towel. Place an 8-pound weight over the cheese and press for 8 hours or over-night at 75°F to 85°F.

6. Make 2 quarts of near-saturated brine (see page 24) and chill to 50°F to 55°F. Remove the cheese from the sack and place it in the brine to soak at 50°F to 55°F for 12 hours, flipping it once to brine evenly. Remove the cheese from the brine and pat dry, then place it on a cheese mat or rack to air-dry at room temperature for 24 hours, or until the surface is dry to the touch. Flip once during this time.

7. Place in a ripening box at 50°F to 55°F and 85 percent humidity and age for 1 week, flipping daily. Then brush with a simple brine solution (see page 24), cooled to 50°F to 55°F, twice a week for 2 weeks.

8. After 2 weeks, rub the cheese with 1¹/₂ tablespoons of the honey to coat, then return it to the ripening box at 50°F to 55°F and 80 percent humidity for 1 week, flipping daily. The honey will form a film, preventing the cheese from drying out. After 1 more week, rub with the remaining 1¹/₂ tablespoons of honey and then with the remaining 1¹/₂ teaspoons of salt. Return the cheese to the ripening box for 2 more weeks, flipping daily, then vacuum-seal or wrap tightly in plastic wrap to protect the coating, and store refrigerated for 1 month up to 1 year.

VARIATION
To make chipotle-rubbed Montasio, combine 1 tablespoon of chipotle powder, ¹/₂ teaspoon of ground cumin, ¹/₄ teaspoon of ground Mexican oregano, ¹/₂ teaspoon of dark brown sugar, ¹/₈ teaspoon of ground white pepper, and 1 teaspoon of fine sea salt in a bowl. Add 1 tablespoon of canola or vegetable oil and mix to form a paste. After brushing with the brine solution for 2 weeks, omit the honey rub. Instead, coat the cheese with the chipotle rub and return to the ripening box for at least 1 month, or longer for a more pronounced flavor. Then vacuum-seal or wrap in plastic to protect the coating, and store refrigerated for up to 1 month.

Rustico Foglie di Noce

Inspired by the robust Pecorino Foglie di Noce from the Emilia-Romagna region of Italy, this hard, round, mixed-milk cheese is wrapped in walnut leaves (*foglie di noce*) and aged for 3 months. You'll need 4 to 6 large dried walnut leaves, stemmed, blanched, and patted dry.

To best emulate the robust flavors that come with the use of sheep's milk, a small amount of cream and a bit of lipase powder are added to the goat's and cow's milks. Make the cheese using the Montasio recipe (page 130), combining 1 cup of heavy cream with the milks. After adding the culture and before adding the calcium chloride and rennet, add a pinch of lipase powder. Follow the directions through the first stage of ripening, prior to rubbing with honey (through step 7). Rub the cheese with olive oil, then sprinkle with kosher salt and rub it into the surface. Though it's not traditional, you can rub the cheese with smoked olive oil alternating with unflavored olive oil for a smoky flavor. The best smoked olive oil comes from the Smoked Olive, www.thesmokedolive.com.

Brush the walnut leaves on both sides with olive oil, then wrap enough leaves around the cheese to cover it fully. Place the cheese in a ripening box at 50°F to 55°F and 75 percent humidity with good air circulation and age for 3 months, flipping daily for the first week, then twice a week thereafter. Rub the cheese daily with olive oil. Consume the cheese once it has aged 3 months, or vacuum-seal or wrap in plastic and store refrigerated for another month. When you're ready to serve these cheeses, allow diners to peel away the leaf wrapping on their portion of cheese.

CHAPTER 4

More Advanced Cheese Making

**Bloomy-Rind and Surface-Ripened Cheeses, Washed-Rind
and Smeared-Rind Cheeses, and Blue Cheeses**

Young Époisses at 2¹/₂ weeks (page 166)

The final cheese making chapter of this book covers some of my favorite styles and families of cheeses. It builds on all that has been presented in the previous chapters. Now that you've become comfortable with the basics of cheese making and have successfully ventured into the world of cultured cheeses in chapter 2, and then pressed, firm, aged cheeses in chapter 3, you are equipped to delve into a few popular types of cheeses that are a bit more

nuanced and finicky: bloomy-rind, surface-ripened, and mold-ripened styles. You'll be working with new molds, bacteria, and secondary cultures that not only flavor the cheese but also work together symbiotically to create colorful, identifiable surfaces, interiors, and aromas. You will learn surface washing techniques, styles of blue mold development, and more cheese ripening methods. Some of the cheeses are easier to make than others. The complex bloom-covered, alcohol-washed, in-your-face stinkers and blue veiners will require more of your attention over the course of their development, with your management affecting the end results. It is with these families of cheeses that the skills of successful cheese ripening are developed. You *will* be tested, but it is worth it. Once you've played in this realm, you will have a clearer understanding of cheese as a living, breathing entity. From this point you can try replicating your favorite cheeses or creating a new one of your own.

Bloomy-Rind and Surface-Ripened Cheeses

Bloomy-rind or surface-ripened (mold- and bacteria-ripened) cheeses include some of the most renowned French cheeses, such as Brie, Camembert, Saint-Marcellin, and Valençay. They are recognizable by their fuzzy white or crinkled "brainy" surface, their creamy or buttery paste under the rind, and a mild to mushroom flavor in the cow's milk cheeses and tangy flavor in the goat's milk cheeses.

These bloomies begin with cow's, goat's, or sheep's milk inoculated with mesophilic starter cultures and *Penicillium candidum* mold. The recognizable velvety, white, bloomy edible rind is created by *P. candidum*, which is sometimes also sprayed on the surface of the cheese to promote the growth. *P. candidum* is used alone or in combination with the mold *Geotrichum candidum*, which aids in rind and flavor development and is responsible for those cheeses with wrinkly, "brainy" surfaces. Bloomy-rind and surface-ripened cheeses ripen from the outside in and become softer and creamier as they age.

Ripened at a relatively high humidity (90 to 95 percent), these cheeses develop the fuzzy white mold on their surface within ten to twelve days. Depending upon the style of the specific cheese, they generally need only ten days to five weeks to develop their flavor. Longer ripening can create a more pungent flavor.

CRÈME FRAÎCHE BRIE

MAKES One 10- to 12-ounce wheel or two 5- to 6-ounce wheels
MILK Pasteurized whole cow's milk
START TO FINISH 4 to 7 weeks: 3 hours to make the cheese; 6 hours to drain; 4 to 7 weeks to ripen

Originally from the Île-de-France region near Paris, this white bloomy-rind cheese is known worldwide and is a very accessible French cheese for Americans. Made in larger wheels than Camembert, Brie is made from cow's milk, which can be whole or skimmed. There are many fantastic artisanal Brie-style cheeses being made in France as well as in America. My version is a rich cousin made with whole milk and homemade cultured crème fraîche. It was inspired by the award-winning triple-cream Brie from Marin French Cheese Company, among others.

....

Penicillium candidum mold powder

Kosher salt (preferably Diamond Crystal brand) or fine flake sea salt

1 gallon pasteurized whole cow's milk

1/4 teaspoon Meso II powdered mesophilic starter culture

Pinch of *Geotrichum candidum* 15 mold powder

1/4 teaspoon calcium chloride diluted in 1/4 cup cool nonchlorinated water

1/2 teaspoon liquid rennet diluted in 1/4 cup cool nonchlorinated water

1 1/2 cups cultured crème fraîche, homemade (page 44) or store-bought, at room temperature

1. Twelve hours before starting, combine a pinch of *Penicillium candidum*, 1/4 teaspoon salt, and 2 cups of cool nonchlorinated water in an atomizer or spray bottle. Store at 50°F to 55°F.

2. In a nonreactive 6-quart stockpot, slowly heat the milk to 86°F over low heat; this should take about 15 minutes. Turn off the heat.

3. Sprinkle the starter, ⅛ teaspoon of *P. candidum* mold powder, and the *Geotrichum candidum* mold powder over the milk and let rehydrate for 5 minutes. Mix well using a whisk in an up-and-down motion for 20 strokes. Cover and maintain 86°F, letting the milk ripen for 30 minutes. Add the calcium chloride and gently whisk in, then add the rennet in the same way. Cover and let sit, maintaining 86°F for 1½ hours, or until the curds give a clean break.

4. Cut the curds into ½-inch pieces and let sit for 5 minutes to firm up the curds. Using a rubber spatula, gently stir for 5 minutes around the edges of the pot to move the curds around. Let the curds rest for 5 minutes; they will sink to the bottom.

5. Ladle off enough whey to expose the curds. Gently ladle the curds into a colander lined with damp butter muslin and let drain for 10 minutes, or until the whey stops dripping.

6. Place the crème fraîche in a bowl and whisk to soften. Using a rubber spatula, gently fold the crème fraîche into the curds to combine. Let drain for 10 minutes, until any residual liquid has drained out.

7. Set a draining rack over a tray, put a cutting board on the rack and a cheese mat on the board, and, finally, place one 8-inch Brie mold or two 4-inch Camembert molds on the mat. Ladle the curds into the mold or molds and let drain for 2 hours. The curds will reduce to about two-thirds the height of the mold. Place a second mat and board over the top of the mold. With one hand holding the board firmly against the mat and mold, lift and gently flip over the bottom board and mat with the mold and place back onto the draining rack; the second board and mat will now be on the bottom and the original mat and board will be on top.

8. Let drain for 2 hours, until the curds are reduced in size by about one-third, then flip again in the same manner and let drain overnight at room temperature. The curds will be about 1½ inches high at this point.

9. Salt the top of the cheese, flip it over, salt the second side, and let drain for 2 more hours. The quantity of salt is hard to pinpoint, but if you imagine salting a steak or tomato well, that is about right. The curds will be about 1 inch high at this point. Remove the mold and spray the cheese lightly (while it is on the draining rack) with the *P. candidum* solution.

10. Place the cheese on a clean cheese mat in a ripening box. Cover loosely with the lid and ripen at 50°F to 55°F and 90 percent humidity. High humidity is essential for making this cheese. Flip the cheese daily, removing any whey that may have accumulated in the ripening box. Keep the box loosely covered to maintain the humidity level.

11. After 2 days, you can lightly spray the cheeses with mold solution again to help ensure proper mold growth, if desired. After about 5 days, the first signs of white fuzzy mold will appear. Remove any undesirable mold with a piece of cheesecloth dipped in a vinegar-salt solution. After 10 to 14 days, the cheeses will be fully coated in white mold. At this point, clean the ripening box, wrap the cheeses in cheese paper, and return them to the ripening box. The cheese will begin to soften within 1 week or so. After a total of 4 weeks from the start of ripening (or 3 weeks if you use Camembert molds), move the wrapped cheeses to the refrigerator and store until they have reached the desired ripeness: firm and mild, or runny and strong. The aging time to desired ripeness will vary depending on the diameter and thickness of the cheese: if a Brie mold was used, count on 4 to 7 weeks total; if 2 Camembert molds, count on 3 to 6 weeks total.

AMERICAN-STYLE BRIE

MAKES 2 pounds
MILKS Pasteurized whole cow's milk, pasteurized heavy cream
START TO FINISH 5 to 6 weeks: 2½ to 3 hours to make the cheese; 13 hours to drain; 5 to 6 weeks to age

American-style Brie differs from its French ancestors in leading a more stable life. This recipe was developed by Nancy Vineyard at the Beverage People for those who like a firmer, less runny Brie. This Brie can sit in your fridge three to four weeks longer than its French cousin before turning into a runny and ever-stronger-tasting cheese. Although making Brie may seem challenging initially, the cooking is straightforward and, with proper attention to ripening the white mold during its first week, the cheese pretty much takes care of itself during maturation. That phase takes place in a regular home refrigerator with the cheese wrapped in cheese paper.

2 gallons pasteurized whole cow's milk

1/2 cup pasteurized heavy cream

Pinch of MA 4001 powdered mesophilic starter culture

1/8 teaspoon Thermo B powdered thermophilic starter culture

1/8 teaspoon *Penicillium candidum* mold powder

1/8 teaspoon *Geotrichum candidum* 15 mold powder

1/4 teaspoon calcium chloride diluted in 1/4 cup cool nonchlorinated water

1/4 teaspoon liquid rennet diluted in 1/4 cup cool nonchlorinated water

Kosher salt (preferably Diamond Crystal brand) or cheese salt

1. Heat the milk and cream in a 10-quart stockpot set in a 102°F water bath over low heat. Bring the milk to 90°F over 10 minutes.

2. Leave the heat on and sprinkle the starter cultures and mold powders over the milk and let rehydrate for 5 minutes. Mix well using a whisk in an up-and-down motion for 20 strokes. Allow the temperature of the milk to rise to 96°F to 98°F. Turn off the heat, cover, and let the milk rest in the water bath for 1½ hours. Add the calcium chloride and gently whisk in, then add the rennet in the same way. Let rest, covered, for 30 minutes, or until the curds give a clean break.

3. Cut the curds into ¾-inch pieces and let sit for 5 minutes. Stir the curds for 10 to 15 minutes, then let them settle for 5 minutes. Ladle off enough whey to expose the curds.

4. Set a draining rack over a tray, put an 8-inch Brie mold (with a bottom) on it, and put the rack in a ripening box. Gently ladle the curds into the mold and let the curds drain for 1 hour, periodically lifting the mold and pouring the whey out of the tray.

5. After 1 hour, gently flip the cheese out of the mold into your hand, turn it over, and return it to the mold. This evens out the drainage and smoothes the surface on both sides. Flip the cheese every hour as you continue to drain and discard whey. Gradually there will only be a few ounces of whey to drain. When there is no more whey, after four or five flips, put a foil cover or lid on the ripening box, vented in two places, and keep the box at room temperature for 8 hours.

6. Drain off the last of the whey and unmold the cheese onto a mat. Salt the top of the cheese, flip it over, and salt the second side. The quantity of salt is hard to pinpoint, but if you imagine salting a steak or tomato well, that is about right. Salting the edges is optional.

7. The blooming phase of ripening begins now and is best carried out at 52°F to 56°F. Put the lid of the ripening box

on askew or cover the middle two-thirds of the pan with aluminum foil, leaving it open at both ends for air circulation. In 3 to 4 days the cheese will bloom, with white mold forming over the surface. Flip the wheel over to bloom the other side. The second bloom will be complete in only 1 or 2 more days.

8. Using cheese paper, wrap the wheel, taping closed any awkward edges. Move the wheel to a clean tray and ripening box with a closed lid. Place 2 wadded damp paper towels at opposite corners of the box to keep the humidity at about

85 percent. Move this box to your refrigerator (set at about 38°F). Moisten the towels as needed and turn the wheel over once or twice during the ripening time.

9. The wheel should be ready to serve after 5 to 6 weeks. You can check by cutting out a small ¼-inch wedge. The cheese should feel soft and begin to ooze out of the rind, and it should taste and smell mild (old Brie will taste very tangy and smell of ammonia). Press a small piece of waxed paper into the cut section before rewrapping. The cheese will keep for 6 to 8 weeks in the refrigerator.

BUCHERON

MAKES Two 8-ounce logs
MILK Pasteurized goat's milk
START TO FINISH 4 to 5 weeks: 30 minutes to make the cheese; 18 hours to ripen;
24 hours to drain; 4 to 5 weeks to age

This log-shaped mold-ripened goat cheese from France's Loire Valley is very popular in America. Mellowed in the ripening, it is soft and creamy just under the rind, while the center remains chalky. The result is a perfect interplay of textures. This version is partially inspired by the French style but also by some amazing versions made by American artisan cheese makers, like Zingerman's Lincoln Log and Redwood Hill's Bucheret. Note that you will need four molds for this recipe: two cylindrical Saint-Maure or bûche molds and two straight-sided molds, such as Camembert molds.

Penicillium candidum mold powder
1¾ teaspoons fine sea salt
1 gallon pasteurized goat's milk
¼ teaspoon Aroma B powdered mesophilic starter culture
Pinch of *Geotrichum candidum* 15 mold powder
¼ teaspoon calcium chloride diluted in ¼ cup cool nonchlorinated water
¼ teaspoon liquid rennet diluted in ¼ cup cool nonchlorinated water

1. Twelve hours before starting, combine a pinch of *P. candidum*, ¼ teaspoon of the salt, and 2 cups of cool nonchlorinated water in an atomizer or spray bottle. Store at 50°F to 55°F.

2. In a nonreactive 6-quart stockpot, heat the milk over low heat to 72°F; this should take about 10 minutes. Turn off the heat.

(continued)

3. Sprinkle the starter, ⅛ teaspoon of *P. candidum* mold powder, and the *Geotrichum candidum* mold powder over the milk and let rehydrate for 5 minutes. Mix well using a whisk in an up-and-down motion for 20 strokes. Add the calcium chloride and gently whisk in for 1 minute, then add the rennet in the same way. Cover and let sit, maintaining 72°F, for 18 hours, or until the curds are a firm mass and whey is floating on top.

4. Place a draining rack over a tray. Steady 2 cylindrical Saint-Maure or bûche molds inside 2 round, straight-sided molds and place on the rack. Gently cut ½-inch-thick slices of curds using a ladle or skimmer and gently ladle the slices into the cylindrical molds to fill. Let drain until more curds can be added to the molds. Do not be tempted to add another mold; the curds will compress as the whey drains out, making room for all of the curds.

5. When all the curds have been ladled into the molds, cover them with a clean kitchen towel and let the cheeses drain for 24 hours at room temperature. Remove any collected whey a few times while draining, wiping out the tray with a paper towel each time. After 6 hours, or when the cheeses are firm enough to handle, gently invert the molds onto your palm to flip the cheeses in their molds. Do this a few more times during the 24 hours to aid in uniform formation of the cheeses and development of the bacteria. At the end of 24 hours, the curds will have reduced to about half the height of the molds.

6. Once the cheeses have stopped draining and the curds have compressed to below the halfway point of the mold, place a mat in a ripening box. Remove the cheeses from the molds and sprinkle ¾ teaspoon of the salt over the entire surface of each cheese.

7. Set the cheeses at least 1 inch apart on the mat in the ripening box and allow 10 minutes for the salt to dissolve, then mist lightly with the *P. candidum* solution. Wipe any moisture from the walls of the box. Cover the box loosely with the lid and let it stand at room temperature for 24 hours.

8. Drain any whey and wipe out any moisture from the box, then ripen the cheese at 50°F to 55°F and 90 percent humidity for 2 weeks. For the first few days, adjust the lid to be slightly open for a portion of each day to maintain the desired humidity level. Too much humidity will create an undesirably wet surface. The surface of the cheese should appear moist but not wet. Each day, wipe out any moisture that may have accumulated in the ripening box. Throughout the ripening period, turn the cheeses one-quarter turn daily to maintain their log shape. After 2 days, very lightly mist with the mold solution. After about 5 days, the first signs of white fuzzy mold will appear. After 10 to 14 days, the cheeses will be fully coated in white mold. Remove any undesirable mold using a piece of cheesecloth dipped in a vinegar-salt solution.

9. Clean and dry the ripening box, wrap the cheeses in cheese paper, and return them to the ripening box. The cheeses will begin to soften within 1 week or so. After a total of 4 weeks from the start of ripening, wrap in plastic wrap and store in the refrigerator. It is best to consume this cheese when it has reached the desired ripeness, between 4 weeks and 5 weeks.

CAMEMBERT

MAKES 1 pound
MILK Pasteurized whole cow's milk
START TO FINISH 6 to 7 weeks: 5 hours to make the cheese; 5 hours to drain; 6 to 7 weeks to age

This recipe is contributed by Aaron Estes, a dedicated cheese head who works at his real job during the day, is a passionate cheesemonger at Lucy's Whey in New York City on weekends, and writes and publishes the fun and informative *Cave-Aged Blog* (see Resources). In between, he makes cheese in his apartment for personal pleasure. The result of Aaron's experimentation, this is an excellent and unconventional recipe for a creamy and wonderfully fragrant Camembert that tastes of fresh milk with a hint of lemon.

3 quarts pasteurized whole cow's milk
¼ teaspoon MM 100 powdered mesophilic starter culture
⅛ teaspoon *Penicillium candidum* mold powder
¼ teaspoon calcium chloride diluted in ¼ cup cool nonchlorinated water
¼ teaspoon liquid rennet diluted in ¼ cup cool nonchlorinated water
5 tablespoons kosher salt (preferably Diamond Crystal brand) or cheese salt

1. In a nonreactive 6-quart stockpot, heat the milk over low heat to 90°F; this should take about 20 minutes. Turn off the heat.

2. Sprinkle the starter and mold powder over the milk and let rehydrate for 5 minutes. Mix well using a whisk in an up-and-down motion. Cover and maintain 90°F, letting the milk ripen for 1½ hours. Add the calcium chloride and gently whisk in, then add the rennet in the same way. Cover and let sit, maintaining 90°F, until the curds give a clean break.

3. Cut the curds into ¼- to ½-inch pieces and let sit for 5 minutes. Gently stir with a rubber spatula to prevent the curd from matting together, then ladle off one-third of the whey. Add the salt and gently stir to incorporate.

4. Ladle the curds into an 8-inch Brie mold set on a draining rack over a tray. Let drain at room temperature until the cheese is firm enough to flip, about 2 hours. Flip the cheese every hour for 5 hours, or until it stops draining.

5. Take the cheese out of the mold and put it in a ripening box. Place a wadded damp paper towel in a corner of the box with the cheese to keep the humidity at about 85 percent. Place the box on the bottom shelf of your refrigerator. Flip the cheese every day. After 5 to 10 days the cheese should have around 75 percent mold coverage. When the cheese is fully covered in white mold, remove it from the box, wrap it in foil or cheese paper, and put it back in the refrigerator for another 5 weeks. It is ready when the center begins to feel soft. Consume within 2 weeks.

VARIATION

Calvados is an apple brandy from the same region of France as Camembert, and macerating the cheese in Calvados yields impressive results. The cheese should be made ahead, but the soaking and finishing should be timed to coincide with cheese service. Make Camembert as above, using 3 Saint-Marcellin molds instead of the single Brie mold. Ripen for 3 weeks, then place the cheeses in a nonreactive container with a lid and pour in 2 cups of Calvados or other apple brandy (or hard apple cider). Soak for 24 hours in a cool but not refrigerated place, flipping once at 12 hours. Spread 1 cup of toasted bread crumbs (or a mixture of bread crumbs and ground walnuts) out on a sheet of parchment paper. Lift the cheeses from the brandy, let them drip dry, and roll them in the crumbs to coat. Decorate each wheel with a walnut half and serve.

COULOMMIERS

MAKES Four 5-ounce cheeses
MILK Pasteurized whole cow's milk
ALTERNATIVE MILK Pasteurized goat's milk
START TO FINISH 8 days to 2 weeks or more: about 2 hours to make the cheese; 15 hours to drain;
1 to 2 weeks or longer to age

Also called Brie de Coulommiers, this lovely, thin-rind, petite relative of other Bries and Camembert is ripened for a short period of time. It is ready to eat when only a few weeks old, and as a result of its youth, it is milder than other Brie cheeses.

Penicillium candidum mold powder

3½ teaspoons kosher or fine flake sea salt

2 gallons pasteurized whole cow's milk

¼ teaspoon MA 4001 powdered mesophilic starter culture

¼ teaspoon calcium chloride diluted in ¼ cup cool nonchlorinated water

¼ teaspoon liquid rennet diluted in ¼ cup cool nonchlorinated water

1. Twelve hours before starting, combine a pinch of of *P. candidum*, ½ teaspoon of salt, and 1 quart of nonchlorinated water in an atomizer or spray bottle. Store at 50°F to 55°F.

2. In a nonreactive 10-quart stockpot, heat the milk over low heat to 90°F; this should take about 20 minutes. Turn off the heat.

3. Sprinkle the starter and ⅛ teaspoon of *P. candidum* mold powder over the milk and let rehydrate for 5 minutes. Mix well using a whisk in an up-and-down motion. Add the calcium chloride and gently whisk in, then add the rennet in the same way. Cover and let sit, maintaining 90°F for 1½ hours, or until the curds give a clean break.

4. Cut the curds into ½-inch thick slices and let sit for 5 minutes to firm up the curds. Using a rubber spatula, gently stir around the edges of the pot for 5 minutes to shrink the curds slightly and keep them from matting.

5. Set a draining rack over a tray, put a cutting board on the rack and a cheese mat on the board, and, finally, place four 4-inch Camembert molds on the mat. Using a skimmer, gently ladle the slices of curds into the molds. Fill the molds to the top, then continue to add slices as the curds drain. When all the curds have been transferred to the molds, cover the molds with a clean kitchen towel and let drain at room temperature for 5 to 6 hours, or until the curds have reduced to almost half the height of the molds. Discard the whey periodically. Place a second mat and cutting board over the top of the molds. With one hand holding the top board firmly against the mat and molds, lift and gently flip over the bottom board and mat with the molds and place back onto the draining rack; the second board and mat will now be on the bottom and the original mat and board will be on top.

6. Let drain for 6 hours, until the curds are about 1½ to 2 inches high, then flip again and let drain for another 3 hours. Stop flipping once the cheeses stop draining; they should be well drained and firm to the touch.

7. Remove the molds and sprinkle about 1½ teaspoons salt over the tops and sides of the cheeses. Leave for 10 minutes, allowing the salt to dissolve. Place the cheeses salt side down on a clean cheese mat in a ripening box and salt the other sides, again using about 1½ teaspoons. Cover the box with the lid slightly open for a little air circulation and ripen the cheeses at 50°F to 55°F and 90 percent humidity. High humidity is essential for making this cheese. Flip the cheeses

daily, removing any whey and any moisture that may have accumulated in the ripening box, as moisture will inhibit the proper white mold development. Once moisture no longer accumulates in the box, cover the box tightly.

8. After 2 days, spray lightly with the mold solution. After about 5 days, the first signs of white fuzzy mold will appear. After 10 to 14 days, the cheeses will be fully coated in white mold. Remove any undesirable mold using a piece of cheese-cloth dipped in a vinegar-salt solution. Clean the ripening box, wrap the cheeses in cheese paper, and return them to the ripening box. The cheese will begin to soften within 1 week or so. It is ready to eat when the center feels soft to the touch; this can be 1 to 2 weeks or slightly longer. Store in the refrigerator until they reach the desired ripeness.

CRAGGY CLOAKED CABRA

MAKES Ten 3-ounce cheeses
MILK Pasteurized goat's milk
START TO FINISH 3 to 4 weeks: 30 minutes to make the cheese; 8 to 10 hours to ripen;
12½ hours to drain and ripen again; 3 to 4 weeks to age

Inspired by the wrinkly rind of French Chabichou and some rumpled American relatives, Bonne Bouche from Vermont Butter & Cheese and Wabash Cannonball from Capriole, this soft-ripened ball-shaped goat cheese looks somewhat disheveled due to the appearance of its cloak. But looks are deceiving. Ripened for only a short period, this ash-dusted cheese is soft under its rumpled bloomy white exterior, while the center remains chalky and tangy.

....

Penicillium candidum mold powder

4¼ teaspoons fine sea salt

1 gallon pasteurized goat's milk

¼ teaspoon Aroma B powdered mesophilic starter culture

Pinch of *Geotrichum candidum* 15 mold powder

¼ teaspoon calcium chloride diluted in ¼ cup cool nonchlorinated water

¼ teaspoon liquid rennet diluted in ¼ cup cool nonchlorinated water

2 tablespoons vegetable ash

1. Twelve hours before starting, combine a pinch of *P. candidum*, ¼ teaspoon of the salt, and 2 cups of cool nonchlorinated water in an atomizer or spray bottle. Store at 50°F to 55°F.

2. In a nonreactive 6-quart stockpot, heat the milk over low heat to 72°F; this should take about 10 minutes. Turn off the heat.

(continued)

3. Sprinkle the starter, ⅛ teaspoon of *P. candidum*, and the *Geotrichum candidum* mold powder over the milk and let rehydrate for 5 minutes. Mix well using a whisk in an up-and-down motion for 20 strokes. Cover and maintain 72°F, letting the milk ripen for 30 minutes. Add the calcium chloride and gently whisk in for 1 minute, then add the rennet in the same way. Cover and let sit, maintaining 72°F for 8 to 10 hours, or until the curds give a clean break.

4. Cut the curds into ½-inch pieces and let sit for 5 minutes. Gently stir for 10 minutes with a rubber spatula, then ladle the curds into a colander lined with damp butter muslin and let drain for 30 minutes. Sprinkle in 1 tablespoon of the salt and gently toss with your hands to incorporate, then make a draining sack from the muslin and let drain for 4 hours, or until the whey stops dripping.

5. Using a scale, portion the drained curds into 10 pieces; each should weigh approximately 3½ ounces. Lightly shape and roll into balls, then place the cheeses at least 1 inch apart on a mat set in a ripening box. Cover the box loosely with the lid and let stand at room temperature for 8 hours.

6. Drain the whey and wipe out any moisture from the box, then ripen the cheese at 50°F to 55°F and 85 percent humidity for 2 days. Adjust the lid to be slightly open for a portion of each day to maintain the desired humidity level. The surface of the cheese should appear moist but not wet.

7. In a small bowl or jar, combine the vegetable ash with the remaining 1 teaspoon of salt. Wearing disposable gloves, use a fine-mesh strainer to dust the cheeses with the vegetable ash, coating them completely. Gently pat the ash onto the surface of the cheeses. Place the dusted cheeses on a clean cheese mat in a dry ripening box. Ripen at 50°F to 55°F and 85 percent humidity, turning the cheeses daily to maintain the round shape.

8. Two days after you have ashed the cheeses, very lightly mist them with the mold solution. Secure the lid on the ripening box. After about 5 days, the first signs of white fuzzy mold will appear through the ash. After 10 to 14 days, the cheeses will be fully coated in white mold. The wrinkled surface will also begin to develop within 10 days.

9. At 2 weeks, clean and dry the ripening box, wrap the cheeses in cheese paper, and return them to the ripening box. The cheeses will begin to soften within 1 week or so. After a total of 3 weeks from the start of ripening, store them in the refrigerator. It is best to consume these cheeses when they have reached the desired ripeness, about 3 to 4 weeks from the start of ripening.

CROTTIN

MAKES Four 3½-ounce cheeses
MILK Pasteurized goat's milk
START TO FINISH 3½ to 4½ weeks: 30 minutes to make the cheese;
18 hours to ripen; 2½ days to drain; 3 to 4 weeks to age

This surface-ripened goat cheese, known as crottin de chèvre in France, was one of the first styles of goat cheese to be emulated by American cheese makers some twenty years ago. The small, two-inch pucks of cheese are soft and mild when young and become firm and a bit salty with aging. A crottin can be eaten fresh (ten days old) or left to age and dry until hard (eight weeks or more), then used as a grating cheese. It's sensational and aromatic when grated and simply dusted on a hot caramelized onion pizza or pissaladière. Laura Chenel, Redwood Hill Farm, and Vermont Butter & Cheese all make excellent versions of crottin.

1 gallon pasteurized goat's milk
¹/₄ teaspoon Meso I or Aroma B powdered mesophilic starter culture
Pinch of *Penicillium candidum* mold powder
Pinch of *Geotrichum candidum* 15 mold powder
¹/₄ teaspoon calcium chloride diluted in ¹/₄ cup cool nonchlorinated water
¹/₄ teaspoon liquid rennet diluted in ¹/₄ cup cool nonchlorinated water
1 tablespoon fine sea salt

1. Let the milk sit at room temperature for 1 hour. In a nonreactive 6-quart stockpot, heat the milk over low heat to 72°F; this should take about 10 minutes. Turn off the heat.

2. Sprinkle the starter and the mold powders over the milk and let rehydrate for 5 minutes. Mix well using a whisk in an up-and-down motion. Add the calcium chloride and gently whisk in for 1 minute, then add the rennet in the same way. Cover and maintain 72°F, letting the milk ripen for 18 hours, or until the curds form a solid mass.

3. Place 4 crottin molds on a draining rack set over a tray. Gently cut ½-inch-thick slices of the curds using a ladle or skimmer and gently ladle the slices of curds into the molds to fill. Drain until more curds can be added to the molds.

(continued)

Fromage à l'Huile

Fromage à l'huile means "cheese [marinated] in oil." Young goat cheeses such as fresh chèvre, crottin, and cabécou are great candidates for marinating because they absorb flavors well. You can make a great version using this crottin. After aging for 2 weeks, the crottin is marinated in walnut oil and aromatics for 1 to 2 weeks. You can substitute cabécou (page 51) or slices of a chèvre log (page 58) for crottin. For additional flavor, lightly smoke the crottin over walnut shells before marinating (see page 27), or experiment with smoked or citrus-infused olive oils.

For each 3¹/₂-ounce crottin, you'll need one sterilized 8-ounce jar with a lid, ¹/₄ cup of coarsely chopped walnuts, ¹/₄ teaspoon of green peppercorns, 3 strips of lemon zest, 4 small sprigs of fresh thyme, and ¹/₂ cup of walnut oil. Slice each crottin into ¹/₂-inch-thick layers. In the jar, layer the slices of cheese with the walnuts, peppercorns, lemon zest, and thyme, then cover with walnut oil to the rim of the jar. Tightly secure the lid and place in a cool, dark cupboard or pantry for 1 to 2 weeks for the flavors to marry. After opening, place in the refrigerator to store. Bring to room temperature to liquefy the chilled oil before serving.

Do not be tempted to add another mold; the curds will compress as the whey drains out, making room for all of the curds.

4. When all of the curds have been ladled into the molds, cover them with a clean kitchen towel and let the cheeses drain at room temperature. Remove any collected whey a few times while draining, wiping out the tray with a paper towel each time. After 12 hours, or when the cheeses are firm enough to handle, gently invert the molds onto your palm to flip the cheeses in their molds. Do this three more times during the next 36 hours to aid in uniform formation of the cheeses and development of the bacteria. After 48 hours, the curds will have reduced to about half the height of the mold.

5. Once the cheeses have stopped draining and the curds have compressed to below the halfway point of the mold, place a mat in a ripening box. Remove the cheeses from the molds and sprinkle the salt over the tops and bottoms of the cheeses. Set them at least 1 inch apart on the mat in the ripening box and allow 10 minutes for the salt to dissolve. Wipe any moisture from the walls of the box.

6. Cover the box loosely with the lid and let it stand at room temperature for 8 hours. Drain any whey and wipe out any moisture from the box, then ripen the cheeses at 50°F to 55°F and 90 percent humidity, flipping the cheeses daily. For the first few days, adjust the lid to be slightly open for a portion of each day to maintain the desired humidity level. Too much humidity will create an undesirably wet surface. The surface of the cheeses should appear moist but not wet.

7. After about 5 days, the first signs of white fuzzy mold will appear. After 10 to 14 days, the cheeses will be fully coated in white mold. Clean and dry the ripening box, wrap the cheeses in cheese paper, and return them to the ripening box. The cheeses will begin to soften within 1 week or so. After a total of 3 weeks from the start of ripening, wrap the cheeses in fresh cheese paper and store in the refrigerator. It is best to consume these cheeses when they have reached the desired ripeness, between 3 and 4 weeks from the beginning of ripening.

Profile: Consider Bardwell Farm

Consider Bardwell Farm was the first cheese making co-op in Vermont, founded in 1864 by Consider Stebbins Bardwell. Since 2000, the farm has been owned by Angela Miller and Russell Glover, who, along with master cheese maker Peter Dixon, revitalized the farm and continue to practice farming and cheese making traditions. The exquisite three-hundred-acre farm covers a portion of the Champlain Valley of Vermont into the eastern corner of New York. Peter's award-winning cheeses are made from raw Jersey cow's milk from a small neighboring farm as well as raw and pasteurized goat's milk from Consider Bardwell's one-hundred-head herd. These small-batch cheeses are handmade and aged on the farm to absolute perfection.

THE GOAT EXPERIENCE

MAKES Four 6-ounce crottin disks
MILK Pasteurized goat's milk
START TO FINISH 2 to 3 weeks: 1 hour to make the cheese;
15 to 20 hours to ripen; 15 to 36 hours to drain; 2 to 3 weeks or longer to age

This recipe is contributed by the renowned Peter Dixon, cheese maker at Consider Bardwell Farm in Vermont (see left). It is made in the style of their Experience goat cheese and is (as Peter describes it) one of the aged, soft-ripened lactic goat cheeses that comprise a very large and diverse group of such cheeses originating in France. They can be served after only ten days of ripening or be aged to make hard grating cheeses. The Goat Experience uses relatively small amounts of starter culture and rennet and a relatively long ripening and coagulating period, and because of its short aging period, it uses pasteurized milk. Note you will need a pH meter or pH strips for this recipe.

2 gallons pasteurized goat's milk
1/8 teaspoon MM 100 or MA 011 powdered mesophilic
    starter culture
Pinch of Choozit CUM yeast
Pinch of *Penicillium candidum* mold powder
Pinch of *Geotrichum candidum* 17 mold powder
1/4 teaspoon calcium chloride diluted in 1/2 cup cool
    nonchlorinated water
1/4 teaspoon liquid rennet diluted in 1/2 cup cool
    nonchlorinated water
2 teaspoons kosher salt (preferably Diamond Crystal
    brand) or cheese salt

1. In a nonreactive 10-quart stockpot, heat the milk over medium heat to 75°F; this should take about 12 minutes. Turn off the heat.

2. Sprinkle the starter, yeast, and mold powders over the milk and let rehydrate for 5 minutes. Mix well using a whisk in an up-and-down motion. Cover and maintain 75°F, letting the milk ripen for 25 minutes. Gently whisk in the calcium chloride for 1 minute, and then add the rennet in the same way. Cover and let sit, maintaining 75°F for 15 to 20 hours, until the pH of the whey is below 4.6 but not lower than 4.4. At this point, the curds will have separated from the sides of the vat and there will be cracks in the body of the curds and a 1/2-inch layer of whey on top of the curds.

3. Set a draining rack over a tray and place 4 crottin molds on the rack. The curd can be ladled in large scoops and drained in damp cheesecloth for 10 to 15 hours and then packed into the crottin molds or gently ladled in small scoops directly into the molds. Either way, once the curds are in the molds, let them drain for 15 to 36 hours at room temperature.

4. Sprinkle 1/4 teaspoon of kosher salt over the top of each cheese in its mold. After about 10 hours of draining, the curds will be firm and hold their shape. After 12 hours total draining time, unmold the cheeses, flip them, and return them to the molds and the rack to drain further. Sprinkle another 1/4 teaspoon of salt over the top of each cheese in its mold.

5. Unmold the cheeses and set them on a cheese mat to air-dry at 60°F to 65°F. Flip the cheeses the next day, then let them sit until there is visible mold growth on the surface; this should take 3 to 5 days. When there is growth, flip the cheeses over and move them to a more humid and colder place, in a ripening box at 45°F to 48°F and 90 percent humidity. Flip the cheeses daily until they are completely covered with white mold; this should happen within 10 days. After a total of 2 weeks from the start of ripening, wrap the cheeses in cheese paper and store in the refrigerator. It is best to consume these cheeses when they have reached the desired ripeness, between 2 and 3 weeks from the beginning of ripening, or longer for a stronger flavor.

Young Mushroom-Infused Camembert at 3 weeks

MUSHROOM-INFUSED CAMEMBERT

MAKES Two 8-ounce cheeses
MILK Pasteurized whole cow's milk
ALTERNATIVE MILK Pasteurized goat's milk
START TO FINISH 4 to 6 weeks: 3 hours to make the cheese; 14 hours to drain;
4 to 6 weeks to age

Camembert is a perfect receptor for added earthy flavors. This is a flavor-enhanced Camembert in which the milk is infused with dried mushrooms. Some mushroom-flavored cheeses have bits of the mushroom added. That works for some firm cheeses, such as Jack or cheddar, but with bloomy-rind, creamy-paste cheeses, the best way to impart added flavor is to infuse the milk before making the cheese. Almost any variety of dried mushrooms can be used, but I prefer dried shiitake because they are the most compatible with the profile of this cheese; porcini would be too overpowering in flavor.

Penicillium candidum mold powder

4¹/₂ teaspoons kosher salt (preferably Diamond Crystal brand), cheese salt, or fine flake sea salt

¹/₂ ounce dried sliced shiitake mushrooms

1 gallon pasteurized whole cow's milk

¹/₄ teaspoon MM 100 powdered mesophilic starter culture

Pinch of *Geotrichum candidum* 15 mold powder

¹/₄ teaspoon calcium chloride diluted in ¹/₄ cup cool nonchlorinated water

¹/₄ teaspoon liquid rennet diluted in ¹/₄ cup cool nonchlorinated water

1. Twelve hours before starting, combine a pinch of *P. candidum*, ½ teaspoon of salt, and 1 quart of cool non-chlorinated water in an atomizer or spray bottle. Store at 50°F to 55°F.

2. In a nonreactive 6-quart stockpot, stir the mushrooms into the milk, then heat over low heat to 110°F to 112°F. Turn off the heat and maintain temperature for 55 minutes. Strain the milk through a fine-mesh strainer, pressing down on the mushrooms to squeeze out any liquid. Discard the mushrooms.

3. Cool the milk to 90°F, then sprinkle the starter, ⅛ teaspoon of *P. candidum* mold powder, and the *Geotrichum candidum* mold powder over the milk and let rehydrate for 5 minutes. Mix well using a whisk in an up-and-down motion. Add the calcium chloride and gently whisk in, then add the rennet in the same way. Cover and let sit, maintaining a temperature of 85°F for 1½ hours, or until the curds give a clean break.

4. Cut the curds into ½-inch pieces and let sit for 5 minutes to firm up. Using a rubber spatula, gently stir around the edges of the pot for 5 minutes to shrink the curds and keep them from matting. Let the curds rest for 5 minutes; they will sink to the bottom.

(continued)

5. Set a draining rack over a tray, put a cutting board on the rack and a cheese mat on the board, and, finally, place the two 4-inch Camembert molds on the mat. Ladle off some of the whey and, using a skimmer, gently ladle the curds into the molds. Let drain for 2 hours, until the curds have reduced to about half the height of the molds. Place a second mat and cutting board over the top of the molds. With one hand holding the top board firmly against the mat and molds, lift and gently flip the molds over and set them back onto the draining rack.

6. Let drain for 2 hours, then flip again. At this point the curds should be 1½ to 2 inches high. Cover and let drain at room temperature for 8 hours or overnight. Flip the cheeses again and let drain for 2 more hours.

7. Remove the molds and sprinkle about 2 teaspoons of salt over the top and sides of the cheeses. Leave for 10 minutes, allowing the salt to dissolve. At this point, spray lightly with the mold solution. Place the cheeses salt side down on a clean mat in a ripening box and salt the other side, using the remaining 2 teaspoons of salt.

8. Cover the box with the lid slightly open for a little air circulation and ripen the cheeses at 50°F to 55°F and 90 percent humidity. High humidity is essential for making this cheese. Flip the cheeses daily, removing any whey and any moisture that may have accumulated in the ripening box. Keep covered to maintain the humidity level.

9. After about 5 days, the first signs of white fuzzy mold will appear. Continue to flip the cheeses daily. After 10 to 14 days, the cheeses will be fully coated in white mold. Wrap them loosely in cheese paper and return them to the ripening box at 50°F to 55°F and 85 percent humidity. The cheeses will begin to soften within 1 week or so. After a total of 4 weeks from the start of ripening, move the cheeses to the refrigerator until they reach the desired ripeness, up to 6 weeks from the start of ripening.

BLOOMY ROBIOLA

MAKES 2 pounds
MILK Pasteurized whole cow's milk, pasteurized goat's milk
START TO FINISH 3 weeks to 3 months: 18 hours to make; 20 hours to drain;
48 hours to ripen; 3 weeks to 3 months to age

There is a broad range of cheeses with many variations that bear the name Robiola. Two styles of Robiola are contributed to this book by Jim Wallace, consultant to New England Cheesemaking Supply. One has a slightly rosy bloom but neither a white nor fuzzy surface and the other is fresh. This recipe is for a mixed milk bloomy-rind Robiola. The fresh version is incorporated into the variation for leaf-wrapped Robiola (see below).

---

1 gallon pasteurized whole cow's milk
1 gallon pasteurized goat's milk
1/8 teaspoon MM 100 powdered mesophilic starter
    culture
1/8 teaspoon *Geotrichum candidum* 15 mold powder
1/4 teaspoon calcium chloride diluted in 1/4 cup cool
    nonchlorinated water
4 drops rennet diluted in 1/4 cup nonchlorinated water
Kosher salt (preferably Diamond Crystal brand)

1. In a nonreactive 10-quart stockpot, heat the milks over low heat to 95°F; this should take about 25 minutes. Turn off the heat.

2. Sprinkle the starter and mold powder over the milks and let rehydrate for 5 minutes. Mix well using a whisk in an up-and-down motion. Add the calcium chloride and gently whisk in, and then add the rennet in the same way. Cover and let sit, maintaining 95°F for 12 to 18 hours, or until the curds give a clean break.

3. Set a draining rack over a tray, followed by a cheese mat. Place 2 Camembert molds on the mat. Using a skimmer, gently ladle the curds into the molds. Let drain at room temperature for 8 to 10 hours, or until the curds have compressed to 1½ to 2 inches.

4. Sprinkle ¼ teaspoon of kosher salt over the top of each cheese in its mold. After 10 to 12 hours of draining, the curds will be firm and hold their shape. Unmold the cheeses, flip them, and return them to the rack to drain further. Sprinkle another ¼ teaspoon of salt over the top of each cheese.

5. Let the cheeses drain for 2 hours, then place the cheeses on a clean cheese mat in a ripening box. Cover the box with its lid and let ripen at 77°F and 92 to 95 percent humidity. Every 8 hours, loosen the lid to allow air to circulate. After 30 to 48 hours (depending on when the whey stops draining), lower the temperature to 55°F and keep the humidity at 92 to 95 percent.

6. After about 5 days, the signs of a creamy white surface will appear. Continue to flip the cheeses daily and remove any excess moisture from the box. After 7 to 10 days, the cheeses will have a rosy surface hue. After 3 to 4 weeks some blue mold may have formed on the surface. At this point the cheese will be very ripe, and barely contained by its thin rind. You may use the cheeses now, wrap and store them in the refrigerator, or continue aging for up to 3 months.

VARIATION

To make leaf-wrapped Robiola, after salting, wrap each cheese in 2 prepared and blanched leaves of savoy cabbage (see page 59) and secure with lengths of raffia. Place in a ripening box at 50°F to 55°F and 80 percent humidity and age for 3 weeks to 1 month.

SAINT-MARCELLIN

MAKES Four 3-ounce rounds
MILK Pasteurized whole cow's milk
ALTERNATIVE MILK Pasteurized goat's milk
START TO FINISH About 2½ to 6½ weeks: 3 hours to make the cheese; 12 hours to ripen;
3½ days to drain; 2 to 6 weeks to age

This small surface-ripened cheese is considered one of France's great culinary treasures. Originally made with goat's milk, this version uses cow's milk and is simplified for the home cheese maker. Soft, spreadable, and petite, Saint-Marcellin has a delicate, barely bloomed rind and is best encased in a crock to safely finish its aging. These crocks can be found at specialty cookware stores (see Resources).

---

3 quarts pasteurized whole cow's milk
⅛ teaspoon Meso II powdered mesophilic starter culture
Pinch of *Penicillium candidum* mold powder
Pinch of *Geotrichum candidum* 15 mold powder
¼ teaspoon calcium chloride diluted in ¼ cup cool nonchlorinated water
6 drops liquid rennet diluted in ¼ cup cool nonchlorinated water
3 teaspoons kosher salt (preferably Diamond Crystal brand) or cheese salt

1.   In a nonreactive 4-quart stockpot, heat the milk over low heat to 75°F; this should take about 12 minutes. Turn off the heat.

2.   Sprinkle the starter and mold powders over the milk and let rehydrate for 5 minutes. Mix well using a whisk in an up-and-down motion. Add the calcium chloride and gently whisk in, then add the rennet in the same way. Cover and let sit, maintaining 72°F to 75°F for 12 hours, or until the curds give a clean break.

3.   Cut the curds into ½-inch slices using a ladle or skimmer. Using a rubber spatula, gently stir around the edges of the pot, then let the curds stand for 5 minutes.

4.   Set a draining rack over a tray, then place 4 Saint-Marcellin molds on the rack. Ladle the curds into a colander or strainer lined with damp butter muslin and let drain for 15 minutes. Ladle the curds into the molds up to their tops, then let drain until more curds can be added to the molds. Do not be tempted to add another mold; the curds will compress as the whey drains out. The process will take about 30 minutes. Drain the curds at room temperature. After 6 hours, flip the cheeses in the molds and sprinkle the tops with 1½ teaspoons of the salt. Let drain for another 6 hours, then flip the cheeses in the molds again and sprinkle the tops with the remaining 1½ teaspoons of salt and drain for another 6 hours.

5.   Unmold the cheeses and place them on a cheese mat in a ripening box. Cover the box loosely and let the cheeses drain at room temperature for 48 hours, flipping the cheeses daily and removing any whey that has accumulated.

6.   Ripen at 55°F and 90 percent humidity for 14 days, or until a white fuzzy mold has developed to cover the cheese, flipping the cheeses daily and continuing to remove the whey. The cheeses are ready to eat at this point, or they can be aged further.

7.   Place each disk in a shallow clay crock and cover with plastic wrap or the crock's lid. If crocks are not used, wrap the cheeses in cheese paper or plastic wrap and store in the refrigerator for up to 6 weeks.

VALENÇAY

MAKES Four 3- to 4-ounce pyramid-shaped cheeses
MILK Pasteurized goat's milk
START TO FINISH About 4 to 6 weeks: 30 minutes to make the cheese;
12 hours to ripen; 48 hours to drain; 4 to 6 weeks to age

This ash-coated goat cheese from the Loire Valley of France is recognizably shaped into an approximately 3-inch-tall trun-cated pyramid, formed by a special mold. Light gray on the bloomy surface due to the vegetable ash peeking through the *Penicillium candidum* bloom, this cheese is firm yet creamy or even oozy just under the thin, edible rind and has a chalky center. The flavor ranges from mild and tangy when young to mushroomy and more salty when aged. A few contemporary American examples made in this style include Andante's Nocturne and Haystack Mountain's Haystack Peak.

1 gallon pasteurized goat's milk
¼ teaspoon Meso I or Aroma B powdered mesophilic
   starter culture
⅛ teaspoon *Penicillium candidum* mold powder
Pinch of *Geotrichum candidum* 15 mold powder
¼ teaspoon calcium chloride diluted in ¼ cup cool
   nonchlorinated water
¼ teaspoon liquid rennet diluted in ¼ cup cool
   nonchlorinated water
¼ cup vegetable ash powder
2 teaspoons fine sea salt

1. In a nonreactive 6-quart stockpot, heat the milk over low heat to 72°F; this should take about 10 minutes. Turn off the heat.

2. Sprinkle the starter and mold powders over the surface of the milk and let rehydrate for 5 minutes. Mix well using a whisk in an up-and-down motion. Add the calcium chloride and gently whisk in for 1 minute, then add the rennet in the same way. Cover and let sit, maintaining 72°F for 12 hours, or until the curds give a clean break.

3. Cut the curds into ½-inch slices using a ladle or skimmer. Using a rubber spatula, gently stir around the edges of the pot for 5 minutes, then let the curds stand for 5 minutes.

4. Set a draining rack on a tray, then place 4 truncated pyramid molds on the rack. Ladle the slices of curds into the molds to fill, then let drain until more curds can be added to the molds. Do not be tempted to add another mold; the curds will compress as the whey drains out. Cover with a dish towel and let the cheeses drain for 48 hours at room temperature, removing any whey a few times while draining and removing any collected whey with a paper towel each time you drain it. Flip the molds after 12 hours or when the cheeses are firm enough to handle, then flip a few more times during the next 36 hours. At the end of 48 hours, the curds will have reduced to about half the height of the mold.

5. Remove the molds and combine the vegetable ash with the salt in a small bowl. Wearing disposable gloves, use a fine-mesh strainer to dust the cheeses with vegetable ash, lightly coating each completely. Gently pat the ash onto the surface of the cheeses.

(continued)

6. Place the cheeses at least 1 inch apart on a clean cheese mat in a ripening box. Cover loosely with the lid and let stand at room temperature for 24 hours. Wipe out any moisture from the box, then ripen at 50°F to 55°F and 90 percent humidity for 3 weeks. For the first few days, adjust the lid to be slightly open for a portion of each day to maintain the desired humidity level. The surface of the cheeses should appear moist but not wet.

7. Continue to flip the cheeses daily. After about 5 days, the first signs of white fuzzy mold will appear through the ash. After 10 to 14 days the cheeses will be fully coated in white mold. As the cheese continues to age, the surface will turn a very light gray.

8. Wrap the cheeses in cheese paper and return them to the ripening box; they will begin to soften within 1 week or so. After a total of 4 weeks from the start of ripening, wrap the cheeses in fresh cheese paper and store them in the refrigerator. It is best to consume this cheese when it has reached the desired ripeness, within 4 to 6 weeks from the start of ripening.

Valençay at 2½ weeks

Washed-Rind and Smeared-Rind Cheeses

Washed-rind cheeses are surface-ripened cheeses that are washed or rubbed over the entire surface with brine, whey, buttermilk, cider, beer, wine, or spirits individually or in some combination, according to the traditions of the region of their origin. Smeared-rind cheeses—also know as the "stinkers"—are cheeses rubbed with a brine that contains a strain of the "red" bacteria *Brevibacterium linens*. The wash attracts desirable bacteria that help break down the curds, so the wash fundamentally alters the cheese rather than just forming a rind. The result is a creamy interior and an often sticky and pungent rind. Many washed-rind and smeared-rind cheeses originated during medieval times in monasteries where monks produced brew, wine, and spirits, as well as cheeses.

Cheeses made in the washed-rind style include Cabra al Vino, Chimay Trappiste, Munster, and Taleggio. Classic stinkers include Époisses and Limburger. Modern American examples include Carr Valley's Mobay, Cato Corner's Hooligan, Consider Bardwell's Dorset and Manchester, Cowgirl Creamery's Pierce Point and Red Hawk, Fiscalini's Purple Moon, Haystack Mountain's Red Cloud, Marin French's Schloss, Meadow Creek's Grayson, and the Mozzarella Company's Blanca Bianca.

Whether the cheese has a washed or a smeared rind, the ripening solution is applied multiple times before the aging to create an edible rind ranging in color from natural to white to light orange to brown, or purple if washed with red wine. Some washed cheeses have a firmer texture due to being pressed before they are washed.

Soft-rind cheeses are ripened at a warm temperature (60°F) and high humidity (90 percent), and aged from three weeks to two months or longer. The pressed cheeses are ripened at 50°F to 55°F and slightly lower humidity (85 percent) and aged for three to six weeks. The flavors of some of the cheeses will become more intense with age.

ALE-WASHED CORIANDER TRAPPIST CHEESE

MAKES 1 pound
MILK Pasteurized whole cow's milk
START TO FINISH 4½ to 6½ weeks: 2½ hours to make the cheese; 16 hours to press;
44 hours to soak and dry; 4 to 6 weeks to age

This cheese is a nod to the Trappist monks who, as part of their daily discipline, grew wheat and raised dairy cows. As a result they made bread, brewed beer, and made washed-rind cheeses, forging an important part of cheese making history. Monasteries in both Europe and the United States are still making cheeses in this tradition. This cheese is not traditional, but it was inspired by that style. The milk is infused with coriander and orange peel, two flavors in the Belgian-style white ale I chose to use as a brine and wash; crushed coriander seeds and dried orange peel are also layered into the cheese. My favorite dried orange peel is from Penzey's Spices (penzeys.com).

....

1 gallon pasteurized whole cow's milk

1½ teaspoons coriander seeds, crushed

1½ teaspoons granulated orange peel

¼ teaspoon Meso II powdered mesophilic starter culture

¼ teaspoon calcium chloride diluted in ¼ cup cool nonchlorinated water

¼ teaspoon liquid rennet diluted in ¼ cup cool nonchlorinated water

Kosher salt (preferably Diamond Crystal brand)

One 12-ounce bottle Belgian ale at room temperature, plus 16 to 24 ounces more for washing

1. In a nonreactive 2-quart saucepan, heat 1 quart of the milk over low heat to 90°F; this should take about 20 minutes. Stir in 1 teaspoon of the coriander and 1 teaspoon of the orange peel, then slowly raise the temperature to 110°F over the course of 10 minutes. Turn off the heat, cover, and let steep for 45 minutes, or until the temperature drops back down to 90°F.

2. Place the remaining 3 quarts of milk in a nonreactive 6-quart stockpot. Pour the steeped milk through a fine-mesh strainer into the larger pot of milk and whisk to combine. Discard the coriander and orange. Bring the milk to 90°F over low heat; this should take 5 minutes. Turn off the heat.

3. Sprinkle the starter over the milk and let it rehydrate for 5 minutes. Mix well using a whisk in an up-and-down motion. Cover and maintain 90°F, allowing the milk to ripen for 30 minutes. Add the calcium chloride and gently whisk in for 1 minute, then add the rennet in the same way. Cover and let sit, maintaining 90°F for 1 hour, or until the curds give a clean break.

4. Still maintaining 90°F, cut the curds into ½-inch pieces and let sit for 10 minutes. Gently stir the curds for 15 minutes to expel more whey, then let settle for another 10 minutes. The curds will shrink to the size of small beans. Meanwhile, heat 2 quarts of water to 175°F. Ladle off enough whey to expose the curds. Add enough hot water to bring the temperature to 93°F. Stir for 10 minutes. Repeat the process of removing whey and adding hot water, this time bringing the temperature to 100°F. Stir for 15 minutes, then let the curds settle for 10 minutes. Cover and let rest for 45 minutes, maintaining 100°F. The curds will mat and form a slab.

(continued)

5. Drain off enough whey to expose the slab of curds. Transfer the slab to a flat-bottomed colander, place it over the pot, and let drain for 5 minutes. Transfer the slab to a cutting board and cut into ⅜-inch-thick slices. Place in a bowl and gently toss with 2 teaspoons of the salt.

6. Line a 5-inch tomme mold with damp cheesecloth and set it on a draining rack. Tightly pack half of the curds in the mold, cover with the cloth tails and the follower, and press at 5 pounds for 10 minutes, just to compact the curds slightly. Peel back the cloth and sprinkle on the remaining ½ teaspoon of coriander and ½ teaspoon of orange peel, then pack in the rest of the milled curds. Cover with the cloth tails and the follower and press at 8 pounds for 6 hours at room temperature. Remove the cheese from the mold, unwrap, flip, and redress, then press again at 8 pounds for 8 hours to thoroughly compress the curds.

7. Pour the bottle of ale into a lidded nonreactive container large enough to hold both ale and cheese. Remove the cheese from the mold and cheesecloth and place in the ale. Soak the cheese, covered, for 8 hours at 55°F, flipping once.

8. Remove the cheese from the ale and pat dry. Reserve and refrigerate the ale and place the cheese on a cheese mat. Air-dry at room temperature for 12 hours. Return the cheese to the ale and soak for another 12 hours at 55°F. Remove, pat dry, and air-dry at room temperature for 12 hours, or until the surface is dry to the touch. Discard the ale.

9. Prepare a brine-ale wash: boil ½ cup of water and let it cool, and combine with ½ cup of ale, then dissolve 1 teaspoon of salt in the liquid. Store in the refrigerator.

10. Place the cheese on a mat in a ripening box and ripen at 50°F and 90 percent humidity for 4 to 6 weeks. Flip the cheese daily for the first 2 weeks, then twice weekly thereafter. After each flip, pour a little brine-ale wash into a small dish, dip a small piece of cheesecloth in it, and use it to wipe the surface of the cheese. Discard any unused brine-ale wash after 1 week and make a fresh batch. Also wipe away any moisture from the bottom, sides, and lid of the ripening box each time you flip the cheese.

11. Wrap the cheese in cheese paper and store refrigerated for up to 1 month. If you vacuum-seal the cheese, remove it from the package and pat it dry before consuming it.

CABRA AL VINO

MAKES 1½ pounds
MILK Pasteurized goat's milk
START TO FINISH 6 weeks: 3 hours to make the cheese; 16 hours to press;
2 days to soak and dry; 6 weeks to age

Cabra al Vino, which originated in Spain, is a pressed, firm goat cheese that is soaked in red wine, creating a beautiful purplish exterior. Typically, this cheese is smooth on the surface, so the mottled appearance of this version is a bit unusual (and, I think, far more interesting). It is achieved by pressing the cheese at a slightly lighter pressure than usual so that a few cracks and crevices are left to soak up the wine flavor. They also provide an opportunity for mold to grow, so monitor the cheese as it ages and wipe away any unwanted growth. If you choose to make a smooth-surfaced version, just press at eight pounds of pressure rather than five.

2 gallons pasteurized goat's milk

¼ teaspoon Meso II powdered mesophilic starter culture

½ teaspoon calcium chloride diluted in ¼ cup cool nonchlorinated water

¾ teaspoon liquid rennet diluted in ¼ cup cool nonchlorinated water

Kosher salt (preferably Diamond Crystal brand)

One 750 ml bottle red wine, chilled to 55°F

1. In a nonreactive 10-quart stockpot, heat the milk over low heat to 90°F; this should take about 20 minutes. Turn off the heat.

2. Sprinkle the starter over the milk and let it rehydrate for 5 minutes. Mix well using a whisk in an up-and-down motion. Cover and maintain 90°F, letting the milk ripen for 30 minutes. Add the calcium chloride and gently whisk in for 1 minute, then add the rennet in the same way. Cover and let sit, maintaining 90°F for 1 hour, or until the curds give a clean break.

3. Still maintaining 90°F, cut the curds into ¾-inch pieces and let sit for 5 minutes. Gently stir the curds for 20 minutes, then let settle.

4. Meanwhile, heat 2 quarts of water to 175°F. Ladle off enough whey to expose the curds. Add enough hot water to bring the temperature to 93°F. Stir for 5 minutes. Repeat the process of removing whey and adding hot water, this time bringing the temperature to 102°F. Stir for 15 minutes, then let the curds settle for 10 minutes. Cover and let rest for 45 minutes, maintaining 102°F. The curds will mat slightly and form a slab.

5. Drain off enough whey to expose the slab of curds. Using a mesh strainer or ladle, gently turn the curds over every 5 minutes for 15 minutes. Place the slab in a bowl and, using your hands, break it into ½-inch pieces and gently toss with 1 teaspoon of the salt.

6. Line an 8-inch tomme mold with damp butter muslin and set it on a draining rack. Fill the mold with the milled curds, cover with the tails of the cloth and the follower, and press at 5 pounds for 8 hours at room temperature. Remove the cheese from the mold, unwrap, flip, and redress, then press again at 5 pounds for 8 hours at room temperature.

(continued)

7. Pour the wine into a lidded nonreactive container large enough to hold both wine and cheese. Remove the cheese from the mold and cloth and place it in the wine. Soak the cheese, covered, for 12 hours at 55°F, flipping once.

8. Remove the cheese from the wine and pat dry. Reserve and refrigerate the wine and place the cheese on a cheese mat. Air-dry at room temperature for 12 hours. Return the cheese to the wine and soak for another 12 hours at 55°F. Remove, pat dry, and air-dry at room temperature for 12 hours, or until the surface is dry to the touch. Discard the wine.

9. Place the cheese on a mat in a ripening box and ripen at 50°F and 85 percent humidity for 6 weeks. Flip the cheese daily for the first 2 weeks, then twice weekly thereafter. After each flip, wipe the surface with a small piece of cheesecloth dipped in a small amount of brine wash: boil ½ cup of water and let it cool, then add 1 teaspoon of salt and stir to dissolve. Store in the refrigerator. The brine wash will control unwanted mold growth. Discard any unused brine wash after 1 week and make a fresh batch. Also wipe away any moisture from the bottom, sides, and lid of the ripening box each time you flip the cheese.

10. After 2 weeks of ripening, you may wax coat the cheese (see page 28) and refrigerate for the duration of the aging time: up to 6 weeks. If you don't want to wax coat, simply keep the cheese in the ripening box for 6 weeks as specified in step 9. After 3½ weeks or so, the cheese will have a musty, winery-meets-cheese-shop aroma.

VARIATION

This cheese can be made with beer instead of wine, in which case it is named Cabra al Birra. Substitute 25 fluid ounces (750 ml) of beer at room temperature for the wine and proceed with the same method.

Cabra al Vino at 5 weeks

DESERT SUNSET PAVÉ

MAKES Two 10-ounce cheeses or one 1½-pound cheese
MILK Pasteurized whole cow's milk
ALTERNATIVE MILKS Pasteurized goat's milk or sheep's milk
START TO FINISH 4 to 6 weeks: 2 hours to make the cheese; 12 hours to drain; 8 hours to soak;
24 hours to dry; 4 to 6 weeks to age

This bright orange pavé (square) washed-rind cheese was inspired by the French sheep's milk Brebirousse d'Argental—and by my cheese making time in Arizona. With flavors reminiscent of Taleggio, Desert Sunset stands an inch and a half tall and has a firm rind and a succulent, creamy paste. First soaked in a brine containing annatto, it is also washed during ripening with an annatto-salt solution to further develop the orange color and the crusty rind.

2 gallons pasteurized whole cow's milk
¼ teaspoon MA 4001 powdered mesophilic starter culture
⅛ teaspoon *Penicillium candidum* mold powder
Pinch of *Geotrichum candidum* 15 mold powder
¼ teaspoon calcium chloride diluted in ¼ cup cool nonchlorinated water
¼ teaspoon liquid rennet diluted in ¼ cup cool nonchlorinated water
Kosher salt (preferably Diamond Crystal brand) for brining and washing
Liquid annatto for brining and washing

1. In a nonreactive 10-quart stockpot, heat the milk over low heat to 90°F; this should take 20 minutes. Turn off the heat.

2. Sprinkle the starter and mold powders over the milk and let rehydrate for 5 minutes. Mix well using a whisk in an up-and-down motion. Cover and maintain 90°F, allowing the milk to ripen for 1 hour. Add the calcium chloride and gently whisk in, then add the rennet in the same way. Cover and let sit, maintaining 90°F for 30 minutes, or until the curds give a clean break.

3. Still maintaining 90°F, cut the curds into ¾-inch pieces and let sit for 5 minutes to firm up. Gently stir the curds for 30 minutes, removing 2 cups of whey every 10 minutes. Then let the curds settle for 10 minutes.

4. Line one 7-inch square Taleggio mold or two 4-inch square cheese molds with damp butter muslin. Place the molds on a draining rack over a tray and gently ladle the curds into the molds, pressing them into the corners with your hand. Cover the curds with the tails of cloth and cover the entire setup with a kitchen towel. Let drain for 6 hours in a warm spot in the kitchen. Remove the cheese from the mold, unwrap, flip, and redress, then let drain for 6 more hours.

5. Two hours before the end of the draining time, make a soaking brine by combining 2½ cups of cool nonchlorinated water, ½ cup of salt, and 8 drops of annatto in a lidded nonreactive container large enough to hold the brine and cheese. Stir to dissolve the salt completely, then cool to 50°F to 55°F. Remove the cheese from the mold and cloth and place it in the brine. Soak the cheese, covered, at 50°F to 55°F for 8 hours, flipping at least once.

Desert Sunset Pavé at 4 weeks

6. Remove the cheese from the brine and pat dry. Air-dry at room temperature on a cheese mat or rack for 24 hours, or until the surface is dry to the touch.

7. Place the cheese on a mat in a ripening box and ripen at 50°F and 85 percent humidity, flipping every other day. At least 2 hours before you flip the cheese the first time, make a brine wash by combining 1½ teaspoons of salt, 3 drops of annatto, and 1 cup of cool nonchlorinated water in a sterilized glass jar; shake well to dissolve the salt, then chill to 50°F to 55°F. After each flip, pour a little brine wash into a small dish, dip a small piece of cheesecloth in it, wring it out, and use it to wipe the surface of the cheese. Discard any unused brine wash after 1 week and make a fresh batch. Also wipe away any moisture from the bottom, sides, and lid of the ripening box each time you flip the cheese.

8. The rind will become crusty and firm, and in 10 to 14 days an orange color will develop; this will deepen as the cheeses age. After 4 weeks, the rind should be slightly moist and the center of the cheese should feel soft; at this point, it's ready to eat. Consume within 2 weeks.

WASHED-RIND TELEME-STYLE

MAKES 2 pounds
MILK Pasteurized whole cow's milk
START TO FINISH 2 weeks to 2 months: 2½ hours to make the cheese; 18 to 20 hours to drain; 2 weeks to 2 months to age

Teleme is a California cow's milk cheese created by the Peluso family in 1919; it was originally known as Peluso's Teleme. Inspired by Peluso's Teleme, this version has a washed rind and the traditional square shape. You may eat it young, at two weeks, if you choose.

2 gallons pasteurized whole cow's milk

½ teaspoon MA 4001 powdered mesophilic starter culture

½ teaspoon calcium chloride diluted in ¼ cup cool nonchlorinated water

½ teaspoon liquid rennet diluted in ¼ cup cool nonchlorinated water

2 tablespoons kosher salt (preferably Diamond Crystal brand) or cheese salt

1. In a nonreactive 10-quart stockpot, heat the milk over low heat to 86°F; this should take 15 minutes. Turn off the heat.

2. Sprinkle the starter over the milk and let it rehydrate for 5 minutes. Mix well using a whisk in an up-and-down motion. Cover and maintain 86°F, allowing the milk to ripen for 1 hour. Add the calcium chloride and gently whisk in for 1 minute, then add the rennet in the same way. Cover and let sit, maintaining 86°F for 30 to 45 minutes, or until the curds give a clean break.

3. Cut the curds into 1½-inch pieces and let sit for 5 minutes. Over low heat, slowly bring the curds to 102°F over a 40-minute period, stirring continuously to prevent them from matting. The curds will release more whey, firm up, and shrink to the size of large lima beans.

4. Once 102°F is reached, remove from the heat, maintain the temperature, and let the curds rest undisturbed for 30 minutes. Heat 2 quarts of water to 120°F. Ladle off enough whey to expose the curds. Add enough hot water to bring the temperature to 104°F. Stir continuously for

15 minutes, or until the curds cling together when pressed in your hand.

5. Line a colander with damp butter muslin and place it over a bowl or bucket large enough to capture the whey, which can be discarded. Gently ladle the curds into the colander and rinse with cold tap water to cool them. Let drain for 5 minutes, then sprinkle in 1 tablespoon of the salt and gently and thoroughly toss with your hands.

6. Place a mat on a draining rack set over a tray, then set a 7-inch square Taleggio mold on the mat. Put the sack of rinsed curds in the mold and press the curds into the corners. Cover the top of the curds with the cloth tails and press with your hands to mat the curds. Let drain at room temperature for 6 hours for moist cheese, or 8 hours for a firmer cheese. Flip the cheese once halfway through this draining period.

7. Remove the cheese from the mold and pat dry. Rub the surface of the cheese with the remaining 1 tablespoon of salt and place it back in the mold without the cloth. Return the mold to the mat on the draining rack for 12 hours, flipping once in that time.

8. Remove the cheese from the mold and place in a ripening box at 50°F to 55°F and 85 percent humidity for at least 2 weeks, flipping the cheese daily for even ripening. After 1 week, wash with a simple brine solution (see page 24) twice a week for up to 2 months of ripening time. When the desired ripeness is reached, wrap and refrigerate until ready to eat.

LEMON VODKA SPIRITED GOAT

MAKES 1½ pounds
MILK Pasteurized goat's milk
START TO FINISH 2 to 3 months: 2½ hours to make the cheese; 13 hours to press; 8 hours to brine;
12 hours to dry; 2 to 3 months to age

Époisses and other spirit-washed cheeses were the inspiration for this unique goat cheese. A tasting at Charbay Distillery in Napa clinched for me which spirit would wash the rind: their Meyer Lemon Vodka. The aromatic vodka and tangy goat's milk work in perfect harmony to develop the flavors in the unctuous finished cheese. I dedicate this cheese to Miles Karakasevic, the proud patriarch, twelfth-generation winemaker, and master distiller at family-owned Charbay Winery and Distillery. You can purchase their spirits online at www.charbay.com.

2 gallons pasteurized goat's milk

1/2 teaspoon MM 100 powdered mesophilic starter culture

1/4 teaspoon Thermo B powdered thermophilic starter culture

Geotrichum candidum 15 mold powder

1/4 teaspoon calcium chloride diluted in 1/4 cup cool nonchlorinated water

1/2 teaspoon liquid rennet diluted in 1/4 cup cool nonchlorinated water

Kosher salt (preferably Diamond Crystal brand) or cheese salt

Pinch of *Brevibacterium linens* powder

1 cup Charbay Meyer Lemon Vodka or other lemon-infused vodka

1. In a nonreactive 10-quart stockpot, heat the milk over low heat to 90°F; this should take about 20 minutes. Turn off the heat.

2. Sprinkle both starters and a pinch of the mold powder over the milk and let rehydrate for 5 minutes. Mix well using a whisk in an up-and-down motion. Cover and maintain 90°F, allowing the milk to ripen for 45 minutes. Add the calcium chloride and gently whisk in for 1 minute, then add the rennet in the same way. Cover and let sit, maintaining 90°F for 30 to 45 minutes, or until the curds give a clean break.

3. Still maintaining 90°F, cut the curds into ½-inch pieces and let rest for 10 minutes. Gently stir the curds for 10 minutes, then let rest for 30 minutes. Slowly raise the temperature to 100°F over 30 minutes, stirring the curds every 5 minutes. Let the curds sit for about 10 minutes; they will sink to the bottom.

4. Ladle out enough whey to expose the curds, then gently ladle the curds into a colander lined with damp butter muslin and let drain for 5 minutes.

5. Line an 8-inch tomme mold or 7-inch square Taleggio mold with damp butter muslin and set on a draining rack. Transfer the curds to the mold, gently distributing and pressing into the mold with your hand. Cover the curds with the cloth tails and a follower and press at 3 pounds for 1 hour.

6. Remove the cheese from the mold, unwrap, flip, and redress, then press at 5 pounds for 12 hours, flipping once at 6 hours.

(continued)

Lemon Vodka Spirited Goat at 5 weeks

7. Make 2 quarts of saturated brine (see page 24) and chill to 50°F to 55°F. Remove the cheese from the mold and cloth and place it in the brine to soak at 50°F to 55°F for 8 hours, flipping at least once during the brining process.

8. Remove the cheese from the brine and pat it dry. Air-dry on a cheese mat at room temperature for 12 hours, or until the surface is dry.

9. Place the cheese on a mat in a ripening box and age at 50°F to 55°F and 90 percent humidity, flipping daily for 1 week. Each time you flip the cheese, wipe any moisture from the bottom, sides, and lid of the box.

10. After 1 week, begin washing the surface with bacterial wash. Twelve hours before the first washing, prepare the solution by dissolving 1½ teaspoons of salt in 1 cup of cool nonchlorinated water in a sterilized glass jar. Add 1 pinch each of *Geotrichum candidum* mold powder and *B. linens* powder, whisk to incorporate, cover, and store at 55°F.

11. When ready to wash, pour 1½ tablespoons of the bacterial wash into a small bowl, preserving the rest for another washing. Dip a small piece of cheesecloth into the solution, squeeze out the excess, and rub it all over the entire surface of the cheese. Using a paper towel, wipe any excess moisture from the ripening box. Flip the cheese over and return it to the ripening box. Discard any bacterial wash left in the bowl.

12. Wash the cheese twice a week for 2 months, alternating the bacterial wash with spirits. To wash with the vodka, pour a little vodka into a bowl, dip a small piece of cheesecloth in it, wring out, and rub it over the entire surface of the cheese. Discard any vodka left in the bowl. The rind will become slightly sticky, and at 10 to 14 days a light orange color will develop, which will deepen as the cheese ages. At 2 months, the rind should be only slightly moist and the cheese should be soft to the touch in the center; it is now ready to eat. The cheese should be eaten within 3 months.

ÉPOISSES

MAKES Two ½-pound cheeses
MILK Pasteurized whole cow's milk
START TO FINISH About 6 weeks: 4 hours to make the cheese; 24 hours to drain;
18 hours to dry; 6 weeks to age

Époisses is the king of all "stinkers," lavishly bathed in Marc de Bourgogne brandy to develop its rind and characteristic "I Am Here" aroma. It is the aristocratic French relative to the Italian Robiola (page 149). Making an Époisses-style cheese at home is challenging and requires a good deal of attention. This adaptation was contributed by Jim Wallace, cheese making consultant for New England Cheesemaking Supply, educator, and passionate hobbyist cheese maker. This recipe uses very little rennet, and like the Robiola recipes and The Goat Experience (page 145), it relies on extended lactic fermentation for curd development. Because pasteurized milk is being used, mesophilic culture is added to replace the bacteria that would be present in raw milk. Époisses is traditionally housed in a round wooden cheese box that both holds and protects the cheese. You can follow tradition by purchasing such a cheese box (see Resources) or recycle one from a store-bought cheese.

1 gallon pasteurized whole cow's milk

¹/₈ teaspoon Meso II powdered mesophilic starter culture

Pinch of *Brevibacterium linens* powder

¹/₄ teaspoon calcium chloride diluted in ¹/₄ cup cool nonchlorinated water

2 drops liquid rennet diluted in ¹/₄ cup cool nonchlorinated water

Kosher salt (preferably Diamond Crystal brand)

3 cups Marc de Bourgogne brandy, other similar pomace brandy, or grappa

1. In a nonreactive 10-quart stockpot, heat the milk over low heat to 86°F; this should take about 15 minutes. Turn off the heat.

2. Sprinkle the starter and *B. linens* powder over the milk and let rehydrate for 5 minutes. Mix well using a whisk in an up-and-down motion. Cover and maintain 86°F, allowing the milk to ripen for 30 minutes. Add the calcium chloride and gently whisk in for 1 minute, then add the rennet in the same way. Cover and let the milk ripen for 4 hours at room temperature, until the curds give a clean break.

3. Over low heat, bring the curds back to 86°F. Cut the curds into ¾-inch pieces and let sit for 5 minutes. At this point the curds will be extremely soft.

4. Line two 4-inch Camembert molds with damp cheesecloth and set on a draining rack over a tray. Gently ladle the curds into the molds, cover with the cloth tails, and cover the entire setup with a kitchen towel. Let drain for 24 hours at room temperature, preferably in a warm spot in the kitchen. Once the drained curds have shrunk to half the height of the molds, flip the cheeses over every 2 hours.

5. Remove the cheeses from the molds and cloth. Rub about 1 teaspoon of salt over the entire surface of each cheese. Air-dry at room temperature on a rack for 18 hours, until the surface is dry to the touch.

6. Place the cheeses on a mat in a ripening box and age at 50°F and 90 percent humidity, flipping every 3 days for 6 weeks. Before you flip the cheese the first time, make a brine wash by dissolving 1 teaspoon of salt in ½ cup of boiled water and cooling it to 50°F to 55°F. Each time you flip the cheese, first use a paper towel to wipe any moisture from the surface of the cheese, then wipe the entire surface of the cheese with a small piece of cheesecloth dipped in the brine wash. Discard any unused brine wash. Also use a paper towel to wipe any moisture from the bottom, sides, and lid of the ripening box each time you flip the cheese.

7. After the first week, begin alternating the brine wash with a wash of diluted brandy (50 percent brandy and 50 percent water). Pour a little of the diluted brandy into a small dish, dip a small piece of cheesecloth in it, and rub it over the entire surface of the cheese. Discard any brandy wash left in the dish. At 3 weeks, begin alternating the brine wash with undiluted brandy.

8. Continue washing and flipping the cheese every 3 days for 6 weeks total. The rind will become slightly sticky and very aromatic, and at 10 to 14 days a pale orange color will develop; this will change to the color of the brandy used and deepen as the cheese ages. At 6 weeks, the rind should be moist but not sticky, the center of the cheese should feel very soft, and the paste should be runny. When the cheese is nearing the desired ripeness, transfer it to the traditional wooden cheese box to finish (see headnote). Move the cheese to the refrigerator when fully ripened, and consume within 2 weeks.

MORBIER

MAKES 1¾ pounds
MILK Pasteurized whole cow's milk
START TO FINISH 2 to 4 months: 3 hours to make the cheese; 13 hours to press;
6 hours to brine; 12 hours to dry; 2 to 4 months to age

Morbier was created hundreds of years ago in France's Franche-Comté region to use surplus curds from making hundred-pound wheels of Comté. The leftover curds from the morning milking were topped with a layer of ash from the wood fire to keep a rind from forming and keep pests away until the evening milking. Topped with the evening batch of curds, the curds with their layer of ash were then pressed and left to ripen for a few months. Today's Morbier is typically made from one batch of milk with the curds separated in the middle by a layer of vegetable ash; that's the method being used here. A small amount of *B. linens* powder in a brine solution is used to develop desirable light brownish mold growth on the rind.

2 gallons pasteurized whole cow's milk

¹⁄₄ teaspoon Meso II powdered mesophilic starter culture

Brevibacterium linens powder

¹⁄₂ teaspoon calcium chloride diluted in ¹⁄₄ cup cool nonchlorinated water

¹⁄₂ teaspoon liquid rennet diluted in ¹⁄₄ cup cool nonchlorinated water

¹⁄₈ teaspoon vegetable ash mixed with ¹⁄₈ teaspoon fine sea salt

Kosher salt (preferably Diamond Crystal brand) or cheese salt

1. In a nonreactive 10-quart stockpot, heat the milk over low heat to 90°F; this should take about 20 minutes. Turn off the heat.

2. Sprinkle the starter and a pinch of *B. linens* powder over the milk and let rehydrate for 5 minutes. Mix well using a whisk in an up-and-down motion. Cover and maintain 90°F, allowing the milk to ripen for 1 hour. Add the calcium chloride and gently whisk in for 1 minute, then add the rennet in the same way. Cover and let sit, maintaining 90°F for 30 to 45 minutes, or until the curds give a clean break.

3. Maintaining 90°F, cut the curds into ¾-inch pieces and let sit for 5 minutes. Over very low heat, slowly raise the temperature to 100°F over 30 minutes, stirring a few times. Let the curds settle for about 10 minutes. Using a measuring cup, remove about half of the whey and replace with enough 110°F water so the curds reach 90°F. Gently stir for 5 minutes, then let the curds settle.

4. Line 2 colanders with damp butter muslin, divide the curds between them, and let drain for 20 minutes. Line a draining rack with damp paper towels, extending the towels a few inches beyond the edges of the rack, and place an 8-inch tomme mold on top. Line the mold with damp butter muslin. Transfer the contents of 1 colander of drained curds to the mold and press the curds into the edges with your hands. Wearing disposable gloves, use a fine-mesh strainer to carefully dust the surface of the curds with ash to within ½ inch of the edge. The dampened paper towels should catch any stray ash. Gently add the second batch of curds on top of the ash layer and press into the edges with your hands. Pull up the cloth and smooth out any wrinkles, then cover the curds with the cloth tails and the follower and press at 5 pounds for 1 hour. Remove the cheese from the mold, unwrap, flip, and redress, then press at 8 pounds for 12 hours or overnight.

5. Make 2 quarts of near-saturated brine (see page 24) and chill to 50°F to 55°F. Remove the cheese from the mold and cloth and place in the brine to soak at 50°F to 55°F for 6 hours, flipping at least once during the brining process.

6. Remove the cheese from the brine and pat dry. Place it on a cheese mat and air-dry at room temperature for 12 hours, or until the surface is dry to the touch.

7. Place the cheese on a mat in a ripening box to age at 50°F to 55°F and 85 to 90 percent humidity for 1 week. Flip daily, using a paper towel to wipe away any accumulated moisture in the box each time you flip the cheese.

8. After 1 week, wash the surface with bacterial wash. Twelve hours before this washing, prepare the solution: Boil ½ cup of water and let it cool in a glass jar, then add 1 teaspoon of kosher salt and stir to dissolve. Add a small pinch of *B. linens* powder, cover the jar with the lid, and gently agitate to dissolve. Set aside at room temperature for the bacteria to rehydrate.

9. When ready to wash, pour 1½ tablespoons of the bacterial wash into a small bowl, preserving the rest for another washing. Dip a small piece of cheesecloth into the solution, squeeze out the excess, and rub it over the entire surface of the cheese. Flip the cheese over and return it to the ripening box. Discard any bacterial wash left in the bowl.

10. Two times a week, wash the cheese with a piece of cheesecloth dipped in simple brine (see page 24) or rub the surface of the cheese with a soft brush dipped in brine. Repeat this process twice a week for 2 months, flipping the cheese each time. The rind will become slightly sticky, and at 10 to 14 days a light orange color will develop, deepening to a tan shade as the cheese ages. After 3 weeks, the paste under the surface at the edges of the cheese will begin to feel soft. Continue to wash or brush for 2 months. At 2 months, the rind should be only slightly moist (not sticky) and the cheese should be soft to the touch; it is now ready to eat. Or, wrap the cheese in cheese paper and refrigerate to age for up to 2 more months if desired.

Mixed-Milk Morbier

This version of Morbier, inspired by Carr Valley's Mobay, is made from half cow's milk and half goat's milk, separated by a layer of vegetable ash. The goat's milk layer will be white and the cow's milk layer will be a light yellow. I've chosen to keep the traditional *B. linens* wash on the rind, but you could opt for a natural rind, looking more like a Jack cheese, by washing with a brine solution of ½ cup water to 1 teaspoon salt, cooled to 55°F, rather than the suggested bacteria solution. If you take the natural rind route, age the cheese for 2 months.

Follow the recipe for Morbier, but use 1 gallon each of pasteurized whole cow's milk and goat's milk, heated in separate 6-quart stockpots. Use the same amount of starter culture, *B. linens*, and calcium chloride, divided between the two pots. For the rennet, use ⅝ teaspoon in all, divided into ¼ and ⅜ teaspoons, each diluted in ¼ cup of cool nonchlorinated water. Add the ¼ teaspoon of diluted rennet to the cow's milk and the ⅜ teaspoon of diluted rennet to the goat's milk. Proceed with the recipe as written.

Wood-Fired Morbier

In early times, Morbier was made in a cauldron over an open fire. The soot that accumulated on the pot or cooled wood ash from the fire was used to coat and protect the curds, and the milk became infused by the smoke. The resulting cheese was deliciously smoky. Today, you can emulate this ancient method by heating the milk for your Morbier in a Dutch oven either in a wood-fired oven or over indirect heat on an open campfire or grill.

To heat the milk in a wood-fired oven, you will need two pots: one for the milk and one to heat the water used to replace the whey. Build a four-log fire. Place the milk in a ceramic-coated Dutch oven or heat-resistant clay pot. After 20 minutes of log burning, place both pots, uncovered, on the floor of the oven about 8 inches from the fire. It will take about 15 to 18 minutes for the milk to reach the desired 90°F, and about 12 minutes longer to heat to 100°F. Carry on to finish the cheese as directed in the recipe.

PORT SALUT

MAKES 1¼ pounds
MILK Pasteurized whole cow's milk
START TO FINISH 4 weeks: 2½ hours to make the cheese; about 12 hours to press; 8 hours to brine;
12 hours to dry; 4 weeks to age

Port Salut is a pressed, orange-colored, washed-rind cow's milk cheese with a rich, buttery aroma and smooth, mild paste. It has no discernable rind, but it does have a firm surface. Its was created in the nineteenth century by Trappist monks at an abbey in Entrammes, Brittany, called Notre Dame du Port-du-Salut. The hand-crafted version of Port Salut now produced by the Trappists is called Entrammes.

---

6 quarts pasteurized whole cow's milk

¼ teaspoon Meso II powdered mesophilic starter culture

Brevibacterium linens powder

¼ teaspoon calcium chloride diluted in ¼ cup cool nonchlorinated water

¼ teaspoon liquid rennet diluted in ¼ cup cool nonchlorinated water

Kosher salt (preferably Diamond Crystal brand) or cheese salt

1. In a nonreactive 8-quart stockpot, heat the milk over low heat to 90°F; this should take about 20 minutes. Turn off the heat.

2. Sprinkle the starter and a pinch of *B. linens* powder over the milk and let rehydrate for 5 minutes. Mix well using a whisk in an up-and-down motion. Cover and maintain 90°F, allowing the milk to ripen for 1 hour. Add the calcium chloride and gently whisk in for 1 minute, then add the rennet in the same way. Cover and let sit, maintaining 90°F for 30 to 45 minutes, or until the curds give a clean break.

3. Cut the curds into ½-inch pieces and let sit for 10 minutes. Meanwhile, heat 1 quart of water to 140°F. Ladle off about one-third of the whey and replace with enough 140°F water to bring the temperature to 92°F. Gently stir for 10 minutes, then let the curds settle for 10 minutes. Repeat the process, again removing one-third of the whey and this time adding enough 140°F water to bring the temperature to 98°F. Gently stir for 10 minutes, then let the curds settle for 15 minutes.

4. Line a colander with damp cheesecloth, ladle the curds into it, and let drain for 10 minutes. Line a 5-inch tomme mold with damp cheesecloth and set it on a draining rack. Transfer the drained curds to the lined cheese mold, pressing the curds into the edges with your hand. Pull up the cloth and smooth out any wrinkles, cover the curds with the cloth tails and follower, and press at 5 pounds for 30 minutes. Remove the cheese from the mold, unwrap, flip, and redress, then press at 8 pounds for 12 hours or overnight.

5. Make 2 quarts of saturated brine (see page 24) and chill to 50°F to 55°F. Remove the cheese from the mold and cloth and place in the brine to soak at 50°F to 55°F for 8 hours, flipping at least once during the brining process.

6. Remove the cheese from the brine and pat dry. Place on a cheese mat and air-dry at room temperature for 12 hours. Place the cheese on a mat in a ripening box and age at 50°F to 55°F and 90 to 95 percent humidity, flipping daily for 1 week. Each time you flip the cheese, wipe any moisture from the bottom, sides, and lid of the ripening box with a paper towel.

7. After 1 week, begin washing the surface with bacterial wash. Twelve hours before the first washing, prepare the solution: Boil ½ cup of water and let it cool in a glass jar, then add 1 teaspoon of kosher salt and stir to dissolve. Add a small pinch of *B. linens* powder, cover the jar with the lid, and gently agitate to dissolve. Set aside at room temperature for the bacteria to rehydrate.

8. When ready to wash, pour 1½ tablespoons of the bacterial wash into a small bowl, preserving the rest for another washing. Dip a small piece of cheesecloth into the solution, squeeze out the excess, and rub the entire surface of the cheese. Flip the cheese over and return it to the ripening box. Discard any bacterial wash left in the bowl.

9. Repeat this process every 2 days, flipping the cheese each time. After you have washed the cheese with bacterial wash 4 times, switch to brine (1 teaspoon of salt dissolved in ½ cup of boiled water, cooled to 50°F to 55°F).

10. The rind will become slightly sticky, and at 10 to 14 days a light yellow-orange color will develop; this color will deepen as the cheese ages. Continue to wash and ripen for 4 weeks total. At this point the rind should be moist but not sticky and the center of the cheese should feel somewhat soft. Consume within 2 weeks of desired ripeness.

REBLOCHON

MAKES Two 1-pound cheeses

MILK Pasteurized whole cow's milk with the highest percentage of milk fat you can find

START TO FINISH 2 to 6 weeks: 2½ hours to make the cheese; 12 hours to press; 2 to 6 weeks to age

Reblochon (see photo on page ii) is a renowned cow's milk cheese from the eastern part of Haute-Savoie in France. Reblochon has *B. linens* added to the milk, which allows the brine-washed rind to develop the desired bacteria. Though developed enough at two weeks to consume, its thin, tannish orange rind and delicious oozy paste are at their best at five to six weeks.

2 gallons pasteurized whole cow's milk

¼ teaspoon Meso II powdered mesophilic starter culture

⅛ teaspoon *Brevibacterium linens* powder

¼ teaspoon calcium chloride diluted in ¼ cup cool nonchlorinated water

¼ teaspoon liquid rennet diluted in ¼ cup cool nonchlorinated water

Kosher salt (preferably Diamond Crystal brand) or cheese salt

1.   In a nonreactive 10-quart stockpot, heat the milk over low heat to 85°F; this should take about 15 minutes. Turn off the heat.

2.   Sprinkle the starter and *B. linens* powder over the milk and let rehydrate for 5 minutes. Mix well using a whisk in an up-and-down motion. Cover and maintain 85°F, allowing the milk to ripen for 30 minutes. Add the calcium chloride and gently whisk in for 1 minute, then add the rennet in the same way. Cover and let sit, maintaining 85°F for 30 minutes, or until the curds give a clean break.

3.   Still maintaining 85°F, cut the curds into ½-inch pieces and let sit for 5 minutes. Slowly warm the curds to 95°F over 30 minutes, stirring every 10 minutes, then remove from the heat and let the curds settle.

4.   Ladle out enough whey to expose the curds. Line two 5-inch tomme molds with damp cheesecloth and set them on a draining rack over a tray. Transfer the curds to the molds; you may have to mound them up in the molds, but

they will all fit in after 10 to 15 minutes of draining. Let drain for 15 minutes, then pull up the cloth and smooth out any wrinkles. Cover the curds with the tails of cloth and the followers. Let drain on the rack for 30 minutes, then flip the cheeses, return them to the molds, and replace the followers. Flip every 20 minutes for 2 hours, then press at 5 pounds for 12 hours or overnight.

5.   Remove the cheeses from the molds and cloth. Sprinkle 1 teaspoon of salt on the top and bottom of each cheese. Place the cheeses on a mat in a ripening box and age at 55°F and 90 percent humidity, flipping every other day. Before you turn the cheese the first time, make a brine wash: boil ½ cup of water and let it cool, then add 1 teaspoon of kosher salt and stir to dissolve. Store in the refrigerator. Each time you flip the cheese, wipe the surface with a small piece of cheesecloth dipped in a small amount of brine wash. The brine wash will control unwanted mold growth. Discard any unused brine wash and make a fresh batch each week. Also wipe away any moisture from the bottom, sides, and lid of the ripening box each time you flip the cheese.

6.   Continue flipping and washing the cheese every 2 days for 2 to 6 weeks. At 10 to 14 days, a light yellow-orange color will develop, deepening as the cheese ages. At 4 weeks, the rind should be moist but not sticky and the center of the cheese should feel soft. Wrap the cheese in cheese paper, refrigerate when at the desired ripeness, and consume within 2 weeks of desired ripeness.

TALEGGIO

MAKES One 2-pound cheese or two 1-pound cheeses
MILK Pasteurized whole cow's milk
START TO FINISH 4 to 5 weeks: 2½ hours to make the cheese; 12 hours to drain; 8 hours to brine;
24 hours to dry; 4 to 5 weeks to age

Taleggio is a washed, thin rind cheese that has been made in Lombardy in Italy for over a thousand years. Due to the *B. linens* bacteria that is added to the milk, the exterior ranges from yellow to orange, darkening as it ages, and the cheese emits a strong odor as it ripens. Taleggio is mild and sweet when young, becoming mushroomy and tangy as it ages.

2 gallons pasteurized whole cow's milk
¼ teaspoon Meso II powdered mesophilic starter culture
Pinch of *Brevibacterium linens* powder
¼ teaspoon calcium chloride diluted in ¼ cup cool nonchlorinated water
¼ teaspoon liquid rennet diluted in ¼ cup cool nonchlorinated water
Kosher salt (preferably Diamond Crystal brand) or cheese salt

1. Heat the milk in a nonreactive 10-quart stockpot over low heat to 90°F; this should take 20 minutes. Turn off the heat.

2. Sprinkle the starter and *B. linens* powder over the milk and let rehydrate for 5 minutes. Mix well using a whisk in an up-and-down motion. Cover and maintain 90°F, allowing the milk to ripen for 1 hour. Add the calcium chloride and gently whisk in for 1 minute, then add the rennet in the same way. Cover and let sit, maintaining 90°F for 30 minutes, or until the curds give a clean break.

3. Still maintaining 90°F, cut the curds into ¾-inch pieces and let sit for 5 minutes. Gently stir the curds for 30 minutes, removing 2 cups of whey every 10 minutes. Then, let the curds rest undisturbed for 10 minutes.

4. Line one 7-inch square Taleggio mold or two 4-inch square bottomless cheese molds with damp cheesecloth and set on a draining rack over a tray. Gently ladle the curds into the molds, pressing them into the edges with your hand. Cover with the tails of cloth and cover the entire setup with a kitchen towel. Let drain for 12 hours at room temperature, preferably in a warm spot in the kitchen. Every 2 hours, remove the cheese from the mold, unwrap, flip, and redress.

5. Make 3 quarts of saturated brine (see page 24) and chill to 50°F to 55°F. Remove the cheese from the mold and cloth and place in the brine to soak at 50°F to 55°F for 8 hours, flipping at least once during the brining process.

6. Remove the cheese from the brine and pat dry. Air-dry at room temperature on a cheese mat for 24 hours, or until the surface is dry to the touch. Place on a mat in a ripening box to age at 50°F and 90 percent humidity, flipping every other day. Before you flip the cheese the first time, make a brine wash: boil ½ cup of water and let it cool, then add 1 teaspoon of kosher salt and stir to dissolve. Store in the refrigerator. Each time you flip the cheese, wipe the surface with a small piece of cheesecloth dipped in a small amount of brine wash. The brine wash will control unwanted mold growth. Discard any unused brine wash and make a fresh batch each week. Also wipe away any moisture from the bottom, sides, and lid of the ripening box each time you flip the cheese.

7. Flip and wash the cheese every 2 days for 4 to 5 weeks. At 10 to 14 days, a light yellow-orange color will develop, deepening as the cheese ages. At 4 to 5 weeks, the rind should be moist but not sticky and the center of the cheese should feel soft. Consume within 2 weeks of desired ripeness.

Blue Cheeses

Some of the most widely recognized old-world cheeses fall in the blue family, including Italian Gorgonzola, French Roquefort, English Stilton, Spanish Cabrales, Irish Cashel Blue, and German Cambozola. Blues are made from cow's, goat's, or sheep's milk or combinations thereof, resulting in a variety of flavor profiles from mellow and sweet to assertive and pungent. The textures vary too, from creamy to crumbly, and shapes range from dense wheels to delicate bloomy logs. It's been said that blue-veined cheeses were born centuries ago, probably resulting from mistakes made when making other cheeses: defects and cracks in the rind would have allowed oxygen into the interior of the cheese, activating molds that had found a place to reside and grow.

The distinctive flavors and blue, green, or grayish veins come from *Penicillium roqueforti* or *Penicillium glaucum* molds; depending on the style of cheese, there may be *Geotrichum* mold added as well. Traditionally, the *Penicillium* mold was grown on rye bread and harvested, and the mold spores were added to the cheese making milk. Now most cheese makers use commercially available molds in powdered form, which are typically added to the milk along with starter cultures.

Many blues are pressed, then pierced to create pathways in which the mold will grow. Some have the *P. roqueforti* mold layered in while the curds are draining; others develop blue rinds; and still others have a kiss of the characteristic blue spiciness in the paste with no signs of blue color. Generally, the more veining—and therefore more blue mold development—the sharper the cheese's flavors, though of course the milks used also have a large influence on the flavor profile. Depending on style, many of the blues ripen at 50°F to 55°F and 85 percent humidity. They typically take four to twelve weeks to ripen and up to a year or more to age.

Today there are many blues being made in a variety of styles, including Jasper Hill Farm Bayley Hazen Blue, Marin French Le Petit Bleu, Mozzarella Company Deep Ellum Blue, Point Reyes Original Blue, Rogue Smokey Blue and Oregonzola, Roth Käse Buttermilk Blue, and Westfield Farm goat's milk Classic Blue Log.

BLOOMY BLUE LOG CHÈVRE

MAKES Two 6-ounce logs
MILK Pasteurized goat's milk
START TO FINISH 4 weeks: 30 minutes to make the cheese;
18 hours to ripen; 24 hours to drain; 4 weeks to age

Inspired by Saint-Maure, Valençay, and a few of my favorite American bloomy goat cheeses, this mild-flavored blue log has just a hint of *P. roqueforti* mold added for the perfect balance with the tangy goat flavor. This cheese can also be made in a round like a Camembert or in a pyramid like a Valençay.

....

1 gallon pasteurized goat's milk
1/4 teaspoon Aroma B powdered mesophilic starter culture
1/8 teaspoon *Penicillium candidum* mold powder
Pinch of *Geotrichum candidum* 15 mold powder
Pinch of *Penicillium roqueforti* mold powder
1/4 teaspoon calcium chloride diluted in 1/4 cup cool nonchlorinated water
1/4 teaspoon liquid rennet diluted in 1/4 cup cool nonchlorinated water
1 tablespoon fine sea salt
1 1/2 tablespoons vegetable ash

1. Heat the milk in a nonreactive 6-quart stockpot over low heat to 72°F; this should take 10 minutes. Turn off the heat.

2. Sprinkle the starter and mold powders over the milk and let rehydrate for 5 minutes. Mix well using a whisk in an up-and-down motion. Add the calcium chloride and gently whisk in for 1 minute, then add the rennet in the same way. Cover and let sit, maintaining 72°F for 18 hours, or until the curds form a firm mass and the whey is floating on the top.

3. Place 2 Camembert or other round, straight-sided molds on a mat on a draining rack over a tray, and steady 2 cylindrical Saint-Maure molds inside them.

4. With a ladle or skimmer, gently cut 1/2-inch-thick slices of curds and layer them in the cylindrical molds to fill. Let drain until more curds can be added to the molds. Do not be tempted to add another mold; the curds will compress as the whey drains out, making room for all of the curds.

5. Cover the molds, rack, and tray with a kitchen towel and let the cheeses drain for 24 hours at room temperature. Remove any accumulated whey a few times while draining, wiping out the tray when you do so. Flip the cheeses after 6 hours, or when they are firm enough to handle, then flip them a few more times during the 24 hours. At the end of 24 hours, the curds will have reduced to about half the height of the molds.

6. Once the cheeses have stopped draining and the curds have compressed to below the halfway point of the molds, remove the molds and sprinkle 2 teaspoons of the salt over the entire surface of each cheese. Set on the rack for 10 minutes to allow the salt to dissolve.

(continued)

Bloomy Blue Log Chèvre at 3 weeks

7.   In a small bowl or jar, combine the vegetable ash with the remaining 1 teaspoon of salt. Wearing disposable gloves, use a fine-mesh strainer to lightly dust the cheeses with vegetable ash, coating them completely. Gently pat the ash onto the surface of the cheeses. Place the dusted cheeses at least 1 inch apart on a clean cheese mat in a ripening box. Cover the box loosely with the lid and let stand at room temperature for 24 hours. Let drain and wipe out any moisture from the box, then ripen the cheese at 50°F to 55°F and 90 percent humidity for 2 weeks. For the first few days, adjust the lid to be slightly open for a portion of each day to maintain the desired humidity level. The surface of the cheese should appear moist but not wet.

8.   Flip the cheeses one-quarter turn daily to maintain their log shape. After about 5 days, the first signs of white fuzzy mold will appear. After 10 to 14 days, the cheeses will be fully coated in white mold. After 3 weeks, some of the dark ash will appear through the white mold. Left a bit longer, more dark ash will appear. After a total of 4 weeks from the start of ripening, wrap in cheese paper and store in the refrigerator. It is best to consume this cheese when it reaches your desired ripeness.

BLUE GOUDA

MAKES 1½ pounds
MILK Pasteurized whole cow's milk
ALTERNATIVE MILKS Blend of raw or pasteurized cow's and goat's milks;
raw or pasteurized sheep's milk
START TO FINISH 6 weeks to 4 months: 1½ hours to make the cheese; 6½ hours to press; 8 hours to brine;
1 to 2 days to dry; 6 weeks to 4 months to age

Gouda is the hallmark cheese of Holland. The plain version (page 94) is perfectly yummy, but blue is even better. This creamy cheese is true to the Gouda style but lightly blue, without any piercing veins. Though this cheese would typically be made with all cow's milk, a fifty-fifty blend of cow's and goat's milks is wonderful. The process of cooking the curds gives the cheese a smooth, elastic paste, and the cheese is waxed so it can be aged without the need to monitor its progress.

2 gallons pasteurized whole cow's milk

¼ teaspoon Meso II powdered mesophilic starter culture

⅛ teaspoon *Penicillium candidum* mold powder

½ teaspoon calcium chloride diluted in ¼ cup cool nonchlorinated water (omit if using raw milk)

½ teaspoon liquid rennet diluted in ¼ cup cool nonchlorinated water

Kosher salt (preferably Diamond Crystal brand) or cheese salt

1. In a nonreactive 10-quart stockpot, heat the milk over low heat to 86°F; this should take 15 to 18 minutes. Turn off the heat.

2. Sprinkle the starter and mold powder over the milk and let rehydrate for 5 minutes. Mix in well using a whisk in an up-and-down motion. Cover and maintain 86°F, allowing the milk to ripen for 45 minutes. Add the calcium chloride and gently whisk in for 1 minute, then add the rennet in the same way. Cover and let sit, maintaining 86°F for 30 to 45 minutes, or until the curds give a clean break.

3. Still maintaining 86°F, cut the curds into ½-inch pieces and let sit for 5 minutes. Then stir for 5 minutes and let stand for 5 minutes. Heat 2 quarts of water to 140°F and maintain that heat. When the curds sink to the bottom of the pot, ladle off 2 cups of the whey, then add enough 140°F water to bring the curds to 92°F. Gently stir for 10 minutes, then let the curds settle. Ladle off enough whey to expose the tops of the curds, then add enough 140°F water to bring the curds to 98°F. Gently stir for 20 minutes, or until the curds have shrunk to the size of small beans. Let the curds settle for 10 minutes; they will knit together in the bottom of the pot.

4. Warm a colander with hot water, then drain off the whey and place the knitted curds in the colander. Let drain for 5 minutes. Line a 5-inch tomme mold with damp cheesecloth and set it on a draining rack over a tray. Using your hands, break off 1-inch chunks of curd and distribute into the mold. Lightly press them into place to fill the gaps. Pull the cloth up tight and smooth, cover the curds with the cloth tails and the follower, and press at 15 pounds for 30 minutes.

5. Remove the cheese from the mold, unwrap, flip, and redress, then press at 10 pounds for 6 hours.

6. Make 1 gallon of saturated brine (see page 24) and chill to 50°F to 55°F. Remove the cheese from the mold and cloth and place it in the brine to soak at 50°F to 55°F for 8 hours, flipping it once during the brining.

7. Remove the cheese from the brine and pat dry. Place on a rack and air-dry at room temperature for 1 to 2 days, or until the surface is dry to the touch.

8. Place on a mat in a ripening box, cover loosely, and age at 50°F to 55°F and 85 percent humidity for 1 week, flipping daily. Remove any unwanted mold with a small piece of cheesecloth dampened in a vinegar-salt solution (see page 25).

9. Coat with wax (see page 28) and store at 50°F to 55°F and 75 percent humidity for at least 6 weeks and up to 4 months. The cheese will be ready to eat at 6 weeks.

BUTTERMILK BLUE

MAKES 10 ounces
MILKS Pasteurized whole cow's milk, cultured buttermilk, heavy cream
START TO FINISH 6 weeks to 3 months: 2 hours to make the cheese; 13 hours to drain and ripen;
6 weeks to 3 months or longer to age

Inspired by the popular, award-winning Buttermilk Blue from Roth Käse in Wisconsin, this tangy yet creamy blue is made with a blend of whole milk, buttermilk, and heavy cream. The buttermilk adds acidity, and its cultures contribute to the cheese's piquant flavor. This pierced cheese is formed without pressing, allowing the curds to drain and compact onto themselves.

2 quarts pasteurized whole cow's milk

1 quart cultured buttermilk, homemade (see page 44) or store-bought

2 cups heavy cream

¼ teaspoon MM 100 powdered mesophilic starter culture

Penicillium roqueforti mold powder

¼ teaspoon calcium chloride diluted in ¼ cup cool nonchlorinated water

½ teaspoon liquid rennet diluted in ¼ cup cool nonchlorinated water

1½ teaspoons kosher salt (preferably Diamond Crystal brand), cheese salt, or fine flake sea salt

1. In a 6-quart stockpot over low heat, heat the milk, buttermilk, and cream to 90°F; this should take about 20 minutes. Turn off the heat.

2. Sprinkle the starter and a pinch of the mold powder over the milk and let rehydrate for 5 minutes. Mix in well using a whisk in an up-and-down motion. Add the calcium chloride and gently whisk in, then add the rennet in the same way. Cover and maintain 90°F for 1½ hours, or until the curds give a clean break.

3. Still maintaining 90°F, cut the curds into 1-inch pieces and let sit for 10 minutes. Then gently stir for 10 minutes to shrink the curds slightly and firm them up. Let stand for another 15 minutes, or until the curds sink to the bottom. Ladle off enough whey to expose the curds.

4. Line a colander with damp butter muslin and gently ladle the curds into it. Let drain for 10 minutes. Tie the corners of the cloth together to form a draining sack and hang for 15 to 20 minutes, or until the whey stops draining.

5. Line a 4-inch Camembert mold with damp butter muslin and place it on a rack over a tray. Gently ladle the curds into the mold, filling it to one-fourth its height and pressing down slightly with your hand to fill the gaps. Measure out ⅛ teaspoon of *P. roqueforti* powder. Lightly sprinkle the curds with one-third of the mold powder, then add more curds to fill the mold halfway, again gently pressing to fill the gaps and sprinkling another one-third of the mold powder over the curds. Repeat to fill the mold with two more layers of curds and one of mold powder; the curds should come up to about 1 inch from the top of the mold. Pull the cloth up tight and smooth and cover the curds with the cloth tails. Let the cheese drain for 4 hours at room temperature, then unwrap, flip, redress, and let drain for 4 more hours.

6. Carefully remove the cheese from the mold, unwrap, and sprinkle one side with ¾ teaspoon of the salt. Flip the cheese and place the cheese mold over it. The cheese will be fairly fragile, so handle it gently. Place it on a mat in a ripening box and sprinkle the remaining ¾ teaspoon of salt on the top.

7. Let drain for 5 hours, then remove the mold. Put the cheese in a ripening box, cover loosely with the lid, and age at 54°F and 75 percent humidity for up to 1 week, or until the whey stops draining. Flip the cheese daily, draining off any whey that may have accumulated in the ripening box and using a paper towel to wipe any moisture from the bottom, sides, and lid of the box.

8. Once the whey has stopped draining, use a sterilized knitting needle or round skewer to pierce the cheese all the way through to the other side, four times horizontally and four times vertically. These air passages will encourage mold growth.

9. Secure the lid of the ripening box and ripen at 50°F and 85 to 90 percent humidity. Blue mold should appear on the exterior after 10 days. Watch the cheese carefully, flipping it daily and adjusting the lid if the humidity increases and too much moisture develops.

10. Over the next 2 weeks, pierce the cheese one or two more times in the same locations to ensure proper aeration and blue vein development. If any excessive or undesirable mold appears on the exterior of the cheese, rub it off with a small piece of cheesecloth dipped in a vinegar-salt solution.

11. Ripen for 6 weeks, rub off any excess mold with dry cheesecloth, then wrap the cheese in foil and store refrigerated for up to 3 more months or longer for a more pronounced flavor.

Buttermilk Blue at 4 weeks

CAMBOZOLA

MAKES Two 10-ounce cheeses
MILKS Pasteurized whole cow's milk, pasteurized heavy cream
START TO FINISH 4 to 6 weeks: 2 hours to make the cheese; 8 hours to drain; 4 to 6 weeks to age

Cambozola is a bloomy-rind blue that was developed less than fifty years ago by the Champignon Company in Germany as a blend of two classics: Camembert and Gorgonzola. Made with whole cow's milk and a fair amount of cream, this version has the blended milks inoculated with the blue *P. roqueforti* mold rather than being injected with it as in the original. Cambozola is one of the more popular styles of blue cheese due to its pleasing bloomy characteristics, hint of blue, and rich mouthfeel.

1/2 gallon pasteurized whole cow's milk

1/2 gallon pasteurized heavy cream

1/4 teaspoon Meso II or C101 powdered mesophilic starter culture

1/8 teaspoon *Penicillium candidum* mold powder

1/4 teaspoon calcium chloride diluted in 1/4 cup cool nonchlorinated water

1/4 teaspoon liquid rennet diluted in 1/4 cup cool nonchlorinated water

1/8 teaspoon *Penicillium roqueforti* mold powder

4 teaspoons kosher salt (preferably Diamond Crystal brand), cheese salt, or fine flake sea salt

1. Combine the milk and cream in a nonreactive 6-quart stockpot set in a 96°F water bath over low heat and gently warm to 86°F; this should take about 10 minutes. Turn off the heat.

2. Sprinkle the starter and *P. candidum* mold powder over the milk and let rehydrate for 5 minutes. Mix in well using a whisk in an up-and-down motion. Cover and maintain 86°F, allowing the milk to ripen for 30 minutes. Add the calcium chloride and gently whisk in, then add the rennet in the same way. Cover and let sit, maintaining 86°F for 1½ hours, or until the curds give a clean break.

3. Cut the curds into ½-inch pieces and gently stir for 5 minutes. Let the curds rest for 5 minutes.

4. Line a colander with damp cheesecloth and gently ladle the curds into it. Let drain for 20 minutes.

5. Line 2 Saint-Maure molds with damp cheesecloth and set them on a draining rack over a tray. Using a skimmer, gently ladle the curds into the molds until half full. Sprinkle the top of each cheese with half of the *P. roqueforti* mold powder, then top off each mold with the remaining curds. Let drain for 6 hours at room temperature, draining off and wiping out any whey that collects. Remove any accumulated whey a few times during draining, wiping out the tray when you do so. When the cheeses are firm enough to handle (after about 8 hours), unmold and unwrap them and discard the cheesecloth, then flip them and return them to the unlined molds. Unmold and flip one more time while the cheeses are draining. The cheeses should drain for 8 to 10 hours total.

6. Once the cheeses have stopped draining, remove them from the molds and place on a clean mat set in a clean, dry ripening box. Sprinkle 2 teaspoons of the salt over the tops of the cheeses and wait 5 minutes for the salt to dissolve. Flip the cheeses over and sprinkle the tops with the remaining 2 teaspoons of salt. Cover the box loosely with its lid. Ripen at 50°F to 55°F and 90 percent humidity. High humidity is essential for making this cheese. Flip the cheeses daily, wiping away any whey that accumulates in the ripening box. When the cheeses are dry on the surface (after about 3 days), cover the box tightly to continue ripening.

7. Continue to flip the cheeses daily and remove any moisture in the box. After about 5 days, the first signs of white fuzzy mold will appear. When the cheeses are fully coated in white mold (after about 8 days), aerate the center of each cheese by piercing horizontally from the sides through the center to the other side using a sterilized knitting needle or skewer. There should be 8 to 10 piercings through each cheese to allow proper development of blue veins. Pierce again in the same places if any holes close up over the next 10 to 12 days.

8. Wrap in cheese paper 10 to 12 days after piercing and return to the ripening box. The cheese will begin to soften within 1 week or so. After a total of 4 weeks from the start of ripening, the cheese should be ready to eat, or continue to ripen to 6 weeks in the refrigerator.

COASTAL BLUE

MAKES Two 1-pound cheeses
MILK Pasteurized whole cow's milk
START TO FINISH 6 weeks to 6 months: 3 hours to make the cheese;
12 hours to drain; 6 weeks to 6 months to age

This blue cheese recipe is from the Giacomini family, owners of Point Reyes Farmstead Cheese Company, and Kuba Hemmerling, the company's exceptionally skilled cheese maker. Fashioned after their cornerstone Original Blue, it is an everyday-style homemade blue cheese.

2 gallons pasteurized whole cow's milk

½ teaspoon MM 100 powdered mesophilic starter culture

⅛ teaspoon *Penicillium roqueforti* mold powder

¼ teaspoon calcium chloride diluted in ¼ cup cool nonchlorinated water

¼ teaspoon liquid rennet diluted in ¼ cup cool nonchlorinated water

1½ teaspoons coarse kosher salt (preferably Diamond Crystal brand)

1. In a nonreactive 10-quart stockpot set in a 96°F water bath over low heat, gently warm the milk to 86°F; this should take about 10 minutes. Turn off the heat.

2. Sprinkle the starter and the mold powder over the milk and let rehydrate for 5 minutes. Mix well using a whisk in an up-and-down motion. Cover and maintain 86°F, letting the milk ripen for 1 hour, stirring every once in a while. Add the calcium chloride and gently whisk in, then add the rennet in the same way. Cover and let sit, maintaining 86°F for 1 to 1½ hours, or until the curds give a clean break.

3. Cut the curds into ½-inch pieces and gently stir for 10 minutes, then let the curds settle to the bottom of the pot. Ladle out 2 quarts of whey and stir the curds for 5 more minutes.

4. Line a colander or strainer with damp butter muslin and gently ladle the curds into it. Let drain for 5 minutes. Line two 4-inch Camembert molds with damp cheesecloth and set them on a draining rack over a tray. Ladle the curds into the molds, pull the cloth up around the curds and cover the top with the tails of the cloth, and let drain for 12 hours at room temperature. Flip the cheeses at least four times to ensure a uniform shape and appearance.

5. Remove the cheeses from the molds and sprinkle the salt over them, coating them evenly. Set the cheeses on a mat in a ripening box and age at 68°F to 72°F and 90 percent humidity. Set the lid ajar a little so there is some air movement. Flip the cheeses daily, wiping away any excess moisture from the box with a paper towel.

6. After 2 days, use a sterilized knitting needle or round skewer to pierce each cheese all the way through to the other side, 4 times horizontally and 4 times vertically. These air passages will encourage mold growth.

7. Place the cheeses back in the box and ripen at 50°F to 56°F and 85 percent humidity for 6 to 8 weeks. Flip the cheeses daily, wiping away any excess moisture from the box with a paper towel. Remove any undesirable mold with a piece of cheesecloth dipped in a vinegar-salt solution.

8. Ripen the cheeses for 6 to 8 weeks. After sufficient blue mold growth is achieved, wrap them in cheese paper and refrigerate for up to 4 to 6 months.

Profile: Point Reyes Farmstead Cheese Company

Northern California's Point Reyes Farmstead Cheese Company is the home of Original Blue cheese, the unique artisan blue cheese that brought the company to prominence in the marketplace in the late 1990s. The Giacomini family's certified organic dairy is the source of all of the milk that goes into their cheeses, thus all of their cheeses are designated as farmstead. In the fifty years since they began making farmstead products, the family (now mother, father, and four daughters) have all been involved in running the business every day, keeping a watchful eye on the quality of the cheese and the marketing of their brand, and now venturing "beyond blue," into other handmade European-style cheeses that reflect the flavors of the region.

GORGONZOLA

MAKES 1½ pounds
MILK Pasteurized whole cow's milk
START TO FINISH 3½ to 5½ months: 3 hours to make the cheese; 14 hours to drain; 8 hours to press;
4 days to salt and drain; 3½ to 5½ months to age

The most famous and possibly the oldest among the Italian blue cheeses, Gorgonzola is a cow's milk cheese named for the town in Lombardy where it is said to have originated. Though it's no longer made in Gorgonzola, it has DOC status in specific areas of Lombardy and Piedmont. Younger varieties are identified as Gorgonzola dolce, while cheeses aged closer to six months are known as Gorgonzola piccante. As with many other blues, Gorgonzola has *Penicillium roqueforti* mold sprinkled in between the layers of curds, and it is then pierced to develop the characteristic blue-green mold veins. Traditionally it was made from evening milk and morning milk (that is, milk from each of the two daily milkings) and molded by alternating layers of curds from the two batches. Both the contrast in bacteria development between the two batches and the ripening procedure contribute to Gorgonzola's unique aromatics and flavors. This formula replicates the tradition by making two batches of curds from the same milk—one drained and ripened overnight and one made the next morning— which are then alternately layered in the cheese molds. You can also accomplish an interesting two-batch contrast by using store-bought pasteurized milk for one batch of curds and raw (then home-pasteurized) milk for the other.

6 quarts pasteurized whole cow's milk
¼ teaspoon MM 100 powdered mesophilic starter
    culture
¼ teaspoon calcium chloride diluted in ¼ cup cool
    nonchlorinated water
½ teaspoon liquid rennet diluted in ¼ cup cool
    nonchlorinated water
⅛ teaspoon *Penicillium roqueforti* mold powder
Kosher salt (preferably Diamond Crystal brand) or
    fine flake sea salt

1. In a nonreactive 4-quart stockpot set in a 100°F water bath, gently warm 3 quarts of the milk to 90°F; this should take about 15 minutes. Turn off the heat.

2. Sprinkle half of the starter over the milk and let it rehydrate for 5 minutes. Mix in well using a whisk in an up-and-down motion. Cover and maintain 90°F, letting the milk ripen for 30 minutes. Add half of the calcium chloride and gently whisk in, then add half of the rennet in the same way. Cover and let sit, maintaining 90°F for 30 minutes, or until the curds give a clean break.

3. Cut the curds into ¾-inch pieces and let rest for 10 minutes, then gently stir for 20 minutes to firm up the curds slightly. Let rest for another 15 minutes, or until the curds sink to the bottom.

4. Ladle out enough whey to expose the curds. Line a colander with damp cheesecloth and gently ladle the curds into it. Let drain for 5 minutes. Tie the corners of the cheesecloth together to form a draining sack and hang at 55°F to let drain for 8 hours or overnight.

5. The next morning, make a second batch of curds in the same manner, using the other half of the milk, starter, calcium chloride, and rennet. Let the curds drain at 55°F for 6 hours. Before the second batch is done draining, bring the first batch to room temperature.

6. Untie the sacks and, keeping the batches separate, break the curds into 1-inch chunks. Line a 4-inch Camembert mold with damp cheesecloth and place it on a draining rack. Using your hands, line the bottom and sides of the mold with a thin layer of the second batch of curds. Press down

slightly to fill the gaps. Layer half of the curds from the first batch in the mold and gently press down to fill the gaps. Sprinkle the top with one-third of the *P. roqueforti* mold powder, then repeat the process two more times until the mold is filled with four layers of curds, alternating first-batch and second-batch curds and finishing with second-batch curds. The mold should be filled to about 1 inch from the top.

7. Pull the cheesecloth up around the curds and cover the top with the tails of the cloth and the follower. Press at 5 pounds for 2 hours, then unmold, unwrap, flip, and redress. Press at 8 pounds for 2 hours. Press at 8 pounds for 6 more hours, unwrapping, flipping, and redressing every 2 hours.

8. Carefully remove the cheese from the mold, unwrap, and sprinkle one side with ¾ teaspoon of salt. Flip the cheese over and place the cheese mold over it. The cheese will be fairly fragile, so handle it gently. Place it on a mat in a ripening box and sprinkle ¾ teaspoon of salt over the top. Let drain for 5 hours, then flip the cheese again. Repeat this process once a day for 3 more days, sprinkling a pinch of salt on each side the first time you flip it each day, then draining for 5 hours and flipping once again. Each time you flip the cheese, drain any accumulated whey and wipe the box dry with a paper towel.

9. After the 4 days of salting, flipping, and draining, remove the mold and cover the ripening box loosely with the lid. Age at 50°F and 75 percent humidity for up to 2 weeks, or until the whey stops draining. Flip the cheese daily, removing any whey that accumulates in the ripening box and wiping any moisture from the sides of the box.

10. Once the whey has stopped draining, use a sterilized knitting needle or round skewer to pierce the cheese all the way through to the other side, 4 times horizontally and 4 times vertically. These air passages will encourage mold growth.

Smoked Brandy-Pecan Gorgonzola

To make a leaf-wrapped Gorzonzola with layers of flavor, cover 4 to 5 pecan leaves with ½ cup of brandy and place in a resealable bag; refrigerate at least overnight or until ready to use. Once the cheese has ripened for 1 month, wrap it in enough macerated leaves to completely encase the cheese. Ripen at 50°F to 55°F and 85 to 90 percent humidity for 2 weeks, flipping daily. Bring the cheese to room temperature, wipe it dry, and cold smoke it for 4 hours (see page 27). Allow to rest for 2 hours, then wrap in plastic wrap or vacuum-seal and refrigerate. Consume within 3 weeks.

11. Secure the lid of the ripening box and ripen at 50°F and 85 to 90 percent humidity. Blue mold should appear on the exterior after 10 days. Watch the cheese carefully, turning it daily and adjusting the lid if the humidity increases and too much moisture develops. Remove any unwanted mold with a piece of cheesecloth dipped in a vinegar-salt solution (see page 25).

12. Over the 2 weeks after the initial piercing, pierce the cheese one or two more times in the same locations to ensure proper aeration and blue vein development.

13. Ripen for 2 months, then wrap the cheese in foil and store refrigerated for 1 to 3 more months.

ROQUEFORT

MAKES 1 pound
MILKS Raw or pasteurized whole cow's milk, heavy cream
ALTERNATIVE MILK Raw or pasteurized sheep's milk
START TO FINISH 6 weeks to 6 months: 3 hours to make the cheese; 24 hours to drain;
6 weeks to 6 months to age

Roquefort, the famous blue-veined cheese originating in the village of Roquefort in southern France, is traditionally made with sheep's milk and aged in the region's limestone caves. The high fat content of sheep's milk results in cheeses with a supremely creamy texture and unique, rich flavor. This recipe uses equal amounts of whole cow's milk and heavy cream to best emulate the fatty richness of sheep's milk; you may add a small amount of lipase powder to bring the flavor closer to the piquant profile of the original. Age this cheese in your cellar or barn or another cool, dark place.

2 quarts pasteurized whole cow's milk

2 quarts heavy cream

1/8 teaspoon MA 4001 powdered mesophilic starter culture

1/8 teaspoon mild lipase powder diluted in 1/4 cup cool nonchlorinated water 20 minutes before using (optional)

1/4 teaspoon calcium chloride diluted in 1/4 cup cool nonchlorinated water (omit if using raw milk)

1/2 teaspoon liquid rennet diluted in 1/4 cup cool nonchlorinated water

1/8 teaspoon *Penicillium roqueforti* mold powder

1 1/2 teaspoons kosher salt (preferably Diamond Crystal brand) or fine flake sea salt

1. In a nonreactive 6-quart stockpot set in a 100°F water bath, combine the milk and cream and gently warm to 90°F; this should take about 15 minutes. Turn off the heat.

2. Sprinkle the starter over the milk and let rehydrate for 5 minutes. Mix well using a whisk in an up-and-down motion. Add the lipase, if using, and gently whisk in, then gently whisk in the calcium chloride and then the rennet. Cover and let sit, maintaining 90°F for 2 hours, or until the curds give a clean break.

3. Cut the curds into 1-inch pieces and let rest for 15 minutes, then gently stir to firm up the curds slightly. Let rest for another 15 minutes, or until the curds sink to the bottom.

4. Ladle out enough whey to expose the curds. Line a colander with damp cheesecloth and gently ladle the curds into it. Let drain for 10 minutes. Tie the corners of the cheesecloth together to form a draining sack and hang at room temperature to let drain for 30 minutes, or until the whey stops dripping. Set a 4-inch Camembert mold on a draining rack and line it with damp cheesecloth. Using your hands, layer one-fourth of the curds into the mold. Gently press down to fill in the gaps. Sprinkle the top of the curds with one-third of the *P. roqueforti* mold powder, then repeat the process until the mold is filled, finishing with a layer of curds. The mold should be filled to about 1 inch from the top.

5. Let drain at room temperature for 8 hours. Once the curds have firmed enough to handle, after about 4 hours of draining, flip the cheese a time or two, keeping it in its cheesecloth. After 8 hours, remove the cheese from the mold, unwrap, flip, and redress, then let drain for 16 hours at room temperature.

6. After 24 hours of draining, carefully remove the cheese from the mold, sprinkle one side with ¾ teaspoon of the salt, then flip it over and place it on a mat in a ripening box. Sprinkle the remaining ¾ teaspoon of salt over the top. The cheese will be fairly fragile at this point, so handle it gently.

7. Cover the box loosely and ripen the cheese at 50°F to 55°F and 85 to 90 percent humidity. Flip the cheese daily for 1 week, draining any accumulated liquid in the ripening box and using a paper towel to wipe any moisture from the box.

8. After 1 week, use a sterilized knitting needle or round skewer to pierce the cheese all the way through to the other side 4 times horizontally and 4 times vertically. These passages will encourage mold growth. Continue to ripen at 50°F to 55°F and 85 to 90 percent humidity. Blue mold should appear on the exterior after 10 days.

9. Once the cheese has stopped draining whey, secure the box's lid to control the humidity. Flip the cheese daily and adjust the lid if the humidity increases and too much moisture develops. Over the 2 weeks after the intial piercing, pierce one or two more times in the same locations to ensure proper aeration and blue vein development. Remove any excessive or unwanted mold with a piece of cheesecloth dipped in a vinegar-salt solution (see page 25).

10. Ripen the cheese for 6 to 8 weeks. When it reaches the desired creamy texture, wrap it in foil and store it, refrigerated, for up to 4 more months.

Roquefort at 4 weeks

STILTON

MAKES 1 pound
MILKS Pasteurized whole cow's milk, heavy cream
START TO FINISH 4 to 6 months: 2 hours to make the cheese; 8 hours to press;
4 days to drain; 4 to 6 months to age

Stilton is probably the best-known blue cheese in the world, having been produced in England since the 1700s. Enriched with cream, it is drier than most other blues and as a result has a slightly flaky texture. Though today it is pierced multiple times about one month into the ripening process to produce blue veining, traditionally the growth of the blue mold happened as a result of the layering process, when slabs of curds formed crevices to encourage this growth. The traditional method is employed here.

1 gallon pasteurized whole cow's milk

1 cup heavy cream

Penicillium roqueforti mold powder

1/4 teaspoon C101 or Meso II powdered mesophilic starter culture

1/4 teaspoon calcium chloride diluted in 1/4 cup cool nonchlorinated water

1/4 teaspoon liquid rennet diluted in 1/4 cup cool nonchlorinated water

4 teaspoons kosher salt (preferably Diamond Crystal brand) or fine flake sea salt

1. In a nonreactive 6-quart stockpot, heat the milk and cream over low heat to 86°F; this should take about 15 minutes. Turn off the heat.

2. Sprinkle 1/8 teaspoon of the mold powder and the starter over the milk and let rehydrate for 5 minutes. Mix well using a whisk in an up-and-down motion. Cover and maintain 86°F, allowing the milk to ripen for 30 minutes. Add the calcium chloride and gently whisk in, then add the rennet in the same way. Cover and let sit, maintaining 86°F for 1½ hours, or until the curds give a clean break.

3. Using a skimmer, slice the curds into ½-inch-thick slabs. Line a colander with damp cheesecloth and set it over a bowl about the same size as the colander. Transfer the curd slices to the colander; the curds should be sitting in the whey caught in the bowl. Cover the colander, maintain

86°F, and let the curds drain for 1½ hours. Then tie the corners of the cheesecloth together to form a draining sack and hang to let drain at room temperature for 30 minutes, or until the whey stops dripping.

4. Set the sack on a cutting board, open the cheesecloth, and gently press down on the curds, forming them into a brick shape. Redress the curds in the same cheesecloth and place on a draining rack. Press them at 8 pounds for 8 hours or overnight at room temperature.

5. Remove the curds from the cheesecloth and break them into approximately 1-inch pieces. Place the curds in a bowl, add the salt, and gently toss to combine.

6. Line a 4½-inch-diameter round cheese mold with damp cheesecloth and set it on a draining rack. Layer half of the curds into the mold. Sprinkle the top with a pinch of *P. roqueforti* mold powder, then layer the remaining curds in the mold. Fold the tails of the cloth over the curds, set the follower in place, and let drain at room temperature for 4 days. Flip every 20 minutes for the first 2 hours, every 2 hours for the next 6 hours, and once a day for the next 4 days. Remove any accumulated whey each time you flip the cheese.

7. After the 4 days of draining, remove the cheese from the mold and cloth and place it on a clean mat in a dry ripening

Stilton at 4 weeks

box. Cover the box loosely with the lid and ripen the cheese at 50°F to 55°F and 85 to 90 percent humidity. High humidity is essential for making this cheese.

8. Flip the cheese daily for 1 week, removing any whey that accumulates in the ripening box and wiping any moisture from the box. Wipe the rind daily with cheesecloth soaked in a simple brine solution (see page 24) for the first week. When the cheese is dry on the surface, secure the lid of the ripening box tightly and continue to ripen at 50°F to 55°F and 90 percent humidity, flipping once or twice a week. After 2 weeks, the cheese should have developed a slightly moldy exterior. At 4 months, wrap the cheese in foil and store refrigerated for up to 2 more months.

CHAPTER 5
Cooking with Artisan Cheeses

Herb Salad with Chèvre- and
Bacon-Stuffed Figs (page 207)

C heese is an extraordinary, inspirational ingredient, capable of transforming even the simplest dishes. However, cooking with cheese successfully requires some forethought. Here are a few guidelines for working with cheese in the kitchen.

1. Always use good quality cheese—the better the cheese, the better tasting the dish will be.

2. Understand the impact of heat, which changes the flavor and texture of a cheese. For example, blue cheese can intensify, while chèvre becomes less intense. Cheese should not be exposed to too fierce a heat unless briefly, in a broiler or wood-fired oven. Too much heat can transform beautiful cheese into a rubbery mass.
   - Fresh cheeses, when gently heated, will melt and become creamy, adding flavor to risottos and pastas.
   - High-fat and soft, moist cheeses are good for melting; for example, on grilled sandwiches and pizza.
   - Low-fat cheeses are higher in protein and have little moisture, so they don't melt well and can become leathery when heated to high temperatures.
   - Harder cheeses can withstand higher temperatures than soft cheeses because more of their protein has been broken down into small fragments in the cheese making process. Their salty flavors will enhance piecrusts, galette doughs, and even biscotti.

3. Incorporated into a dish (rather than used as a topping), cheese blends into a dish best when:
   - It is at room temperature and is cut, grated, or crumbled into small pieces
   - It is added slowly and stirred only until the cheese is melted and incorporated
   - It is added in small amounts
   - It is cooked at relatively low temperatures for a short period of time, typically toward the end of the cooking process

4. Add grated cheese as a topping to a casserole or baked dish in the final 5 to 10 minutes to keep it creamy.

5. To prevent curdling or stringiness when adding cheese to a hot liquid, such as a cheese sauce or fondue, gently stir it in while the dish is off the heat and make sure a starch (flour, cornstarch, or arrowroot) is present. Adding a little acid (dry white wine, liqueur, vinegar, or, especially, lemon juice) while stirring over low heat will prevent the protein in the cheese from curdling and create a smooth sauce.

6. In long-cooking cheese dishes such as casseroles, the cheese won't separate if you toss a little flour or cornstarch with the grated cheese (use 1 rounded tablespoon of starch per pound of cheese).

7. The rinds of soft-ripened or washed-rind cheeses are most easily removed when the cheeses are cold. Rinds of aged cheeses such as Parmesan can be added to soups or stocks to impart delicious flavor. Also, when grating cheese, chill it first to firm it up.

MAPLE-PLANKED BRIE WITH MUSHROOM-WALNUT RAGOUT

Serves 8

Roasting or grilling on aromatic wood planks is an easy, flavor-enhancing way of cooking. This method can be done on the stovetop in a cast-iron grill pan, but it is better still on a wood-fired grill or in a wood-fired oven, and it can even be done on a campfire. The planks are soaked in water or in a spirit-infused liquid, and then lightly charred on one side to release the aromatic oils in the wood. The food to be cooked is set on the charred side and roasted or grilled. For this simple planked dish, a beautiful bloomy-rind Brie is served on toast with a mushroom-walnut ragout that cooks while the cheese grills.

1½ pounds fresh meaty mushrooms, such as shiitake, royal trumpet, or oyster
4 cloves garlic, thinly sliced lengthwise
1 cup lightly toasted walnut pieces
Four ¼-inch strips lemon zest
Kosher salt
Freshly ground black pepper
Olive oil
2 long sprigs fresh thyme
1 bay leaf
1 cup dry white wine
2 wheels firm, ripe Brie, about 5 to 6 ounces each (page 136), at room temperature
Four ½-inch-thick slices artisan whole wheat raisin or currant bread

Submerge two 6-inch-square, ½-inch-thick maple planks in water and soak for 1 hour.

Preheat a grill to medium heat (400°F), with areas for both direct and indirect heat. When hot, place a clay baking vessel or cast-iron skillet on the grill to preheat.

Clean and trim the mushrooms, then cut lengthwise into thick slices. Put them in a bowl, add the garlic, walnuts, lemon zest, and some salt and pepper and toss to combine. Drizzle with olive oil just to moisten.

Place the mixture in the preheated pan and add the thyme, bay leaf, and wine. Place on the grill over indirect heat to roast until the mushrooms are golden, about 30 minutes, covering the grill. Taste and add more salt and pepper as needed. Keep warm until ready to serve.

While the ragout cooks, take the maple planks out of the water and let them drain for 10 minutes. Carefully cut the top rinds off the Brie and place them back on the wheels as lids (these will be removed later).

Toast one side of each plank over direct heat until well marked and fragrant, 5 to 7 minutes. Place a wheel of Brie on the marked side of each plank and place on the grill over indirect heat. Close the lid and grill the Brie for 10 minutes. Remove the top rinds from the cheeses and discard, close the lid, and continue to cook for another 5 minutes, or until the surface of the cheese is golden brown and the interior is soft and oozy but the rind is intact. Grill the bread on both sides while cooking the Brie, then cut the toasts in half diagonally and keep them warm.

Remove the planked Brie from the grill and let cool for a few minutes. Take the planks to the table and spoon the roasted mushrooms over the cheeses. Smear the Brie on the toasts and load them up with ragout.

SMOKED MOZZARELLA–EGGPLANT FRITTERS
with Roasted Tomato–Herb Sauce
Makes 18 to 20

Who can resist melted, gooey smoked mozzarella? These cheese-filled crispy appetizers are like eating eggplant Parmesan in just two bites. The fritters can be prepared ahead of time and then fried at party time. If tomatoes are out of season, make the sauce with fire-roasted canned tomatoes.

2 globe eggplants (about 1½ pounds), diced small

Kosher salt

Olive oil

1 yellow onion, diced small

1 red bell pepper, roasted, peeled, seeded, and diced

½ cup oil-cured black olives, pitted and coarsely chopped

3 cloves roasted garlic, minced

½ teaspoon sugar

1½ teaspoons dried thyme

2 tablespoons toasted pine nuts, coarsely ground

Freshly ground black pepper

2 large eggs

¾ cup grated Parmesan (page 108) or other hard cheese

1¼ cups plain dried bread crumbs

6 ounces smoked mozzarella or Scamorza (page 88), cut into ¾-inch cubes, chilled

2½ tablespoons all-purpose flour

Canola oil for frying

Roasted Tomato–Herb Sauce (recipe follows)

Place the diced eggplant in a colander and sprinkle with 1 teaspoon of salt. Let drain over the sink or a bowl for 10 minutes to remove any bitterness. Quickly rinse under cold water and pat dry with paper towels. Set aside. Line a baking sheet with paper towels.

In a large, deep cast-iron skillet over medium-high heat, heat ¼ cup of olive oil. Add the onion and sauté until translucent, about 7 minutes. Add the eggplant and sauté until golden, about 10 minutes. Remove the eggplant mixture with a

slotted spoon to the lined baking sheet to drain, then transfer to a bowl. Add the bell pepper, olives, garlic, sugar, thyme, and pine nuts. Mix well, add salt and pepper to taste, and set aside to cool.

In a medium bowl, whisk together 1 of the eggs, the grated cheese, and ¼ cup of the bread crumbs. Stir in the eggplant mixture. Shape the mixture into 1½-inch balls, pressing 1 cube of mozzarella into the center of each ball and covering the cheese with the eggplant mixture to enclose completely. Chill for 2 hours to firm up slightly, or refrigerate overnight and finish the next day.

Preheat the oven to 350°F.

Place the remaining 1 cup of bread crumbs on a plate for dredging. In a separate bowl, whisk together the remaining egg and the flour. Dip the balls into the egg batter one at a time, then roll in the bread crumbs to coat. Set aside on a baking sheet and place in the refrigerator to chill for 30 minutes.

Set a draining rack over a baking sheet and set it by the stove. Heat 1½ inches of canola oil in a medium skillet over medium-high heat. The oil is hot enough when a wooden spoon handle dipped in the oil sends up bubbles. Test with 1 eggplant ball for proper sizzling, signaled by robust bubbling when submerged in the hot oil, before frying the rest. Working in batches, add a few balls at a time to the hot oil; don't add too many at once or the oil temperature will drop too much for proper browning. Use a slotted spoon to turn them a few times to brown evenly to a dark golden color and crispy exterior. Transfer to the rack to drain and keep warm in the oven until ready to serve. Sprinkle with salt and serve hot with the sauce on the side for dipping.

ROASTED TOMATO-HERB SAUCE
Makes about 3 cups

4 large Roma or seasonal tomatoes (about
    1^1/$_2$ pounds), halved, cored, and seeded
2 unpeeled shallots, halved
Olive oil
Kosher salt
Freshly ground white pepper
1 cup basil leaves, chopped
^{1}/$_4$ cup mint leaves, chopped
Juice of 2 lemons
Red pepper flakes (optional)

Preheat the oven to 350°F.

In a bowl, combine the tomatoes and shallots, drizzle with olive oil to moisten, season with salt and pepper, and toss. Place the tomatoes and shallots cut side down on a baking sheet and roast for 30 minutes, or until they are softened and their skins have shriveled. When cool enough to handle, remove the skins from the tomatoes and shallots. Coarsely chop the tomatoes and shallots, then transfer them to a bowl along with all their juices.

Add the basil, mint, lemon juice, and ½ cup of olive oil to the tomato mixture, then season with salt, pepper, and red pepper flakes, if using. Transfer to a food processor or blender and pulse until pureed to the desired consistency. Set aside for 20 minutes at room temperature to allow the flavors to come together. Taste and adjust the seasonings. Serve warm or at room temperature. The sauce can be stored in the refrigerator in a closed jar for 1 week. Allow cold sauce to return to room temperature before serving.

GRILLED GRAPE LEAF GOAT CHEESE TOASTS
with Citrus Tapenade

Serves 8 as an appetizer

Fresh or brined grape leaves are used throughout their growing regions for wrapping rice, fish, or poultry before placing them on the grill. Here, the leaves encase disks of seasoned chèvre, which are then popped on the grill for a quick char. For additional flavor, you can macerate the grape leaves in lemon vodka or other spirits before wrapping. Use two leaves if one is too small to thoroughly encase the cheese. While still warm, the grape leaf packages are opened; the cheese is slathered onto grilled toast and topped with brightly colored citrusy tapenade. Any extra tapenade can be refrigerated for use at a later time.

8 to 16 large fresh grape leaves, stems removed,
    blanched, and patted dry
Flake sea salt
12 ounces chèvre (page 58), shaped into a
    2-inch-diameter log
1 teaspoon herbes de Provence
Olive oil
Eight 1/2-inch-thick slices rustic country-style bread
2 cloves garlic, peeled
Citrus Tapenade (recipe follows)

Lay the grape leaves out on baking sheets, ribbed side up. Lightly season with sea salt.

Slice the chèvre log into 8 portions and shape into patties about 2½ inches across. Combine the herbs de Provence with ½ cup of olive oil and dip each chèvre patty into it to coat.

Place a chèvre patty in the center of each grape leaf (use two overlapping leaves if one isn't big enough), then fold the sides over the cheese, burrito-style: fold up the bottom to cover, then fold the sides in, and, lastly, fold the top over. Place the packets flap side down on one of the baking sheets. Lightly brush the packets with some of the remaining herbed olive oil, then chill for 1 hour.

Preheat a grill to medium-high heat (450°F), with areas for both direct and indirect grilling. Lightly oil the grill grates.

Prepare the bread by rubbing both sides of each slice with the garlic, then place on a baking sheet. Put about 2 tablespoons of olive oil in a small bowl and set on the baking sheet with the bread slices and a brush for swabbing the bread. Place the wrapped chèvre rounds on the grill, flap side down, over direct heat. Close the lid and cook for 2 minutes, or until the leaves are slightly charred. Turn the packets over and move them to indirect heat, close the lid, and cook for another 2 to 3 minutes, or until the cheese softens but isn't melted and the leaf is charred. At the same time, brush one side of each slice of bread with olive oil and place oiled side down on the direct-heat portion of the grill to toast for a few minutes. Brush the top side with olive oil and turn over for a few minutes. Remove the toasts, cut them in half diagonally, and place them in a basket to keep warm.

Serve 1 grape leaf packet and 2 pieces of toast per person, with the tapenade on the side. Eat the grape leaves if they are tender, or simply open the packet and smear chèvre on the toasts and top with some tapenade.

VARIATION
Macerate the grape leaves in ½ cup of citrus-flavored vodka in a resealable plastic bag overnight; lay flat and refrigerate. Drain and pat the leaves dry before using. Reserve the leftover vodka for a martini!

CITRUS TAPENADE
Makes about 4 cups

2 small oranges
½ red onion, coarsely chopped
¼ cup unseasoned rice vinegar
8 ounces green olives in brine, rinsed, pitted, and chopped
1 fennel bulb, finely chopped
1 tablespoon salted capers, rinsed and drained
3 cloves roasted garlic, minced
½ cup Italian parsley leaves, minced
2 anchovy fillets, finely minced (optional)
½ cup olive oil
Kosher salt
Finely ground white pepper

Zest one or both of the oranges and mince the zest to make 2 tablespoons. Remove the peels and pith of both oranges with a knife and cut between the membranes to section. Cut the sections into small chunks.

For a chunky relish, toss the chopped onion in rice vinegar in a small bowl and set aside. In a medium bowl, toss together the olives, fennel, capers, and garlic. Add the parsley, anchovy, if using, ¼ cup of the olive oil, the orange chunks, and the zest. Drain the onion, discarding the vinegar, and add it to the orange mixture. Stir in the remaining ¼ cup of olive oil and season with salt and white pepper to taste.

For a smoother tapenade, you can skip a lot of the mincing and simply pulse the ingredients together in a food processor to the desired consistency.

Either way, set aside for at least 30 minutes for the flavors to come together before serving. Tapenade may be stored in an airtight container in the refrigerator for up to 1 week.

TALEGGIO FONDUTA

Serves 6

Rich, unctuous *fonduta* is Italy's answer to fondue. It's used as a dip for roasted vegetables and rustic toasts or as a sauce for gnocchi, or is stirred into polenta. Here I suggest you serve it with roasted mushrooms and potatoes and sweet, crisp apples, but you can add roasted baby artichokes or artichoke hearts or even roasted brussels sprouts to the assortment. Gruyère or Havarti can also be used for this dish, in place of the Taleggio or Fontina. Serve in individual dipping dishes or in one communal pot. A lightly dressed salad is a nice accompaniment.

1 pound Taleggio (page 173) or Fontina (page 92)

3 large apples, cored and cut into 8 wedges each

Juice of 1 lemon

1 pound mixed robust-flavored mushrooms, such as chanterelles, porcini, shiitake, or maiitake

Olive oil

Kosher salt

12 to 18 small red creamer potatoes

2 large sweet potatoes, skin on, cut in half lengthwise and then into chunks

6 tablespoons butter, melted

6 egg yolks, lightly beaten

1½ cups whole milk

½ teaspoon truffled or smoked olive oil (optional)

1 loaf rustic bread, sliced and toasted

Preheat the oven to 350°F.

Trim the rind from the cheese, then cut the cheese into ½-inch cubes. Keep in a cool but not cold place until needed. Submerge the apple wedges in a bowl of cool water combined with the lemon juice and set aside until the *fonduta* is ready to serve.

Remove the ends of the stems from the mushrooms (or the entire stems of the shiitake). Cut or tear the mushrooms into generous bite-size pieces. Toss with 1 or 2 tablespoons of olive oil and some salt and place on a baking sheet. Toss the red potatoes and sweet potatoes with 2 or 3 tablespoons of olive oil, salt them lightly, and place cut side down on a separate baking sheet. Put both pans in the oven. Roast the mushrooms for 20 minutes, or until they have released their liquid and it has evaporated. Roast the potatoes for about 30 minutes, or until they are tender and the cut side is slightly crispy. After removing each pan from the oven, cover with aluminum foil to keep warm. Reduce the oven heat to 250°F and place 6 individual clay or ceramic crocks or one larger cast-iron pot or fondue pot in the oven to warm while you finish making the *fonduta*.

While the mushrooms and potatoes are roasting, bring 1 inch of water to a low boil in a medium saucepan. In a medium stainless steel bowl that will sit on the saucepan to create a double boiler, whisk together the butter, egg yolks, and milk to combine, then set the bowl over the saucepan. Cook the mixture while whisking slowly but constantly. When it has thickened slightly, stir in the cheese and continue to stir until melted and thickened into a creamy sauce, about 20 minutes. If adding truffled or smoked olive oil, stir it into the sauce. Whisk the sauce until smooth, then pour it into the warmed crocks.

Drain the apples and pat dry. Serve the apples, mushrooms, and potatoes in separate bowls or on one platter, along with the toasted rustic bread, all for dipping into the *fonduta*.

GRILLED CUMIN FLATBREADS *with Tomato-Ginger Chutney and Crème Fraîche Cottage Cheese*

Makes 6 rustic flatbreads

Flatbreads are a staple food in most cultures around the world, and they make a fantastic backdrop for fresh cheeses like the cultured cottage cheese used here. This basic recipe easily adjusts to your flavor or cuisine preferences—change the cumin to fennel seed or rosemary, or include a bit of whole wheat flour. I think flatbreads taste best when they are a bit charred from the grill. If you don't have a grill, you can use a cast-iron stovetop grill pan and cook the flatbreads on the ribbed side. Note that you should prepare the chutney a day before the flatbreads.

4 cups all-purpose flour
2 teaspoons active dry yeast
2 teaspoons kosher salt
1 teaspoon cumin seeds
1½ cups water, plus more as needed
Olive oil
Canola oil
Coarse sea salt
Crème Fraîche Cottage Cheese (page 55)
Tomato-Ginger Chutney (recipe follows)

Combine the flour, yeast, salt, and cumin in a stand mixer and mix on low speed for 2 minutes. Slowly add the water and mix at a slightly higher speed for 5 minutes, and then on slow speed for another 2 minutes to start the formation of the gluten. Alternatively, to mix by hand, in a large bowl combine the flour, yeast, salt, and cumin and mix well for 2 minutes. Slowly add the water and mix to combine until well incorporated. Put the dough on a lightly floured work surface and knead for 1 minute. If the dough is not coming together to form a ball, add more water. Cover the dough and let it rise for 2 hours or until doubled in size.

Punch the dough down, then form it into a large ball and cut the ball into 6 equal pieces. Shape the individual balls by gently stretching and tucking under, then rolling the ball to keep the "belly button" on the bottom. Set on a floured sheet pan and lightly brush the tops of the balls with olive oil. Cover with a damp towel or plastic wrap to prevent the surface of the balls from drying out and let rest for at least 1 hour and up to 2 hours.

Heat a grill to medium-high heat (450°F to 500°F) or place a stovetop grill pan over high heat. Lightly brush the grill grates or grill pan with canola oil just before grilling.

When ready to make the flatbreads, flour a wood peel and, working on the peel, stretch and shape a dough ball into an 8- to 10-inch round or oblong shape. Brush with more of the olive oil, being careful not to get oil on the peel. Lightly dust the edges of the dough with coarse sea salt and flip it onto the grill over direct heat, oiled side down. Repeat the process with the other dough balls, grilling 2 or 3 flatbreads at the same time if you have the space, over direct heat.

Close the lid of the grill, or if using the stovetop method, place an inverted skillet over each flatbread to act as a lid. When the dough puffs up and there are good grill marks on the dough, about 4 minutes, lightly brush the top of each flatbread with olive oil and flip over to grill the other side for about 5 minutes. Transfer the flatbread to a cooler spot, over indirect heat, to finish cooking the interior.

Remove the flatbreads from the grill as they finish cooking, place on a cutting board, and cut into wedges. Serve hot with the cottage cheese and chutney.

TOMATO-GINGER CHUTNEY

Makes about 2 cups

1 cup golden or mixed cherry tomatoes, halved

1 red bell pepper, roasted, peeled, seeded, and finely chopped

4 cloves garlic, blanched and thinly sliced into strips

1/4 cup olive oil

3 tablespoons golden raisins, plumped in hot water and drained

1 tablespoon minced fresh ginger

2 tablespoons red wine vinegar

Zest from 1 orange

Juice of 1 orange

1 teaspoon cumin seeds

1/4 teaspoon fennel seeds

1/2 teaspoon turmeric

1/4 teaspoon ground cinnamon

1/2 teaspoon kosher salt

1/4 teaspoon freshly ground black pepper

Combine all of the ingredients in a saucepan and bring to a low boil over medium heat. Cook for 5 to 6 minutes, stirring frequently. Adjust the salt and pepper to taste. Remove from the heat, cool, cover, and refrigerate overnight to allow the flavors to come together. Bring to room temperature before serving.

GOAT CHEESE AND CHIVE FALLEN SOUFFLÉS
with Herb-Citrus Vinaigrette
Serves 8

Cheese soufflés are delicious and easy to make, and this version is foolproof, since they are intentionally allowed to fall before serving! Because of this, they can even be made ahead and reheated. My favorite combination is the one presented here with tart fresh goat cheese and chives, served with a citrus vinaigrette, but you can substitute other cheeses, such as grated Gruyère, Asiago, Jack, dry Jack, or even a favorite blue. Play with other herb combinations as well.

1/4 cup plus 1/3 cup finely grated Parmesan cheese
   (page 108)
2 teaspoons dried thyme
3 tablespoons finely chopped chives
1/2 cup Italian parsley leaves, finely chopped
1/2 teaspoon kosher salt
1/4 teaspoon freshly ground white pepper
3 tablespoons unsalted butter
3 tablespoons all-purpose flour
1 1/2 cups whole milk at room temperature
Pinch of freshly grated nutmeg
3 egg yolks, beaten
1/2 cup crumbled chèvre (page 58)
5 egg whites
4 cups baby salad greens
Herb-Citrus Vinaigrette (recipe follows)

Spray a 2-quart oval baking dish or 8 individual 4-ounce ramekins with olive or canola oil. Combine the ¼ cup of Parmesan and the thyme and dust the baking dish or ramekins with this mixture. Combine the chives, parsley, salt, and pepper and set aside.

Preheat the oven to 375°F.

In a medium saucepan over medium heat, make a roux by melting the butter, then adding the flour and stirring for 3 minutes to cook the flour. Slowly pour in the milk while stirring. Stir in the nutmeg and continue to cook, stirring occasionally, for about 20 minutes, or until the sauce is thickened to the consistency of pancake batter. Remove from the heat and add the parsley mixture.

Stir the egg yolks into the sauce, then add the crumbled chèvre. In a large bowl or stand mixer, beat the egg whites until stiff peaks form when the beater is lifted. Fold one-third of the egg whites into the mixture, and then repeat until all of the whites have been added. Spoon the mixture into the prepared pan or ramekins. Sprinkle the tops with the ⅓ cup of Parmesan.

Place the soufflé dish or ramekins on a rimmed baking sheet, place on the middle rack of the oven, and fill the baking sheet halfway with warm water. Bake for 25 to 30 minutes, or until golden and firm to the touch. Remove the baking dish or ramekins from the water and let stand for 15 minutes to allow the soufflés to fall.

Dress the greens with some of the vinaigrette, then divide them among 8 serving plates. Scoop out servings of soufflé or turn out individual soufflés onto the greens, placing them top side up.

HERB-CITRUS VINAIGRETTE
Makes about 1½ cups

2 shallots, unpeeled

Olive oil

1 teaspoon minced orange zest

1 teaspoon chopped tarragon leaves

2 tablespoons chopped parsley

2 oranges, peeled

¼ cup champagne vinegar

1 tablespoon freshly squeezed orange juice

2 teaspoons honey

½ to ¾ cup fruity olive oil

Kosher salt

Freshly ground white pepper

Preheat the oven to 350°F. Lightly rub 2 whole skin-on shallots with olive oil. Place the shallots in a small skillet and roast in the oven, turning once or twice, until the skins are well marked and the interiors of the shallots are slightly soft, 20 to 25 minutes. Let the shallots cool before removing the skins and finely chopping.

Combine the orange zest, shallots, tarragon, and parsley. Working over a small bowl, holding an orange in one hand, section the oranges by cutting between the flesh and the membrane of each section with a sharp knife to release the orange sections. Cut the orange flesh into small chunks and put them in a separate bowl.

Combine the champagne vinegar, orange juice, and honey in a bowl and stir to dissolve the honey. Add any reserved orange juice from the orange-sectioning process. Slowly pour in the olive oil, whisking continuously to create an emulsion. Season with salt and white pepper to taste. Just before dressing the greens, whisk again to incorporate all of the ingredients, then stir in the orange chunks.

MANCHEGO AND SAFFRON FLAN

Serves 6

This creamy custard side dish features two of Spain's notable ingredients, aromatic saffron and aged Manchego cheese. Dry Jack, Romano, and Asiago are also good options. Serve the flan on a bed of baby greens or top with dressed microgreens. This is a nice side for roasted chicken or grilled fish.

1½ cups whole milk

8 threads saffron

¼ cup crème fraîche (page 44)

3 eggs, beaten

2 egg yolks, beaten

¼ teaspoon smoked paprika

½ teaspoon kosher salt

¼ teaspoon freshly ground white pepper

4 ounces six-month-aged Manchego, finely grated

Preheat the oven to 350°F. Butter six 5-ounce ramekins or one 1½-quart baking dish.

Over medium-low heat, bring the milk to a simmer. Add the saffron threads. Remove from the heat and steep for 15 minutes. Whisk in the crème fraîche. Cool for 10 minutes, then whisk in the beaten eggs and egg yolks to mix well. Add the paprika, salt, and pepper and whisk to combine. Stir in the Manchego.

Pour the mixture into the prepared ramekins or baking dish, leaving ¼ to ½ inch of space at the top edge. Place the ramekins or baking dish in a larger baking dish of the same depth. Pour in enough hot water to fill the larger dish to a depth of 1 inch. Bake until the flans are slightly puffed and firm to the touch on top, about 30 to 35 minutes for ramekins, or 5 minutes longer if baking in one dish.

Carefully remove the larger pan from the oven, leaving the flan in the hot water for another 5 minutes to set up. Remove the flan from the water bath and set aside to cool for 10 minutes. Run a paring knife around the edges to release the flan. When ready to serve, invert the ramekins to release each flan into your hand, then quickly turn it over and place, top side up, on a serving plate, or serve the larger flan in its baking vessel.

HERB SALAD WITH CHÈVRE- AND BACON-STUFFED FIGS

Serves 6

Drizzled with an orange-thyme syrup, this is an absolutely beautiful yet simple salad. The classic food partnerships here among fresh goat cheese, fines herbes (a blend of chervil, chives, parsley, and tarragon), orange, thyme, and smoky bacon all ring harmoniously in the presence of fresh, ripe figs. Make this dish when figs are at their prime—if they are slightly underripe, place them in a shallow baking dish and heat through in a 300°F oven. When figs are out of season, use poached pears on baby salad greens for an equally delicious dish.

SYRUP

1 cup freshly squeezed orange juice
1 tablespoon orange zest
1/4 cup sugar
Pinch of freshly ground white pepper
3 sprigs thyme

SALAD

1 1/2 cups arugula leaves, stems removed
1 cup baby red lettuce leaves
1/2 cup basil leaves
1/4 cup mint leaves
2 tablespoons chervil

1/2 cup softened chèvre (page 58) (about 4 ounces)
1 teaspoon dried fines herbes
1/4 teaspoon sea salt, plus more for dressing
2 teaspoons fruity olive oil, plus more for dressing
4 ounces thick-sliced applewood-smoked bacon, finely chopped
1/4 cup finely minced shallot
6 large firm, ripe black or green figs
Freshly ground white pepper

To make the syrup, combine the orange juice, zest, sugar, and pepper in a small saucepan and bring to a boil. Add the thyme, then lower the heat to medium-high and cook, stirring occasionally, until the liquid is reduced by half, about 10 minutes. Remove from the heat, discard the thyme, and set aside to cool.

To make the salad, tear the leaves of the arugula, red lettuce, basil, and mint into a bowl, add the chervil, and toss to combine. Set aside in the refrigerator to chill.

In a small bowl, mix together the goat cheese, fines herbes, and 1/4 teaspoon of salt. Set aside in the refrigerator to chill. Heat the 2 teaspoons of olive oil in a small skillet over medium heat, add the bacon, and cook, stirring often, until nearly crispy. Add the shallots and cook, stirring occasionally, until they soften, about 2 minutes. Remove from the heat and let drain on a paper towel.

Cut the figs in half lengthwise, press the center of each to make a small cavity for the filling, and divide the bacon and shallots among the figs, mounding the filling slightly. Spoon a small amount of the goat cheese mixture over the filling. Lightly dress the greens with more of the olive oil, sea salt, and white pepper, and divide them among 6 serving plates. Place the stuffed figs atop the greens and drizzle with the syrup, then serve.

BOCCONCINI AND ROASTED TOMATO PASTA SALAD

Serves 6

Caprese salad is a favorite from Capri featuring fresh mozzarella, sliced ripe tomatoes, and basil. This dish reimagines caprese, adding pasta, bocconcini (bite-size mozzarella pieces), roasted tomatoes, and aromatic smoked olive oil. The type of oil I prefer comes from the Smoked Olive (www.thesmokedolive.com); feel free to substitute plain extra virgin olive oil. Serve the salad family-style in a shallow bowl or on a platter.

12 Roma tomatoes, halved, cored, and seeded

3 tablespoons olive oil

1 tablespoon balsamic vinegar

3 cloves garlic, thinly sliced

Sea salt

Freshly ground white pepper

1 pound small shaped dried pasta, such as farfalle, gemelli, orecchiette, or a mixture

1 pound bocconcini balls, drained (page 79)

1/4 cup smoked olive oil or extra virgin olive oil

15 large basil leaves

1/4 teaspoon red pepper flakes

Preheat the oven to 375°F.

Toss the tomatoes in 3 tablespoons of olive oil, then place them cut side up on a baking sheet and roast for 20 minutes, or until they are softened. When cool enough to handle, transfer the tomatoes to a bowl (reserve any juices from the pan for the pasta), add the balsamic vinegar and garlic, season with salt and pepper, and toss to combine.

Cook the pasta in boiling salted water until al dente. Meanwhile, tear 4 of the bocconcini balls into shreds and toss with sea salt and a drizzle of the smoked olive oil. Stem and shred 3 of the basil leaves. When cooked, drain the pasta and toss with the reserved tomato juices, the shredded cheese, the remaining smoked olive oil, the shredded basil, salt to taste, and the red pepper flakes. Place in a shallow serving bowl or on a platter.

Toss together the roasted tomatoes and the remaining whole bocconcini and arrange them over the pasta. Tuck in the remaining 12 whole basil leaves and serve at room temperature.

SPINACH SALAD WITH CHARRED RICOTTA SALATA AND CARAMELIZED ORANGES

Serves 6

Salt, sweetness, smoke, and a hint of bitterness all come together here to create a sensational salad. Caramelized oranges are absolutely perfect with the grilled ricotta salata, and together they brighten the slightly tannic spinach and earthy olives.

10 ounces ricotta salata, drained (page 67)

10 tablespoons olive oil

3 large oranges

1/2 cup sugar

4 cups packed spinach leaves, stems removed, patted dry

1/2 teaspoon sea salt

6 cloves garlic, blanched and slivered

Pinch of red pepper flakes

1/2 cup green olives, pitted and slivered lengthwise

1/4 cup oil-cured olives, pitted and coarsely chopped

Dried mint for garnish

1/4 cup shelled salted pistachios, coarsely chopped, for garnish (optional)

Cut the ricotta salata into 3/4-inch cubes, toss in a bowl with 5 tablespoons of the olive oil, and set aside. Cut the ends off 2 of the oranges. Remove the peels and pith with a knife by following the curvature of the orange, carving below the pith to reveal the flesh. Trim off any remaining pith. Cut each orange into 4 or 5 horizontal slices. Spread on a baking sheet and sprinkle the tops with 1/4 cup of the sugar. Set aside. Zest the remaining orange and mince the zest, then set both the zest and the orange aside.

Heat a cast-iron griddle pan over high heat. Place the cubes of ricotta salata on the hot griddle and cook for 5 to 10 seconds, just long enough to char. Turn over on the opposite side and repeat until charred on the second side. Remove the cheese from the pan immediately and place on a baking sheet to cool.

Heat a 10-inch cast-iron skillet over medium-high heat and spread the remaining 1/4 cup of sugar over the bottom of the pan. When the sugar begins to melt, place the orange slices sugar side down into the melting sugar. Do not move the oranges for 1 to 2 minutes to allow the syrup to set, but if the sugar is caramelizing before the oranges are slightly softened and lightly caramelized, lower the heat. Return the oranges, caramelized side up, to the baking sheet to cool.

Pour the cooked sugar syrup from the pan into a bowl. Squeeze the juice from the zested orange into the skillet and stir to deglaze. Add the orange juice to the sugar syrup, then stir in the zest and any sweet juices that the cooling orange slices have exuded. Slowly whisk in 3 tablespoons of the olive oil to make a vinaigrette.

Just before serving, using the same skillet used for the oranges, warm the remaining 2 tablespoons of olive oil over medium-low heat until heated through. Add the spinach, salt, garlic, and red pepper flakes, then quickly stir to slightly wilt the spinach. Do not overcook, and promptly drain off any liquid.

Working quickly, divide the hot spinach among 6 individual serving plates. Top each serving with caramelized orange slices, dividing them evenly among the salads. Top each salad with a few pieces of charred ricotta salata, drizzle with the vinaigrette, and sprinkle the olives, dried mint, and chopped pistachios, if using, over the oranges. Serve right away.

COBB SALAD *with Buttermilk Blue Dressing*

Serves 6

Created as a way to use leftovers by Bob Cobb, the owner of Hollywood's Brown Derby restaurant, Cobb salad became the benchmark composed salad of the 1920s. I consider it the American salade niçoise. The original salad of chopped chicken or turkey, bacon, hard-boiled eggs, tomatoes, avocado, cubed cheddar cheese, and chopped iceberg lettuce was dressed with a simple vinaigrette. This version uses a variety of lettuces, crumbly artisan blue cheese, and smoky bacon. The creamy blue cheese dressing seconds the flavors of the cheese and complements the chicken and bacon, making for a luxurious salad.

2 tablespoons olive oil
$^1/_2$ teaspoon smoked paprika
Pinch of kosher salt
Pinch of freshly ground white pepper
1 pound boneless, skinless chicken breast
Canola oil
4 leaves Bibb lettuce
3 leaves romaine lettuce
4 leaves frisée
6 slices applewood-smoked bacon, cooked until crisp
  and crumbled
6 radishes, quartered
3 hard-boiled eggs, chopped
1 cup cherry tomatoes, halved
$^1/_3$ cup mixed marinated or kalamata olives, drained
  and pitted
2 tablespoons finely chopped chives
$^1/_2$ cup Buttermilk Blue Dressing (recipe follows)

Combine the olive oil, paprika, salt, and pepper in a small bowl. Rub the chicken with the mixture. Heat a cast-iron grill pan over medium-high heat and lightly oil with canola oil. Cook the chicken breasts until well marked on both sides and cooked to an internal temperature of 175°F, 5 to 8 minutes per side. Remove from the pan to cool, then cut into bite-size cubes and set aside.

Remove any thick stems from the lettuce leaves and tear them into bite-size pieces, then toss them together and place on a serving platter. Arrange the chicken, bacon, radishes, eggs, tomatoes, and olives in decorative rows on top of the lettuce. Sprinkle the chopped chives over the top. When ready to serve, drizzle the entire platter with about half of the dressing. Serve the remaining dressing on the side. Let your guests plate their own salads with the ingredients of their choice, drizzling and tossing with more dressing if they desire.

BUTTERMILK BLUE DRESSING
Makes about 1¼ cups

$^3/_4$ cup buttermilk (page 44)
$^1/_4$ cup mayonnaise
1 teaspoon champagne vinegar or white wine vinegar
Pinch of sugar
$^1/_4$ teaspoon freshly ground white pepper
2 ounces crumbled blue cheese (pages 175–191)

Combine the buttermilk, mayonnaise, vinegar, sugar, pepper, and 1 ounce of the blue cheese in a blender and blend until smooth. Transfer to a bowl and adjust the seasonings, then fold in the remaining blue cheese. Set aside in the refrigerator to chill slightly.

MOROCCAN CHICKPEA SOUP *with Harissa and Yogurt Cheese*

Serves 6 as a main course

This hearty, rustic soup is filled with healthy legumes and flavored with Moroccan spices. The spicy chile-based Tunisian condiment harissa is stirred into the soup to build the level of heat you desire. Harissa can be purchased ready-made in the Middle Eastern foods section of markets, but I encourage you to make your own to keep on hand for use in this and other dishes. The counterpoint to the heat and spiciness of the soup is easy-to-make yogurt cheese with mint, shaped into balls and floated on top of the soup. The cheese can be eaten in bites with the soup or spread onto seed crackers or crisp flatbreads.

3 tablespoons olive oil

1 white onion, diced

2 carrots, peeled and diced

1/2 teaspoon kosher salt

7 cups chicken or vegetable stock

Two 14-ounce cans diced fire-roasted tomatoes

1 1/2 teaspoons sugar

1 1/2 cups cooked chickpeas or one 15-ounce can chickpeas, drained and rinsed

3/4 cup brown or green lentils, picked over

1 teaspoon dried mint

1 teaspoon toasted cumin seeds

1/2 teaspoon ground ginger

1/2 teaspoon ground cinnamon

1 teaspoon turmeric

Freshly ground white pepper

1/4 cup cilantro leaves, chopped

1/2 teaspoon freshly squeezed lemon juice

Yogurt Cheese with Mint (page 48)

Harissa (recipe follows)

In a Dutch oven or clay pot, heat the olive oil over medium heat, then add the onion and carrots and sauté for 5 minutes, or until the onions are translucent. Add the salt, stock, tomatoes with their juice, and sugar, and bring to a simmer. Add the chickpeas and lentils, cover, and cook until the lentils are al dente, about 20 minutes. Stir in the mint, cumin, ginger, cinnamon, and turmeric, cover, and cook for another 15 minutes, or until the lentils are soft but not mushy. Season with pepper to taste, add more salt if needed, then stir in the cilantro. Add the lemon juice, taste, and add more if needed—just to brighten the flavor, not to make it taste lemony. Heat the soup through and serve it in soup bowls with a few balls of yogurt cheese floating on top and the harissa on the side to season the soup.

HARISSA

Makes about 1/2 cup

6 to 8 dried hot red chiles (preferably New Mexico), seeded

2 cloves garlic, crushed

1/2 teaspoon sea salt

1 teaspoon toasted cumin seeds

1/2 teaspoon ground coriander

1/2 cup olive oil

Soak the chiles in hot water for 30 minutes to hydrate, then drain and squeeze out the excess water. Place the drained chiles and the remaining ingredients in a blender and process to form a paste. Store in a jar, covered with a thin layer of olive oil, in the refrigerator for up to 1 month.

TORTILLA SOUP *with Grilled Shrimp, Cotija, and Avocado-Tomatillo Salsa*

Serves 6 as a main course

This Mexican soup is a meal in itself, bursting with color and flavor, and healthy to boot. Many of the steps can be done ahead, including grilling the vegetables and shrimp and making the chicken-shrimp stock. You can also forgo the soup and simply serve the skewered shrimp with the salsa and toasted tortillas.

GRILLED SHRIMP

1 quart water

1/3 cup kosher salt

1/2 cup sugar

1 pound extra-jumbo (16/20) shrimp, shells on

4 cloves garlic, finely minced

Zest from 1 lemon

1/2 teaspoon red pepper flakes

1/4 cup white wine

Juice from 2 lemons

1/4 cup olive oil

SOUP

6 cups chicken stock

2 corn tortillas

Canola oil

1 guajillo chile, toasted, stemmed, and seeded

1 cup canned diced fire-roasted tomatoes

6 cloves garlic

1 tablespoon dried Mexican oregano

1 teaspoon ground cumin

1/4 cup freshly squeezed lime juice

2 tablespoons corn oil

1 poblano chile, roasted, peeled, and seeded

1 serrano chile, seeded and diced

1 cup diced white onion

Kosher salt

Freshly ground white pepper

2 tablespoons cilantro

Avocado-Tomatillo Salsa (recipe follows)

1 cup crumbled Cotija (page 65)

To prepare the shrimp, combine the water, salt, and sugar in a tub with a lid and stir to dissolve the salt and sugar. Place the shrimp in the brine, cover, and refrigerate for 20 minutes, then remove the shrimp, rinse, and pat dry.

Submerge bamboo skewers (2 for every 3 shrimp) in water and soak for 20 minutes. Whisk together the garlic, lemon zest, red pepper flakes, wine, lemon juice, and olive oil and toss with the shrimp. Marinate for 20 to 35 minutes in the refrigerator. While the shrimp are marinating, begin making the Avocado-Tomatillo Salsa (recipe follows); you can grill the vegetables for the salsa as you are grilling the shrimp.

Preheat a grill to medium-high heat (450°F) and lightly oil the grill grates.

Remove the shrimp from the refrigerator and let them come to room temperature. Drain the skewers. Thread 3 of the shrimp on each pair of skewers. Grill for 2 minutes per side, or until the shrimp start to turn pink but remain slightly translucent inside. When cool enough to handle, remove the shells. Set the shrimp aside and reserve the shells for the soup.

To make the soup, combine the chicken stock and shrimp shells in a pot and bring to a boil over medium heat. Remove from the heat, cool slightly, then discard the shells.

(continued)

Cut the corn tortillas into ⅛-inch strips. Heat ½ inch of canola oil over medium-high heat. Add the tortilla strips and gently stir to brown and crisp, about 3 minutes. Drain the strips on paper towels and set aside.

Break the toasted guajillo into small pieces and place in a blender or food processor with the tomatoes, garlic, oregano, cumin, lime juice, and corn oil. Pulse a few times just to chop the tomatoes, garlic, and guajillo. Pour half of the mixture into the stock and puree the rest. Add the pureed mixture to the stock. Place over medium heat and bring to a low boil.

Cut the poblano into strips and add it to the pot, along with the serrano and onion. Cook for 5 minutes, then season to taste with salt and pepper.

Ladle into 6 warmed shallow soup bowls and place 3 shrimp in each. Garnish with the fried tortilla strips, cilantro, a dollop of salsa, and Cotija.

AVOCADO-TOMATILLO SALSA
Makes about 1½ cups

1 red onion, unpeeled, cut in half
2 ripe but firm avocados, halved and pitted
4 tomatillos, husks on
¼ cup finely diced red bell pepper
1 serrano chile, seeded and diced
½ teaspoon kosher salt
Freshly ground white pepper
Grated zest of 1 lime
2 teaspoons freshly squeezed lime juice
2 tablespoons chopped cilantro

Preheat a grill to medium-high heat (450°F) and lightly oil the grill grates. Over direct heat, grill the onion and avocados, cut side down, until well marked, about 7 minutes. Remove them from the grill, put the tomatillos on the grill, close the lid, and toast until the husks are charred and the tomatillos are just soft, about 7 minutes. Take the tomatillos off the grill. Remove the husks from the tomatillos and the skins from the onion and avocados. Coarsely chop the tomatillos, onion, and avocados and place in a bowl along with the red pepper and serrano chile. Add the salt and pepper and toss to combine. Add the lime zest and juice and mix well. Cover and set aside for 30 minutes. Just before serving, toss in the cilantro.

CURRIED SAAG PANIR

Serves 6

Saag panir (or saag paneer) is a classic Indian dish, and it's the one that first got me hooked on Indian food. Panir is a very firm traditional Indian cheese that keeps its shape and texture in the cooking process. Here it's coated with turmeric, then slightly toasted before being added to the curried spinach mixture. Use mild or hot curry powder depending on your taste. This is wonderful served with aromatic basmati rice and grilled flatbread slathered with clarified butter (try the Grilled Cumin Flatbreads on page 202).

1 tablespoon plus 2 teaspoons turmeric powder

1 tablespoon plus 1 teaspoon kosher salt

12 ounces panir (page 37), cut into 3/4-inch cubes

4 tablespoons canola oil

1 white onion, finely chopped

2 tablespoons minced fresh ginger

3 serrano chiles, seeded and minced

5 cloves garlic, minced

1 teaspoon cumin seeds

2 teaspoons ground coriander

1 1/2 teaspoons mild or hot curry powder

1 1/2 pounds fresh spinach leaves, stemmed, washed, and drained, or two 10-ounce packages frozen spinach, thawed and well drained

1 1/2 cups reduced fat (2 percent) milk at room temperature

2 1/2 cups low-fat plain yogurt, at room temperature

2 1/2 teaspoons cornstarch

In a small bowl, combine the 1 tablespoon of turmeric with the 1 tablespoon of salt. Add the panir and toss until evenly coated. Place on a paper towel.

Heat 2 tablespoons of the oil in a large cast-iron skillet over medium-high heat. Add the panir, making sure the pieces don't touch, and brown the cubes on all sides. Set the panir aside on a paper towel to let drain. Repeat the process with any remaining panir.

Without cleaning the skillet, add the remaining 2 tablespoons of oil, scrape up any bits from the bottom of the pan, and heat to medium-high. Add the onion, ginger, and chiles and sauté until soft, about 7 minutes. Add the garlic and sauté for another 5 minutes. Lower the heat to medium and stir in the cumin, coriander, curry powder, and the remaining 2 teaspoons of turmeric. Cook for 2 minutes. Stir in the spinach and season with the remaining 1 teaspoon of salt. Cover and simmer for 3 minutes to cook the spinach. Remove from the heat, cool slightly, then place the spinach mixture in a blender or food processor. Add the milk, and puree until only slightly chunky. Adjust the salt to taste. Return the mixture to low heat until it is bubbling slightly.

While the spinach is heating, whisk the yogurt and cornstarch together in a small bowl until the cornstarch is thoroughly dissolved. (The cornstarch will prevent the yogurt from separating when heated.) Stir this into the bubbling spinach mixture. Set the browned panir on top of the spinach, cover, and heat for 2 minutes. Gently stir to incorporate, then cover and continue to simmer for 10 minutes, or until completely heated through.

GRILLED CHILES RELLENOS STUFFED WITH QUESO OAXACA, MUSHROOMS, AND SWEET POTATO

Serves 8

Cheese-filled chiles rellenos are one of my favorite Mexican dishes. I love to grill them rather than batter-fry them—it lends a smoky, charred flavor. In this version, wonderful, fresh queso Oaxaca is the base for the earthy, spicy-sweet filling combining mushrooms and sweet potato. Achiote paste is made with annatto seeds, garlic, and other spices and is used in many Hispanic dishes to give rich, deep flavors. Annatto seeds are used to make the liquid annatto, which is used to color certain cheeses. I serve this dish with a side of rice and simple tossed greens.

8 large poblano chiles

Kosher salt

12 ounces queso Oaxaca (page 79), chilled

Juice of 1 lime

2 large sweet potatoes (about 14 ounces total), cooked, peeled, and mashed

1 1/2 teaspoons achiote paste, crumbled

Zest of 1 lime

3 tablespoons olive oil

1 small white onion, diced

4 cloves garlic, minced

8 ounces shiitake mushrooms, stemmed and coarsely chopped

1/4 cup mirin or dry white wine

1/4 cup cilantro, coarsely chopped

Cut a 3-inch slit down one side of each poblano to allow for stuffing. Remove the veins and most of the seeds. Lightly salt the insides and set aside on a baking sheet.

Coarsely shred the cheese into a medium bowl and drizzle the lime juice over it. Sprinkle with 1/2 teaspoon of salt, rub the salt into the cheese, then toss to combine.

In a separate bowl, combine the mashed sweet potato, achiote paste, and lime zest. Season with salt to taste and set aside.

Heat the olive oil in a skillet over medium heat, add the onion, and sauté until translucent. Add the garlic and mushrooms and continue to sauté for 5 minutes. Add the mirin and cook until the mushrooms are soft and the liquid has been absorbed, about another 10 minutes. Remove from the heat and stir in the cilantro.

Preheat a grill to medium-high heat (450°F), with areas for both direct and indirect grilling. Lightly oil the grill grates.

Using a spoon, smear the inside walls of each poblano with about 1/4 cup of the sweet potato mixture. Follow with a handful of the seasoned queso Oaxaca, then top the cheese with a generous spoonful of the mushroom mixture. Place on a baking sheet and brush with olive oil.

Place the chiles over direct heat on the grill. Cover and grill, turning occasionally, until the skins are blistered and slightly charred, about 5 minutes. Move to indirect heat and continue cooking until the cheese is hot and melted, about 5 more minutes. Alternatively, roast the chiles in a 375°F oven for 30 minutes. Transfer to a platter and serve.

BLUE CHEESE, BACON, AND PEAR GALETTE

Makes one 10-inch tart

This savory galette combines salty-sweet bacon with maple-coated pears and an earthy blue cheese, all cozily housed in a golden, nutty almond crust. An herbaceous rosemary glaze is the crowning touch to a real crowd-pleaser.

DOUGH

2 cups all-purpose flour

1/4 cup almond flour or almond meal

1 1/2 teaspoons sugar

1/2 teaspoon kosher salt

1/2 cup unsalted butter, cut into small pieces and chilled

About 3/4 cup ice water

FILLING

2 tablespoons olive oil

4 ounces bacon, cut crosswise into narrow strips

1 yellow onion, thinly sliced into wedges

3 large shallots, thinly sliced into wedges

1/4 cup maple syrup

1/2 teaspoon pure vanilla extract

1/2 teaspoon ground cardamom

2 large pears, peeled, cored, and cut into 12 wedges each

3 ounces mild blue cheese or Coastal Blue (page 184), cut into 8 thin wedges

GLAZE

Reserved maple syrup mixture

1/4 cup sugar

1/4 cup water

1 teaspoon chopped rosemary leaves

To make the dough, combine the all-purpose flour, almond flour, sugar, and salt in a bowl. Using a pastry cutter, cut the cold butter into the dry ingredients until the pieces are the size of a pea and still visible. Slowly add 6 tablespoons of the ice water and stir to incorporate, adding more water as needed until the dough comes together and forms a ball. You may not need the full amount of water. Do not over-work the dough. Once the dough holds together, form it into a 6-inch disk, wrap tightly in plastic wrap, and refrigerate for 30 minutes or up to overnight.

Preheat the oven to 375°F.

To make the filling, in a large skillet over medium-high heat, heat the olive oil, then add the bacon and cook, stirring often, until the bacon is crispy and the fat is rendered, about 7 minutes. Set aside on paper towels to drain. Remove half of the fat from the pan, add the onion and shallots, and sauté until lightly caramelized, about 7 minutes. In a bowl, combine the maple syrup, vanilla, and cardamom. Toss the pear wedges in the syrup mixture to coat, then leave them to soak in the mixture.

Working on a sheet of parchment paper, roll out the dough into a rough 14-inch circle. Lift the parchment with the dough onto a baking sheet. Leaving a 2-inch border, evenly distribute the bacon-onion mixture over the the dough. Place the pear wedges in a decorative pattern over the bacon-onion mixture, overlapping if needed. Fill in the center with small pieces of pear. Reserve the maple syrup mixture to use in the glaze.

(continued)

Moving around the tart, fold the edges of the dough toward the center and over the filling, pleating it as you go to securely enclose the filling. Place on the lower rack of the oven and bake until golden, 20 to 25 minutes. Top with the wedges of blue cheese and bake for another 10 minutes, or until the crust is crispy and very golden and the pears are caramelized.

Meanwhile, make the glaze. Combine the reserved maple syrup mixture, sugar, water, and chopped rosemary in a small skillet over medium-high heat. Bring to a low boil and cook until the sugar is melted and a slightly thick syrup is created, about 10 minutes. Remove from the heat and allow to cool for 5 minutes. Using a pastry brush, spread the glaze over the top of the galette. Let cool for 15 minutes, then cut and serve.

GRILLED APPLE, JACK, AND CURRY SANDWICH

Serves 2

To me, all grilled cheese sandwiches are winners, but this is one of my favorites. Originally created by chef John Ash for his namesake restaurant in Northern California, it's now one of the most popular combinations at John's food cart business, Hot Cheese. Make it even more delicious by including one or more of the suggested add-ons listed in the Variations, below. Since curry powders vary widely in flavor and power, use your favorite and adjust to your own taste.

1/4 cup mayonnaise

2 teaspoons honey

1 teaspoon Dijon mustard

1 teaspoon Madras-style curry powder

4 thick slices rustic whole wheat, multigrain, or seeded bread

2 apples (Gravensteins are good), peeled, cored, and thinly sliced

8 ounces coarsely grated Jack cheese (pages 96 or 98)

2 tablespoons butter

2 tablespoons olive oil

Combine the mayonnaise, honey, mustard, and curry and mix until smooth. Taste and adjust the balance of flavors if necessary. Liberally spread the mixture on 1 side of the bread slices. Top 2 of the bread slices with a layer of apples. Arrange a mound of the cheese over the apples and top with the remaining slices of dressed bread.

Melt the butter and oil together in a heavy-bottomed or cast-iron skillet and cook the sandwiches until golden on both sides. Cut in half diagonally and serve immediately.

VARIATIONS

- *4 strips applewood-smoked bacon, crisply fried or baked*
- *Slices of good ham or salumi*
- *Almond or any other nut butter that you like*
- *Major Grey or any other chutney that you like*

YOGURT AND DILL NO-KNEAD BREAD

Makes one 1½-pound loaf

This very simple bread recipe, adapted from my book *Wood-Fired Cooking*, is baked in a covered Dutch oven or clay pot, a centuries-old technique. The yogurt adds a light tangy flavor and also tenderizes the dough. Add 1 tablespoon of minced lemon zest to the dough just before folding for even more layers of flavor.

3 cups all-purpose flour, plus more for dusting
½ cup whole wheat flour
¼ teaspoon instant yeast
1½ teaspoons kosher salt
½ cup whole (page 47) or low-fat yogurt
1¼ cups plus 2 tablespoons water
1½ tablespoons minced fresh dill or
    1½ teaspoons dried
1 teaspoon fine cornmeal (optional)
Coarse sea salt

In a large bowl, combine the all-purpose flour, whole wheat flour, yeast, and kosher salt. Using a whisk, combine the yogurt and water, then stir in the dill. Fold this into the dry mixture until blended. Add another tablespoon of water if the dough is dry; it should be rough looking and a bit sticky. Place the dough in an oiled container, cover, and let rest for 12 to 18 hours at an ambient temperature of about 70°F. The dough is ready when bubbles appear on the surface.

Gently turn the dough out onto a lightly floured work surface. Dust the dough with flour, then, using a bowl scraper or bench scraper, fold the dough over on itself two times. Cover with a kitchen towel and let rest for 15 minutes.

Line a bowl large enough to hold the risen dough with a flour sack or smooth kitchen towel. Generously coat the portion of the towel that is inside the bowl with all-purpose flour or a combination of flour and the cornmeal.

Flour your hands and the work surface (if needed) and gently shape the dough into a ball, then quickly place it, seam side down, in the floured bowl. Cover the dough with the ends of the towel and let rest for about 2 hours, or until doubled in size.

This bread can be baked in a conventional oven or over a wood fire. Half an hour before baking, set an empty 4-quart lidded baking pot (cast-iron, ceramic, or clay) and lid over the fire to preheat; if baking indoors, 1½ hours into the rising time place the baking pot and lid in the cold oven and preheat the oven to 500°F.

When the dough has risen, remove the pot from the oven or fire, and gently turn the dough out into the pot, seam side up. Any ragged edges are fine. They will become crispy and crunchy during baking. Sprinkle with coarse sea salt.

If cooking over coals, cover the pot with a sheet of foil and put the lid in place over the foil. Put 10 or so hot coals on top of the lid and put the pot over the fire. Bake for 20 minutes. If cooking in a conventional oven, place the heated lid on the pot and bake for 30 minutes.

Remove the lid and bake for another 15 minutes or more, until the loaf is a deep golden color. Slide the bread out of the pot and cool it on a rack. It tastes best if left to rest for 1 hour before serving.

CHEDDAR AND CHIVE SCONES

Makes 12 scones

Though scones are often thought of as sweet, savory versions are equally delicious, especially served warm with a dollop of crème fraîche. Combining sharp cheddar with chives makes these scones a perfect match with everything from a citrusy summer salad to a hearty cold-weather potato and bacon soup. You can play with different flavored cheddars in this recipe; try Irish-Style Cheddar (page 123) paired with fresh English thyme instead of chives. If you prefer a round shape to a wedge, cut into two- or three-inch rounds with a biscuit cutter and bake for a shorter length of time—fourteen to seventeen minutes.

3 cups all-purpose flour, plus more for dusting

1½ tablespoons baking powder

1 teaspoon baking soda

2 teaspoons kosher salt

¼ teaspoon sugar

10 tablespoons unsalted butter, cut into ½-inch cubes and chilled

About 1¼ cups cultured buttermilk (see page 44)

1¾ cups coarsely grated sharp cheddar cheese (page 123) (about 7 ounces)

2 tablespoons finely chopped chives

1 teaspoon grated lemon zest

Place the flour, baking powder, baking soda, salt, and sugar in a mixing bowl and stir to combine. Place the bowl in the refrigerator to chill for 10 minutes. Add the cubed butter and blend it into the flour mixture, breaking the butter into large flakes that remain visible. Combine 1 cup plus 2 tablespoons of the buttermilk, 1½ cups of the cheddar, and the chives and gently stir the mixture into the flour. The dough should have only enough moisture to just hold it together; add a few drops more buttermilk if needed. Do not overwork the dough or the scones will be tough.

Place the dough on a floured work surface and lightly dust with flour. With floured hands, shape the dough into two 8-inch disks about ¾ inch thick. Place the disks on a parchment-lined baking sheet, cover, and chill for at least 1 hour or up to overnight.

Preheat the oven to 400°F.

Cut each disk into 6 wedges and place on a freshly lined baking sheet. Lightly brush with some of the remaining buttermilk and sprinkle with a bit of the remaining ¼ cup of grated cheese. Bake for 20 to 25 minutes, or until lightly golden. Cool on a rack for 10 minutes, then serve warm. Store cooled scones in an airtight container for up to 3 days or freeze for up to 1 month.

BLUE CHEESE AND TOASTED WALNUT FUDGE BROWNIES

Makes sixteen 2-inch brownies

It may sound crazy, but blue cheese and chocolate, two seemingly mismatched partners, dance together deliciously. In this brownie, crunchy toasted walnuts work with the saltiness of the blue cheese, which in turn complements the bittersweet chocolate. This is my adaptation of the fudge brownie recipe from Michael Recchiuti and Fran Gage's book *Chocolate Obsession*. Because these are very rich, I cut them into small squares to serve. Trust me: try this one. You will be the hit of the party!

$^1/_2$ cup toasted walnut pieces

5 ounces 70 percent bittersweet chocolate, coarsely chopped

6 tablespoons unsalted butter

4 ounces crumbled mild blue cheese (page 186)

$^2/_3$ cup all-purpose flour

$^1/_2$ teaspoon kosher salt

3 eggs

1 teaspoon pure vanilla extract

1$^1/_4$ cups sugar

Preheat the oven to 325°F. Line the bottom and 2 sides of an 8-inch square baking pan with aluminum foil, then coat with cooking spray.

Break the larger walnut pieces into small bits. Divide the chocolate into 2 equal portions. Put 2 inches of water in a small pot and bring it to a simmer. Place half of the chocolate and the butter in a small stainless steel bowl and set it over the pot. Turn off the heat. Stir occasionally until the chocolate and butter melt and are fully combined. Stir in 2 ounces of the blue cheese until well combined and smooth. Set the bowl aside.

Sift the flour and salt together into a bowl. In a separate bowl, whisk the eggs and vanilla together until blended, then whisk in the sugar. Whisk the egg mixture into the chocolate mixture. Stir the flour and the remaining chocolate chunks into the batter and mix well. Using a spatula, fold in the remaining 2 ounces of blue cheese and the walnuts.

Pour the batter into the prepared baking pan and spread evenly with an offset spatula. Place on the middle rack of the oven and bake until the top gives only slightly when you touch it with a finger, about 30 minutes. At this point, test with a skewer for doneness. The skewer should have a slight amount of batter on it; the brownies will finish baking as the pan cools. Place on a rack to cool completely, then cover with plastic wrap and refrigerate until cold and set up.

Run a knife around the edges of the pan and lift the whole brownie out of the pan on the foil. Place it on a work surface and, using a sharp knife, cut into sixteen 2-inch brownies. Store refrigerated in an airtight container for up to 2 weeks.

CARAMELIZED APPLE TART WITH CHEDDAR CRUST

Makes one 9- to 10-inch tart

This tart uses cheddar in the crust for a spin on the classic cheddar–apple pie pairing. The crust is actually a cheddar cookie recipe from my friend Nick Malgieri, the author of *Bake!* and numerous other cookbooks. You'll have some dough left after filling the tart pan, so you can either use that dough to make decorative cutouts to add to the top of the tart or cut it into squares and bake it as crackers. This dough is also wonderful in a savory tart.

DOUGH

1¼ cups all-purpose flour

½ cup unsalted butter, cubed and chilled

4 ounces grated sharp cheddar

¼ teaspoon kosher salt

Pinch of white pepper

FILLING

¼ cup unsalted butter

2 or 3 large apples (1½ pounds), peeled, cored, and sliced into wedges

3 tablespoons brown sugar

Pinch of anise seeds

Pinch of freshly grated nutmeg

2 ounces grated sharp cheddar

To make the dough, combine the flour, butter, cheddar, salt, and pepper in a food processor and process until the dough comes together to form a ball. Place the dough on plastic wrap, cover with more plastic wrap, and immediately roll out to ⅛ inch thick. Place the dough in a removable-bottom tart pan and gently press into the bottom and up the sides of the pan. Trim any extra dough from the edge of the pan and reserve for another use. Place the pan in the refrigerator.

Preheat the oven to 350°F.

To make the filling, melt the butter in a heavy-bottomed skillet over medium heat, then add the apples and brown sugar and cook, gently stirring on occasion, until slightly softened, about 10 minutes. Remove from the heat and stir in the anise seeds and nutmeg. Set aside to let cool.

Toss the grated cheese into the cooled mixture, then distribute the filling over the bottom of the tart crust. Place on the lower rack of the oven and bake for 30 to 35 minutes, until the top is slightly caramelized and the cheese has melted. Cool on a rack, then remove from the tart pan. Cut into wedges and serve.

VANILLA BEAN FONTAINEBLEAU *with Pistachio Brittle*

Serves 8

If you are a fan of frothy desserts such as zabaglione or sabayon, you will love this version of Fontainebleau, the very airy, creamy dessert typically made from fromage blanc and heavy cream. I love the combination of crème fraîche and goat's milk yogurt used here. The preparation time is minimal, yet the results will garner applause. You can substitute cow's milk yogurt for the goat's milk yogurt, though the lovely tang from the goat's milk will be missing. Reserve the scraped vanilla bean pod to infuse sugar or spirits. Annie Simmons, my amazing kitchen assistant and talented pastry chef, created the crunchy pistachio brittle that accompanies the Fontainebleau. When making the brittle, have fun playing with different nut mixtures, adding chopped candied orange peel, or stirring in a bit of chopped chocolate as the brittle cools.

2/3 cup goat's milk yogurt

2/3 cup crème fraîche (page 44)

Seeds from 1/2 split and scraped vanilla bean

1 teaspoon grated orange zest

1 1/2 teaspoons orange flower water (optional)

4 tablespoons granulated sugar or vanilla-infused superfine sugar

1 egg white

Pistachio Brittle (recipe follows)

12 lightly toasted pistachios, finely chopped

Drain the yogurt and crème fraîche in separate fine-mesh strainers until the liquid stops dripping from them. Combine the crème fraîche, vanilla seeds, orange zest, orange flower water, if using, and 2 tablespoons of the sugar in a chilled bowl. Using a whisk or an electric mixer, whip until firm peaks are formed. Whisk some air into the yogurt to make it a bit fluffy, and then fold it into the whipped crème fraîche to incorporate.

In a separate dry bowl, whip the egg white until fluffy, then add the remaining 2 tablespoons of sugar and whip until soft but firm peaks form. Using a rubber spatula, gently fold the egg white into the crème fraîche mixture until well combined.

Line a strainer or small colander with fine cheesecloth or butter muslin and place over a bowl for draining. Spoon the mixture into the strainer, cover with plastic wrap, and place in the bottom of the refrigerator for 6 hours, or up to overnight to drain and set up. The finished consistency should be like a mousse.

Spoon or pipe the Fontainebleau into chilled parfait glasses and garnish with a shard of pistachio brittle and a sprinkling of finely chopped pistachios. Serve promptly, as the shape will only hold for about 20 minutes.

PISTACHIO BRITTLE

Makes about 12 ounces

1 teaspoon unsalted butter, softened
2 cups sugar
Pinch of cream of tartar
1/4 cup water
1 cup lightly toasted pistachios
1 teaspoon flake sea salt

Line a rimmed 10 by 14-inch baking sheet or jelly roll pan with aluminum foil and use the butter to grease the foil. Set the pan aside.

In a heavy-bottomed saucepan, whisk together the sugar, cream of tartar, and water. Bring to a boil over medium-high heat and cook for 3 to 5 minutes, until steam no longer evaporates off the boiling sugar mixture. Turn the heat down to medium and allow the mixture to caramelize, swirling the pan once or twice, until the caramel is a medium amber color. Add the pistachios to the caramel and immediately pour the mixture into the prepared baking sheet, gently tilting the sheet to even out the distribution of the brittle. Be very careful at this step, as the sugar is very hot. Set the pan of brittle on a rack, sprinkle with the salt, and allow to cool completely before breaking into pieces of desired sizes. The brittle can be stored in an airtight container for up to 3 days.

RICOTTA-FILLED CHOCOLATE CREPES
WITH NUTELLA AND SOUR CHERRY PRESERVES

Makes 12 dessert crepes

Though you're used to seeing ricotta in lasagna, this recipe showcases the versatility of this creamy cheese. Here it fills chocolate crepes that have been spread with the decadent hazelnut-cocoa spread Nutella and topped with sour cherry preserves and chopped hazelnuts. The crepes can be made a day ahead. Stack them with plastic wrap between them and refrigerate in a resealable plastic bag. They will keep refrigerated for 1 week or frozen for about 1 month. Warm them before using.

CREPES
- 1½ cups all-purpose flour
- ½ cup unsweetened cocoa powder
- 6 tablespoons confectioners' sugar
- ¼ teaspoon kosher salt
- 2¼ cups whole milk
- 2 large eggs
- 6 tablespoons unsalted butter, melted
- ½ teaspoon pure vanilla extract

FILLING AND TOPPING
- 2 cups fresh ricotta (page 39), drained for 1 hour
- 1 teaspoon confectioners' sugar
- 1½ cups Nutella hazelnut-cocoa spread
- 1½ cups sour cherry or red raspberry preserves, warmed
- ¾ cup chopped toasted hazelnuts

To make the crepes, in a medium bowl sift together the flour, cocoa, sugar, and salt. In a separate bowl or in a blender, whisk together 2 cups of the milk, the eggs, 2 tablespoons of the butter, and the vanilla. Add one-third of the dry ingredients to the blended liquid and blend until smooth. Repeat twice to blend in the rest of the dry ingredients. Cover and refrigerate the batter for 30 minutes or overnight. When ready to use, whisk the batter thoroughly and add up to ¼ cup more milk if the batter is thicker than runny pancake batter.

Preheat a 10-inch nonstick skillet over medium-high heat. Brush the bottom with melted butter. Ladle enough batter (about ¼ to ⅓ cup) into the pan to just cover the bottom. Immediately lift the pan off the heat and swirl the batter around to cover the bottom of the pan as though you were making an omelette. Cook for about 1 minute, until the edges start to look dry but not crispy and a few steam holes appear in the center. This tells you that there's enough structure to the crepe to be able to flip it over. Using an offset spatula, turn the crepe over and cook for about 30 seconds. Slide the crepe from the pan onto a plate. Continue the process, brushing the pan with melted butter each time and stacking the crepes until all the batter is used.

To make the filling, put the ricotta and sugar in a bowl and stir until well combined. Spread half of each open crepe with 2 tablespoons of Nutella. Crumble or spread the ricotta over the Nutella. Fold the plain half over the filled half and then fold again into a wedge. Place on a serving plate, top each with 2 tablespoons of preserves and 1 tablespoon of chopped hazelnuts, and serve.

STONE FRUIT PHYLLO TARTS
with Mascarpone-Cardamom Ice Cream
Serves 8

This not-too-sweet dessert has it all: soft, juicy fruit, a crunchy crust, and cardamom-infused ice cream to top it off. Mascarpone, a rich Italian cultured cream, is what makes the ice cream sensational. Cardamom pods work best for infusing the milk, as they keep the color pure, but ground cardamom can also be used. You can use any seasonal ripe, firm stone fruit, though apricots or nectarines are especially wonderful with the cardamom and pistachios.

....

4 or 5 large ripe but firm nectarines or other stone
    fruit (1½ pounds)
Juice of 1 orange
1¾ cups unsalted butter
12 sheets phyllo dough
2 teaspoons ground cardamom
2 teaspoons ground cinnamon
4 teaspoons plus ¾ cup granulated sugar
⅓ cup pistachios, finely chopped
2 tablespoons unbleached all-purpose flour
Grated zest of 1 orange
1 tablespoon turbinado sugar
Mascarpone-Cardamom Ice Cream (recipe follows)

Blanch the nectarines in a pot of simmering water for 30 seconds, then place in a water bath to cool slightly. Remove the skins, cut the flesh into quarters, and discard the pits. Brush the fruit with orange juice so it does not brown.

Melt 1 cup of the butter in a small saucepan. Lay the sheets of phyllo out on a baking sheet and cover with a slightly damp towel. Combine the cardamom and cinnamon and the 4 teaspoons of granulated sugar in a small bowl.

Lay out 1 sheet of phyllo on a work surface and brush with the melted butter. Sprinkle with some of the sugar-spice mixture, then lay another sheet of phyllo on top, brush with butter, and sprinkle with the sugar-spice mixture. On top of this second sheet, also sprinkle some of the chopped pistachios. Cover with a third layer of phyllo and brush the top with butter. Cut off enough phyllo to form one square large enough to fit into a shallow 10-inch round baking dish with 1½ inches extending over the edges of the dish. Gently place the stack of phyllo into the baking dish and press down into the edges. Leave the excess to encase the fruit before baking. Repeat the layering process three more times. (For individual tarts, cut each stack of 3 sheets into two 7 by 7-inch squares so that you have 8 squares of 3 layers each. Gently place each square into a shallow 4-inch baking ramekin and press down into the edges.)

Preheat the oven to 350°F.

Melt the remaining ¾ cup of butter and the ¾ cup of granulated sugar together in a saucepan, stir to combine, and cook over low heat until the sugar dissolves and then begins to caramelize, about 20 minutes. Whisk in the flour, then stir in the zest. Add the nectarines and toss to coat in the mixture, then cook for 5 minutes. Remove from the heat and let the mixture cool for 5 minutes, then spoon into the phyllo-lined baking dish (or spoon a portion into each phyllo-lined ramekin). Fold the excess phyllo over the fruit, brush with any remaining melted butter, and sprinkle with the turbinado sugar. Place the baking dish or ramekins on a baking sheet and bake for 15 to 20 minutes, until the pastry is golden brown. Serve warm, topped with the ice cream.

MASCARPONE-CARDAMOM ICE CREAM
Makes about 1½ quarts

2 cups whole milk

2 cups heavy cream

6 cardamom pods, crushed, or 1 teaspoon
    ground cardamom

½ split and scraped vanilla bean or 1 teaspoon
    pure vanilla extract

9 large egg yolks

¾ cup sugar

1 cup mascarpone (page 36)

¼ cup finely chopped pistachios (optional)

Place the milk and cream in a nonreactive saucepan. Warm over medium-low heat to just below the boiling point. Turn off the heat and add the cardamom pods and vanilla bean, if using, cover the pan, and allow the mixture to steep for 40 minutes. Pour the mixture through a fine-mesh strainer into a medium bowl, pressing firmly against the cardamom pods to release their flavor. Discard the pods and reserve the vanilla bean for another use. Return the flavored milk mixture to the saucepan.

Place the pan over medium-low heat and reheat the mixture to just below the boiling point. In a bowl, whisk the egg yolks together with the sugar. Whisking constantly, slowly add about 1 cup of the hot milk mixture to the yolks to temper the eggs. Pour the yolk mixture into the saucepan and cook over medium heat, stirring constantly with a wooden spoon, until the custard thickens and coats the back of the spoon (it will be at about 170°F). Do not let the mixture boil, as the eggs will curdle. Remove from the heat and immediately pour the mixture through a fine-mesh strainer set over a stainless steel bowl. Set the bowl in an ice bath and gently stir the custard for a few minutes to cool it slightly. Whisk in the mascarpone and the vanilla extract, if using. Remove the bowl from the ice bath, cover with plastic wrap placed directly on the custard's surface, and refrigerate until well chilled. (At this point you have a crème anglaise—a delicious dessert sauce.)

After the custard has chilled, freeze it in your ice cream maker according to the manufacturer's directions. Immediately transfer the ice cream to a storage container, cover, and freeze. Serve within 1 hour of freezing, or allow it to soften slightly before serving. Sprinkle with the pistachios before serving, if using.

ACKNOWLEDGMENTS

I owe a great deal of gratitude to passionate American cheese makers who were inspired and courageous enough to venture into the world of hand-crafted cheese making. Thank you to these who I consider to be the godmothers and godfathers of the American artisan cheese movement: Jennifer Bice, Laura Chenel, Allison Hooper, Mary Keehn, Paula Lambert, Judy Schad, Tom and Ig Vella, and Celso and Pete Viviani. The crafting of handmade cheese in America began with them. All have generously shared their cheeses, passion, and cheese making expertise over the years and have mentored a new wave of cheese makers. They are the foundation of the American cheese community and continue to contribute daily to its nourishment and sustainability. These artisans are my inspiration for teaching cheese making, making cheese myself, and writing this book.

In addition I want to thank these folks for their support:

Lynne Devereux, for your constant encouragement and unwavering support throughout the years.

David Viviani and Lou Biaggi, of Sonoma Jack, for inviting me to create cheeses with you.

Ted Reader and Napoleon Grills, for showing me how food *really* should be smoked.

Peter Dixon and Jim Wallace, for lifting the veil on many of the mysteries of cheese making.

Laura Werlin, for making cheese so popular.

Fran Gage and Michael Recchuiti, for your chocolate genius.

Nick Malgieri, for your baking expertise and advice.

Hugs and kisses to the cheese maker contributors: Jill Giacomini Basch and Kuba Hemmerling of Point Reyes Farmstead Cheese, Jacquelyn Buchanan of Laura Chenel's Chevre, Angela Miller and Peter Dixon of Consider Bardwell Farm, Stan Biasini of Mt. Mansfield Creamery, Kurt Dammeier and Brad Sinko of Beecher's Handmade Cheese, Paula Lambert and her ladies of Mozzarella Company, Judy Schad of Capriole, Allison Hooper of Vermont Butter & Cheese, and serious hobbyists Aaron Estes, Nancy Vineyard, and Jim Wallace. Thank you for allowing me to include you.

To my incredible cooking recipe testing team: Kay Austin, team manager, and James Cribb, Suzy Foster, Nancy Lang, Lisa Lavagetto, Annie Simmons, and Sue Simon. Thank you for contributing your practiced palates to my recipes once again.

To my *amazing* cheese testing team: Sally McComas, team manager, and Lori Bowling, Gabe Jackson, and Robyn Rosemon. Thank you for bringing your cheese making expertise to this project. You are awesome!

A special nod to Sally McComas, for being my cheese assistant extraordinaire. Her thoughtful suggestions and well-honed managerial skills kept me moving forward.

Applause for the Beverage People in Santa Rosa for their staunch support and contributions. Thank you to Bob and Nancy for taking my cheese making class. Thank you for supporting hobbyist cheese makers. Hugs to Robyn, the Cheddar Queen, for her love for all things cheese. Kudos to Gabe Jackson, Maestro pH, for his adventuresome spirit and investigative mind.

Thanks also to the following people:

Bert Archer, my biggest fan, for years of love and coaching.

John Ash, for years of love, encouragement, and generosity.

Bud and Lorrie Polley, for your willingness to taste my cheeses and for years of friendship.

Peter Reinhart, for being there.

Richard and Karen Silverton, for feeding me the scoop on artisan cheese makers.

Liz Thorpe, Sasha Ingram, and Michael Anderson at Murray's Cheese, for educating cheese-hungry enthusiasts, and approaching cheese with respect and humor.

Annie Simmons, my photo shoot assistant; your acute professionalism made the shoot effortless.

Ed Anderson, photographer, for your artistic eye and wicked humor.

Aaron Wehner, Melissa Moore, and the creative team at Ten Speed Press, for welcoming my vision and producing a beautiful book.

Ricki Carroll, for having the idea way back that cheese making at home would be embraced.

All of the cooking schools who recognize that do-it-yourselfers want to learn to make cheese. Thank you to all who come to my classes.

GLOSSARY

Acidification. Development of acid (and corresponding drop in pH) in milk or cheese as lactic bacteria convert lactose to lactic acid.

Acidity. In cheese making, the concentration of all acid components in milk, curds, cheese, or whey; usually measured on the pH scale.

Affinage. The process of caring for, aging, and developing a cheese to its highest potential; from the French *affiner* (refine, polish, mature).

Aged. Refers to cheese that has been held under cellar conditions to achieve a desirable balance of texture, flavor, and aroma.

Aging. Holding of a cheese, usually in cavelike conditions, for best development; *see also* affinage.

Ambient temperature. The warmth (or coolness) all around; the temperature of aging in a cellar or other enclosed place.

Annatto. An extract of achiote fruit and seeds; a naturally derived orange or yellow dye often used in liquid form in the production of cheddar or similar cheeses.

Aroma mesophilic culture. A lactic bacteria culture growing at moderate (mesophilic) temperatures; particularly valued for contributions to cheese aromas through production of diacetyl and other aromatic compounds.

Artisan. Made by hand in small batches, as contrasted with large-scale industrial manufacturing.

Bacteria. Autonomous microscopic organisms that can produce positive or negative effects. In cheese making the most important positive group is lactic bacteria, which convert lactose into lactic acid.

Bandaging. Wrapping of cheese with cloth to protect the surface and promote ripening.

Bloomy-rind. Descriptive of cheeses that develop a white, downy rind through growth of mold species such as *Penicillium candidum* or *Geotrichum candidum.*

Blue-veined. Characteristic of pierced-cake cheeses in which blue mold (*Penicillium roqueforti*) is encouraged to grow.

Brevibacterium linens. The bacteria characteristic of cheeses known as "stinkers," such as Limburger and Muenster cheeses; a red "smear" bacterium.

Brine. In cheese making, a salt solution used for soaking cheese, sometimes incorporating whey or calcium chloride.

Brining. The soaking of a cheese in a salty solution to flavor the cheese and develop desirable surface characteristics, as contrasted with dry salting.

bST. Bovine somatotropin, a naturally occurring growth-promoting hormone in cattle. Controversy surrounds the genetically engineered version, rbST or recombinant bovine somatotropin. In natural or synthetic form, it supports milk production in the dairy cow.

Butterfat (aka milk fat). The combination of fatty acids and triglycerides that constitutes the fatty portion of milk.

Buttermilk. The milk left after butter is churned. Naturally or by culturing, it undergoes a lactic fermentation, producing sour flavors and coagulating proteins, which thickens its texture.

Butter muslin. A fine, woven cotton cloth used in draining whey from some cheeses.

Calcium. An alkaline earth chemical element; important in cheese making as the calcium ion, Ca++, which is critical for curd formation.

Calcium chloride. A common salt consisting of one calcium ion and two chloride ions, CaCl2; in solution form, a convenient way to add calcium to milk for cheese production.

Casein. A major protein in milk. When acted upon by acid or rennet, it precipitates from milk to form the primary structure of curds.

Cave. Any cool, moist chamber for the aging of cheese.

Cheddaring. Cutting of curds into strips and draining them while stacked into slabs, prior to pressing the cheese; a distinguishing process in the production of cheddar cheeses.

Cheesecloth. A cotton cloth used for draining whey from curds; usually loosely woven, unless specified otherwise.

Cheese mat. A mat made of any open-weave impervious material, such as nylon mesh or bamboo sushi mats; used to support drying or aging cheese.

Citric acid. A naturally occurring carboxylic acid, $C_6H_8O_7$, characteristic of citrus fruits; used to directly acidify milk in some applications, such as quick mozzarella.

Clabber. Verb: to coagulate or curdle. Noun: a somewhat thick soured milk, originally from naturally occurring lactic bacteria, but now cultured due to pasteurization of most milk. German quark and French crème fraîche are similar.

Clean break. The point in the solidification of curds that a finger, thermometer, knife, or spoon can be used to lift some curd and it falls away sharply, looking like a miniature cliff face.

Coagulation. Solidification of proteins forming curd.

Curd knife. A long, thin-bladed knife used for cutting curds; generally rounded at the end to avoid scratching the pot.

Curds. The solid part of cheese as it's being made, as compared with the liquid whey. Curd structure is formed from protein and it contains fat, moisture, salts, and other milk components.

Cutting. Passing a knife or other narrow blade through a curd mass to divide it into smaller chunks; encourages the release of whey.

Dairy thermometer. A glass or stainless steel instrument for measuring the temperature of milk, curds, or whey.

Denaturing. Degradation and cross-linking of protein strands, caused by the addition of acid, heat, enzymes, or solvent. In the kitchen, the process yields nonsoluble solid materials such as cheese curd or cooked egg white.

Diacetyl. A fermentation compound which contributes a desirable buttery aroma to a cheese; gas production: refers to cultures that produce CO_2.

Direct-set culture. Bacteria or mold organisms prepared in a form for direct addition to milk for production of cheese; usually sold as a freeze-dried granular powder kept cold for storage.

Double boiler. An arrangement of a large outer pot containing water and a smaller inner pot containing the material to be cooked, as milk for cheese, allowing for gentler and more gradual heating than direct heat might; *see also* water bath.

Double-cream. High-fat cheeses (60 percent butterfat by dry weight).

Drying. In cheese making, reducing the moistness of cheese by placing it in a drier atmosphere.

Dry salting. Sprinkling or coating directly with salt, as contrasted with brining.

Enzymes. Biologically active proteins that break or form chemical bonds in specific environments; for example, the action of the enzymes in rennet on the milk protein casein.

Eyes. Openings or bubbles in a finished cheese created by bacterial production of carbon dioxide during aging; characteristic of Swiss and similar cheeses.

Farmstead cheese. Cheese produced at the same location as the milk from which it's made.

Fat content. Percent by weight of butterfat (milk fat) in milk or cheese.

Fermentation. Conversion by micro-organisms of a specific substance into a desired product; for example, production of alcohol from fruit sugar or lactic acid from lactose.

Finishing. The name for a process in commercial cheese production: the stirring of curds and their removal from the tank; similar stirring is used in some home cheese recipes.

Follower. A snug-fitting plug or cap inserted into a cheese press or mold on top of the curds, to which pressure or weight is applied. This insert "follows" the curds down into the mold as they are being pressed.

Food grade. A level of quality recognized in food service as being food safe.

Fresh cheeses. Cheeses not subjected to aging or affinage; usually ready to eat immediately or within days of production.

Geotrichum candidum. One of the white mold species important to bloomy-rind cheeses as Valençay, Camembert, and Brie.

Grana style. Hard cheese with a granular structure that is broken apart with a blunt knife rather than sliced; for example, Grana Padano.

Heat-treated milk. Milk that has been pasteurized or sterilized by exposure to high temperatures.

Herd share. An agreement in which a consumer pays a farmer for a share of a dairy herd (or individual animal) in exchange for a share of the milk.

Homogenization. The mechanical reduction of the size of fat particles in milk to form a stable emulsion.

Hygrometer. An instrument for measuring relative humidity in the air.

Inoculating. Introducing living organisms onto or into a growth medium; for example, the addition of bacterial or mold cultures to milk.

Lactic. A reference to the fermentation of lactose (milk sugar) into lactic acid.

Lactic acid. A carboxylic acid of formula C3H6O3; the natural acid produced in the fermentation processes involved in cheese making.

Lactic bacteria. Microorganisms capable of converting lactose into lactic acid.

Lactose. Milk sugar; a disaccharide (twelve-carbon sugar) consisting of the two monosaccharides glucose and galactose.

Lipase. An enzyme from the gut of a juvenile milk-producing mammal that breaks down fat into aromatic short-chain fatty acids.

Mat. *See* cheese mat.

Matting. The knitting together of warm curds; the result of letting curds settle untouched in whey or the binding together in the curd draining process.

Mesophilic bacteria. Microorganisms that thrive on "middle" temperatures from about 70°F to 90°F.

Microflora. A term for the collective microorganisms, usually bacteria and molds, native to a substance (such as milk) or place (either geographical, as a region, or biological, as the gut).

Milk fat. *See* butterfat.

Milling. Cutting or breaking finished curds prior to forming them into cheese.

Mold. (1) A form of perforated plastic or stainless steel used for draining and shaping a cheese; (2) fungal microorganisms that grow in multicellular filaments.

Molding. Forming or shaping a cheese in a mold.

Mold-ripened. Cheese in which fungal growth has been encouraged through inoculation and/or through the conditions of aging.

Natural rind. A relatively solid surface of a cheese, formed by the cheese itself during aging.

Nonreactive. Refers to cookware used for ripening milk that does not react to the acid being added to the milk. Examples: stainless steel, ceramic-coated cast iron, glass, enamel-coated canning pots, clay.

Overripe. The condition of cheese aged past its prime; often accompanied by unpleasant ammonia odors and equally unpleasant taste.

Paste. The interior portion of a cheese.

Pasteurization. Heat treatment of milk to reduce the population of viable microorganisms; intended to eliminate pathogens, or disease-causing organisms.

Pasteurized milk. Milk that has been heat-treated to destroy pathogens.

Penicillium candidum. A white mold common in the production of Camembert and Brie.

Penicillium roqueforti. A blue and/or green mold present in the production of blue cheese.

pH. A measure of acid content in a substance, measured on a scale of 0 (completely acidic) to 14 (completely alkaline/basic, or nonacidic), with 7 being the neutral midpoint.

pH meter. An electronic instrument for the measurement of pH.

Piercing. Puncturing a cheese to create air channels, encouraging growth of aerobic molds such as *Penicillium roqueforti*.

Pressing. Applying weight or pressure to a cheese to help expel whey and achieve a desired texture.

Protein. A long-chain molecule made up of peptides, which in turn are made up of amino acids. Proteins are the structural building blocks of cheese curds.

Proteolytic. Protein-degrading enzymes that contribute to the development of desirable flavor and texture in virtually all aged cheeses.

Raw milk. Milk that has not been pasteurized and thus retains its full complement of microflora.

rbST. *See* bST.

Redressing. Removing a cheese from the press, unwrapping it from its cheesecloth, flipping it, and rewrapping it in the same cloth before pressing again.

Rennet. An enzyme extract from the gut of an infant ruminant animal or from specific plants or fungi and used as a coagulant. Its most active cheese-curdling component is the enzyme rennin, or chymosin. Defined as animal, vegetable, or microbial rennet.

Ricotta basket. A plastic or wicker basket for draining ricotta curds.

Rind. The surface layer of a cheese.

Ripe. Mature and ready to eat; the end point of cheese affinage.

Ripening. (1) Allowing the enzymatic, chemical, and moisture changes to bring cheese to a desired endpoint; (2) manipulating temperature and bacterial growth to prepare the milk for coagulation.

Ripening bacteria. Microorganisms that are active during various phases of affinage.

Room temperature. As defined in this book, refers to an ambient temperature of 68°F to 72°F.

Salting. Adding (usually) sodium chloride to a cheese; *see also* brining and dry salting.

Secondary culture. A bacteria, mold, or yeast used alone or in combination with other secondary cultures that make their contributions in the ripening phase of the cheese's development.

Semisoft. Cheeses that are resilient or rubbery but not soft enough to spread.

Setting. Allowing curds to stand undisturbed during coagulation and finishing.

Sharp. Pungent; in cheese making, usually denotes an elevated acid level in a finished cheese.

Skimmed milk. Milk from which the fat has been removed.

Skimmer. A handled, perforated tool used to remove foam or residue from the top of a liquid; useful in cheese making for slicing curds and transferring curds to a mold or strainer for draining.

Smear bacteria. Bacteria applied to the surface of a smeared-rind cheese to encourage desirable bacteria development.

Squeakers. Curds that give a characteristic squeaky feel when bitten.

Starter culture. A preparation of living organisms suitable for inoculating milk to develop cheese.

Sterilize. To destroy all living microorganisms, usually with high heat.

Surface-ripened. Cheese that has matured through development of aerobic microbes growing on the surface or rind, gradually spreading their influence into the paste.

Terroir. A French term denoting the total influence of climate, sunlight, soil, and moisture on a finished agricultural product such as cheese or wine.

Thermophilic bacteria. Microorganisms that thrive at warmer temperatures, usually 104°F to 122°F.

Tomme press. A small- to medium-size press suitable for making tomme (French Alpine) and similar pressed cheeses.

Triple-cream. A very high-fat cheese (75 percent butterfat by dry weight).

Ultra-pasteurized. Milk and cream treated at very high temperature to produce a long shelf life; generally not suitable for cheese making due to protein damage during the process.

Vegetable ash. The black dusting powder made from activated charcoal (often referred to as ash); used to coat the exterior surface of certain cheeses such as Valençay or to dust layers of pressed curds to define milk batches in cheeses such as Morbier.

Washed curds. Curds that have been rinsed after being cut and prior to final cheese formation. The process generally reduces the lactose level in the finished cheese.

Washed-rind. Descriptive of a cheese whose rind has been rubbed with a liquid (such as brine or spirits) as part of its aging.

Water bath. A pot or tank containing hot water in which a smaller production pot or tank is fitted, allowing for gentle indirect heating of milk for cheese production.

Waxed. Coated with paraffin or similar sealing material.

Whey. The watery lactose-carrying solution that is drained from curds during cheese production; the part of milk that does not become cheese.

RESOURCES

Cheese Making Supplies

The Beverage People • www.thebeveragepeople.com

Dairy Connection • www.dairyconnection.com

Glengarry Cheesemaking and Dairy Supply
www.glengarrycheesemaking.on.ca

Grape and Granary • www.grapeandgranary.com

New England Cheesemaking Supply • www.cheesemaking.com

Schmidling CheesyPress • www.schmidling.com/press.htm

Miscellaneous Supplies

The Cheesemaker • www.thecheesemaker.com
Wood cheese boxes

The Cheese Saver • www.cheesesaver.com
Ripening box and humidor

Formaticum • www.formaticum.com
Cheese paper and cheese journal

Junket Desserts • www.junketdesserts.com
Junket rennet tablets

Tagines • www.tagines.com • Thistle blossoms

Whole Spice • www.wholespice.com • Dried herbs and spices

Cheese Smokers and Cookware

The Big Green Egg • www.biggreenegg.com
Ceramic cooker/smoker

Cooking.com • www.cooking.com
Carbon steel wok, burner ring, and lid; Joyce Chen 6-inch
bamboo steamer

Napoleon Grills • www.napoleongrills.com
Apollo 3-in-1 Smoker Grill

Cheese Making Classes and Cheese Workshops

Carr Valley Cheese Cooking School • La Valle, WI
www.carrvalleycheese.com

The Cheesemaker • Cedarburg, WI
www.thecheesemaker.com

The Fork Culinary Center, Point Reyes Farmstead Cheese
Point Reyes, CA • www.theforkatpointreyes.com

Great News! Cooking School • San Diego, CA
www.great-news.com

New England Cheesemaking Supply • South Deerfield, MA
www.cheesemaking.com

Peter Dixon Consulting • Westminster West, VT
www.dairyfoodsconsulting.com

Ramekins Culinary School • Sonoma, CA • www.ramekins.com

Relish Culinary Center • Healdsburg, CA
www.relishculinary.com

Shelburne Farms • Shelburne, VT • www.shelburnefarms.org

Vermont Institute for Artisan Cheese • Burlington, VT
www.nutrition.uvm.edu/viac

Cheese Festivals and Events

American Cheese Society Festival of Cheese
www.cheesesociety.org

Artisan Cheese Festival
www.artisancheesefestival.com

Oregon Cheese Festival • www.oregoncheeseguild.org

Seattle Cheese Festival • www.seattlecheesefestival.com

Vermont Cheesemakers Festival • www.vtcheesefest.com

Wisconsin Original Cheese Festival • www.wicheesefest.com

Regional Cheese Organizations

California Artisan Cheese Guild ▪ www.cacheeseguild.org

Maine Cheese Guild ▪ www.mainecheeseguild.org

New York State Farmstead and Artisan Cheesemakers Guild
www.nyfarmcheese.org

Oregon Cheese Guild ▪ www.oregoncheeseguild.org

Pacific Northwest Cheese Project
www.pnwcheese.typepad.com

Southern Cheesemakers' Guild ▪ www.southerncheese.com

Vermont Cheese Council ▪ www.vtcheese.com

Wisconsin Dairy Artisan Network
www.wisconsindairyartisan.com

Milk Resources

American Dairy Association ▪ www.adadc.com

California Milk Advisory Board ▪ www.realcaliforniamilk.com

California Real Milk Association (CReMA)
www.californiarawmilk.org

Campaign for Real Milk ▪ Raw milk laws, cow shares
www.realmilk.com and www.realmilk.com/cowfarmshare.html

Eat Well Guide ▪ www.eatwellguide.org

Northeast Organic Farming Association ▪ www.nofa.org

Rural Vermont ▪ www.ruralvermont.org

Small Dairy ▪ www.smalldairy.com

Cheese Publications

Cheese Enthusiast newsletter ▪ www.cheeseenthusiast.net

Culture magazine ▪ www.culturecheesemag.com

Artisan Cheese Retailers

Bi-Rite Market ▪ San Francisco, CA ▪ www.biritemarket.com

The Cheese Board Collective ▪ Berkeley, CA
www.cheeseboardcollective.coop

Cowgirl Creamery ▪ Northern CA and Washington, DC
www.cowgirlcreamery.com

Katzinger's ▪ Columbus, OH ▪ www.katzingers.com

Lucy's Whey ▪ New York, NY ▪ www.lucyswhey.com

Murray's Cheese ▪ New York, NY ▪ www.murrayscheese.com

Oliver's Markets ▪ Santa Rosa, CA ▪ www.oliversmarket.com

Scardello ▪ Dallas, TX ▪ www.scardellocheese.com

Wisconsin Cheese Mart ▪ Milwaukee, WI
www.wisconsincheesemart.com

Zingerman's Delicatessen ▪ Ann Arbor, MI
www.zingermansdeli.com

Websites and Blogs

Author's blog at http://homecraftedcheese.com
and website at www.artisancheesemakingathome.com

blog.artisanalcheese.com

caveagedblog.wordpress.com

curdnerds.com

Artisan Cheese Producers

Beecher's Handmade Cheese ▪ Seattle, WA
www.beechershandmadecheese.com

Capriole Farmstead Goat Cheeses ▪ Greenville, IN
www.capriolegoatcheese.com

Consider Bardwell Farm ▪ West Pawlet, VT
www.considerbardwellfarm.com

Laura Chenel's Chèvre ▪ Sonoma, CA ▪ www.laurachenel.com

Mozzarella Company ▪ Dallas, TX ▪ www.mozzco.com

Point Reyes Farmstead Cheese Company ▪ Point Reyes Station,
CA ▪ www.pointreyescheese.com

Vermont Butter and Cheese Creamery ▪ Websterville, VT
www.vermontcreamery.com

BIBLIOGRAPHY

Armein-Boyes, Debra. *200 Easy Homemade Cheese Recipes*. Toronto: Robert Rose, 2009.

Barthelemy, Roland. *Guide to Cheeses of the World*. London: Octopus Publishing Group, 2005.

Brennan, Terrance. *Artisanal Cooking*. Hoboken, NJ: John Wiley & Sons, 2005.

Carroll, Ricki. *Home Cheese Making*, 3rd edition. North Adams, MA: Storey Publishing, 2002.

Dixon, Peter. *Farmstead Cheesemaking Collection Newsletter* (Summer 1999–2006).

Dixon, Peter. *Farmstead Cheesemaking Newsletter* (Summer 2007–Fall 2008).

Herbst, Sharon Tyler, and Ron. *The Cheese Lover's Companion*. New York: William Morrow, 2007.

Jenkins, Steven. *Cheese Primer*. New York: Workman Publishing, 1996.

Jordi, Natalie. "It's a Wrap." *Culture* volume 1, issue 3 (Summer 2009), 70–77.

Kaufelt, Rob. *The Murray's Cheese Handbook*. New York: Broadway Books, 2006.

Kindstedt, Paul. *American Farmstead Cheese*. White River Junction, VT: Chelsea Green Publishing, 2005.

Kosikowski, Frank V. *Cheese and Fermented Milk Food*, 3rd edition. Brooktondale, NY: F. V. Kosikowski and Associates, 1982.

Lambert, Paula. *The Cheese Lover's Cookbook and Guide*. New York: Simon & Schuster, 2000.

Le Jaouen, Jean-Claude. *The Fabrication of Farmstead Goat Cheese*. Ashfield, MA: Cheesemakers' Journal, 1987.

McCalman, Max, and David Gibbons. *Cheese*. New York: Clarkson Potter, 2005.

McCalman, Max, and David Gibbons. *Mastering Cheese*. New York: Clarkson Potter, 2009.

McGee, Harold. *On Food and Cooking*. New York: Scribner, 2004.

Mendelson, Anne. *Milk*. New York: Alfred A. Knopf, 2008.

Michelson, Patricia. *Cheese: Exploring Taste and Tradition*. Layton, UT: Gibbs Smith, 2010.

Ogden, Ellen Ecker. *The Vermont Cheese Book*. Woodstock, VT: The Countryman Press, 2007.

Percival, Frances, and Bronwen. "Animal Meets Vegetable." *Culture* volume 2, issue 2 (Spring 2010), 39–45.

Peters-Morris, Margaret. *The Cheesemaker's Manual*. Lancaster, ON, Canada: Glengarry Cheesemaking, 2003.

Planck, Nina. *Real Food: What to Eat and Why*. New York: Bloomsbury USA, 2007.

Roberts, Jeffrey P. *The Atlas of American Artisan Cheese*. White River Junction, VT: Chelsea Green Publishing, 2007.

Rubino, Roberto, Pierre Sardo, and Angelo Surrusca (editors). *Italian Cheese*. Cuneo, Italy: Slow Food Editore, 2005.

Schmid, Ron. *The Untold Story of Milk*, revised and updated. Washington, DC: NewTrends Publishing, 2009.

Smith, Tim. *Making Artisan Cheese*. Gloucester, MA: Quarry Books, 2005.

Thorpe, Liz. *The Cheese Chronicles*. New York: HarperCollins Publishers, 2009.

Werlin, Laura. *Laura Werlin's Cheese Essentials*. New York: Stewart, Tabori, and Chang, 2007.

INDEX

Copyright © 2011 by Mary Karlin
Foreword copyright © 2011 by Peter Reinhart
Photographs copyright © 2011 by Ed Anderson

Published in the United States by Ten Speed Press,
an imprint of the Crown Publishing Group, a
division of Random House, Inc., New York.
www.crownpublishing.com
www.tenspeed.com

Ten Speed Press and the Ten Speed Press colophon
are registered trademarks of Random House, Inc.

Library of Congress Cataloging-in-Publication Data
Karlin, Mary.
    Artisan cheese making at home : techniques and
recipes for mastering world-class cheeses / Mary
Karlin ; photography by Ed Anderson.
        p. cm.
    Summary: "A contemporary guide to making 100
artisan cheeses at home, with an extensive primer on
ingredients, equipment, and techniques"—Provided
by publisher.
    Includes bibliographical references and index.
    1. Cheesemaking. 2. Cookbooks. I. Title.
    SF271.K37 2011
    641.3'73—dc22

                          2011004548

ISBN 978-1-60774-008-7

Printed in China

Design by Katy Brown

10 9 8 7 6 5 4 3 2 1

First Edition